£2

THE
BIRD
THAT
NEVER
FLEW

The Bird That Never Flew

JOHN
STEELE

SINCLAIR-STEVENSON

First published in Great Britain by
Sinclair-Stevenson Limited
7/8 Kendrick Mews
London SW7 3HG England

The publisher acknowledges subsidy from the Scottish Arts
Council towards the publication of this volume

British Library Cataloguing in Publication Data
A CIP catalogue record for this book is available from the
British Library.

ISBN: 1 85619 124 9

Typeset by Butler & Tanner Ltd
Printed and bound in Great Britain by
Butler & Tanner Ltd, Frome and London

FOREWORD

Was it me who came into this world to face the
strange and new?
Was it me who stood with arms unfurled and
knew not what to do?
Was it me, or was it you?

Was it me who grew up in your cage
always longing to be free?
Was it you who flew into a rage because
one couldn't see,
but was it you or me?

I dedicate this book to my best friend my mother, and anyone
like her. And to my family and friends who continued to show
their loyalty and love towards me, giving me strength and
hope, especially Daniel Lafferty and Honeybugs, Caroline and
Irene, the three ladies who came into my life in the latter part
of my sentence, who shared my pain and who imprisoned
themselves through loving me.

I've been told by those in authority that I shall be punished
if I seek to have this book published; punished because I
refused to let the Prison Department read it beforehand: it
may set the prison system back many years, it wouldn't be fair

to any governors wishing to write a book or a thesis on the prison system ... and I'll be punished should I cause the Secretary of State any further embarrassment.

It is time we opened our eyes. Our prison system is geared to torment its human stock, to lock us away in concrete tombs and cages, degrade us, strip us of our identity, punish us mentally and physically, and leave us to rot and die a thousand deaths in the space of years or even months. With its constant misery, pain, deaths, psychiatric hospitals, and of course riots and escapes, the system has failed prisoners and society. Who, I wonder and ask, does it serve a purpose to? And what reason is there to encourage and condone such a system? One doesn't need to be a philosopher to help solve the problem, but one would certainly have to be unstable to want to keep it as it is. There is no room or time for any of us to become embarrassed, there's got to be change now for a more humane system, one that can prepare us for our eventual release, not this madness that has proved worthless and destructive. I have spoken to many politicians who tell me they would like to make the necessary changes, but society would be up in arms to think of prisoners getting humane treatment. But isn't taking away freedom enough in itself?

Such a humane system does indeed exist in the Scottish Penal System – the Barlinnie Special Unit. Men are sent there, mental and physical wrecks from the mainstream prison and the Unit helps them recover and live as normal a life as possible. Those of us who pass through this Unit owe our lives to the guards there for helping us and understanding our problems and needs (even though some of them at one time had played a part in the earlier system that helped to destroy us). We owe our lives to Dr Peter Whatmore who helped set up the Unit and to the Secretary of State for Scotland and his ministers for allowing the Special Unit to continue to serve its purpose. The Unit opened in 1972. Since that date no one has escaped or attempted to escape, no prison guard has been taken hostage or stabbed or slashed, no riots, hunger strikes or work strikes, no brutality nor solitary confinement. It offers humane rehabilitation. It is not my intention to embarrass

viii

particular individuals, only to help those working for change within the penal system to take a clearer view of the dinosaur which has swallowed us all up and made the worst come out in us. I take this opportunity to thank the pals I had while I was struggling to survive, and those who helped me and those who suffered along with me. Bless them who never made it, and those of you still struggling.

John Steele
H.M. Prison, Perth

17.11.91.

CONTENTS

PART TWO

PART ONE

1 JOHNNYBOY

There's one thing that hurts people more than anything else, and that is waste. Anything of value that goes to waste: human life, for instance.

As a kid I learned a little rhyme which belongs to Glasgow's coat of arms. We would chant it while out playing and even in the classroom:

The bird that never flew,
The tree that never grew,
The bell that never rang,
The fish that never swam.

I was born on 27 March 1956 at my grandmother's home in Carntyne in Glasgow's East End. Glasgow, as far as Glaswegians are concerned, is the flower of Scotland. Our motto – 'Let Glasgow Flourish' – seems to say it all, but there are parts of Glasgow that will never flourish. When I was born Glasgow was full of slums, but there was wealth in every street – the neighbours flourished while Glasgow decayed.

In the street where I was born there was nothing but houses: tenement buildings three storeys high. We lived on the second floor: we had two bedrooms, a living room, a kitchenette known as the 'scullery', and a bathroom. At the bottom of the street, about twenty yards from my close, stood the massive steel gates of the main entrance of the greyhound-racing track. Our playground was the streets and back courts and sometimes the racing track – which was forbidden and, as far as we kids were concerned, all the better as a result.

The streets and back courts were filthy with broken bottles, cans, burst drains and bits of old furniture. Each back court had a rubbish tip known as a midden, which we kids sometimes used as gang huts. All the neighbours in our close were regarded as uncles, aunts and cousins.

I reckon we kids were spoiled, and better off than most in the neighbourhood. I was happy when I was very young, and it seems as if everybody was happy then. More often than not we had a lot of people staying in our house, which was one of the most notorious houses in the city, since almost all my relations were thieves, mostly safe-blowers, and most of them had been to gaol.

My mother had long black hair, and I can remember everyone saying how pretty and young-looking she was. She had five brothers; Uncle Alec was the oldest, and he lived with my Aunt Chrissie and their children Betty, Alec and Christine in another part of the city. My Uncle Tam, who used to stay with us at Carntyne, had a reputation as a safe-blower, and the tips of some of his fingers were missing. My mother's brother John lived next door with his family; he also had a reputation for blowing safes. Though all Ma's brothers were good-looking, Uncle Billy was said to be the most handsome; small and wiry, he too was a safe-blower. He lived elsewhere in the city with his family, but would often come to visit. His son Peter and I would go wandering (or 'gallivanting', as Ma put it), trying to catch pigeons. Ma's youngest brother Arthur, or Atty, was a soldier and, unlike the others, he wasn't a thief. When he came home he would sleep in the same room as me and my older brother, Jim, and tell us stories. In all, my uncles were well known and very well liked.

My dad, Andy Steele, was a country boy, born in Blantyre, the birthplace of David Livingstone. I don't remember seeing much of Dad's mother, or even of his sisters and brother. They kept very much to themselves and worked hard. When my dad was in Borstal he met and became pally with two of Ma's brothers. They decided they would get together when they were released and crack open safes, which they did. Then my dad fell in love with Ma and they got married. My dad had a considerable reputation as a safe-blower, robber and gangster. Jim and I – and often a couple of uncles as well – slept in the same bedroom, which faced the street. The other room was occupied by my mother, my younger sister, Lana, and my grandmother. I can't remember my dad being there at this time – whenever I asked about him I was told he was in the army. The only soldier I can remember was my Uncle Atty; he would come home in tartan uniform and everybody was proud of him.

Although she was blind my grandmother, Elizabeth Padden, was one of the finest people I have ever known. She was very much a mother to everyone – so much so that she was universally known as 'Maw'. As a kid I used to ask 'Maw' why she couldn't see: she told me she had fallen out of a train when she was a little girl, but I found out in later life that she went blind after the birth of her first child. If you had met her you would have sworn that she could see. She would walk about the house, make dinner when Ma was out and do the washing, never letting her handicap get the better of her.

Maw and her family had moved to Carntyne from the Gorbals, on the south side of Glasgow. My grandad, an Irishman named Harry, died when he was quite young. The Gorbals was full of slums and condemned buildings. Rats would come into their house during the night and frighten Maw, and my ma, till her sons got up and killed them. Maw told me stories about the Gorbals; how all the neighbours knew each other and were always ready to help each other whenever anyone was in need – and they were all in need of something. When people cannot get what they need, many of them turn to crime, and that's what my uncles did. They started off very young, going through approved schools, remand homes, Borstal and finally prison.

In Carntyne I was too young to know all this. I would play in the back court with Jim and our pals, climbing the dykes or playing hide-and-seek. We did everything and anything to amuse ourselves. We used to bang on doors and then run away, with our neighbours shouting and threatening to tell our parents – or else they'd laugh and tell us to 'chap' on so and so's door and annoy them. Once one of our neighbours called Tommy joined us and people came out shouting at him, saying that he should have more sense than to run about chapping doors and running away with a bunch of kids.

Tommy was admired and loved and trusted by everybody who knew him. He was a hawker, collecting rags with his horse and cart. He would pick the best of the rags and go round the neighbours asking them if they would like anything for themselves or their kids. He wouldn't take a penny for them, though everybody knew that if he took them to the rag store he could make a couple of pounds. Tommy was the kind of guy who, if he had four loaves and four fishes, would work a miracle. He was very poor and often had to use candles because he couldn't pay his electricity bill. One evening, when his electricity had been cut off, he tried to put it back on by tampering with the cables in his close. He had us kids watching for the police – two of us at the bottom of the street, two at the top and others scattered at strategic points here and there. We shouted to him to let him know that it was all clear, and he disappeared into the close with his shirt sleeves rolled up. All of a sudden there was a bang and a blue flash. All the windows in the street went up and the neighbours were leaning out. We kids met in the middle of the street, terrified because someone was shouting that poor Tommy was dead.

We looked down the close and saw Tommy lying there. His face was all black, and he looked as if he was dead. The next thing we knew more people were lifting up their windows and shouting that their lights had fused. By now all the neighbours were in the close, and we kids had been pushed aside and told to go home. One woman was making the sign of the cross and shouting for an ambulance, others were saying that he was dead. There was a lot of excitement – still more so when Tommy stood up and told them all to stop their whining or they would have the police in the street in a minute. Everybody began to laugh – even those who had had their lights fused.

As for Tommy, he wasn't dead – he had simply fainted when he heard the bang.

My particular pal at that time was Danny McGlachlan, who lived a couple of closes down from us. We'd go hunting for rabbits in the dog tracks, or collect the empty beer bottles that were lying around. We'd take them to the pub, saying our fathers had sent us with them, and make twopence a bottle. Danny was like me in many ways: we were the same size and build – both of us were skinny, with light fair hair. Everybody called him Dannyboy, and I was called Johnnyboy. We would go and rake the middens with all the other guys in our area. We went to what we called the toffs' houses. It was rumoured that they even threw out old money, as well as toys of every sort. Whenever they saw us marching along their street singing and shouting they used to shout to us not to go near their middens or they would set their dogs on us, but that didn't deter us. It was like a gold rush, with all of us leaping over fences and through closes and into these 'lucky middens', as they were known. I guess almost every kid in Glasgow has done this. Dannyboy and I would share whatever we got.

We invented a new game called 'daredevils'. We would climb up drainpipes and on to the roofs, or else we would climb up high bridges, far above the road, and crawl along the steel beams. Passers-by would stare at us in disbelief. If you fell off and didn't kill yourself by the fall, the chances were you'd get run over by a vehicle, so all the traffic would stop and the drivers come out, some cursing us and others telling us not to move till the fire brigade came. We'd be off and away before they knew what was happening.

Sometimes Dannyboy stayed with Jim and me and we'd be up all night talking about what we would like to do and what we would like to be when we grew up. My ma would hear us talking and call out to us to get to sleep and if we didn't keep the noise down Dannyboy wouldn't be allowed to stay with us again.

One day we kids asked Tommy if he'd help us make a go-cart. Go-carts were all the thing at the time. We made them out of old pram wheels and a plank of wood. We would take a cart to the top of a hill and let it freewheel down and on to the main road, sometimes with as many as four boys aboard. Occasionally we were caught by angry motorists, slapped about the head or taken back to our parents, who would skelp us and threaten us with the police and the priest. This was no deterrent, as go-carts were our fun. It was easier to live dangerously than not to live at all.

Tommy took us into his barely furnished living room, gave us tea and biscuits and he started telling us about the hazards of go-carts. In the end he said no, but he had something else for us. He wouldn't say what. He told us to come back during the week. We all left very excited, wondering what he had for us.

When we next knocked at his door we were told to come in and make ourselves at home. Picks and shovels and spades were lying all over his living-room floor.

'How many of you can swim?' he asked us.

We all swore blind that we were great swimmers; but the truth was that half of us had never seen a swimming-pool, and Tommy knew it.

'Are we going to the baths, Tommy?' I asked. He laughed and said we weren't going to any baths: we were going to dig a big hole in his garden and make our own swimming-pool. It must have taken him about ten minutes to quieten us down as we grabbed the shovels and picks and ran into the garden. My shovel was bigger than I was.

After a while Tommy sent us all home for tea and said he would wait for us. We made him promise that he wouldn't do any digging till we got back.

Ma took one look at me and said I was to have a good scrub before tea. I told her about Tommy's swimming-pool, and she said I wouldn't be going into any filthy swimming pool. I begged her to let me go in, and promised that I would take a bath when I got out. Uncle Billy spoke up and said, 'Let him go and have a bit of fun.' But my ma shouted that she wasn't letting her son into a muck-hole. Maw said that we'd be eaten alive by rats, and that God knows what else was down there. I was heartbroken – and so was everybody else, as they had

8

been told the same by their parents. Eventually Tommy told us that the whole thing was off, as there were too many gas pipes under the ground – and that was the end of the swimming-pool.

Near our home was a coal bing, and in the winter Tommy would struggle up the street with a huge bag of coal on his back. He'd make this trip several times each night, and then he would come round asking if we needed any coal.

My ma used to make big pots of soup, and when we had had our fill of it, the pot would go to the neighbours; nothing went to waste. And our neighbours did the same for us.

I had a budgie named Joey and an Alsatian dog named Major. Every morning I'd let Major out to roam, and Joey would be let out of his cage to fly about the house. Sometimes he landed on my head and everyone laughed at his antics.

Every now and then Maw would give me a sixpence and I would go and buy some sweets to share them with her. She only had one tooth with which to break and chew her toffee.

I used to take her for walks and she would ask me how many closes there were in the street, or what the shops were like. She told me that I was her eyes, and that once I could read I should read her books and newspapers. She told me that I could come and stay with her when I was older and that we would have a great time; but as far as I was concerned I would be staying with her for ever, and I told her so. She was just like a mother to me, and the thought of going to live with someone else and leaving my blind Maw behind did something to me.

Sometimes Uncle Atty would come home on leave from the army, grabbing us kids, giving us bear-hugs and throwing us up in the air. He would take us down to the shop and order us anything we wanted – bottles of ginger beer, sweets and cakes. We'd be too full to eat our supper and Atty would laugh and tell my ma that we had forced him to buy us the sweets. When he went back to the army we all wanted to go with him, and we'd follow him till he was out of sight.

Jim and I and often an uncle or two all slept in the same bed, and occasionally one of us wet the bed and soaked everybody to the skin. As the youngest, I got the blame, and my ma would laugh and say: 'I know my poor wee Johnnyboy gets the blame of everything.' When it was just me and Jim in the bed he used to wake up during the night, feel that his shirt was soaking and run in and tell my ma that I had wet the bed and that he was soaking wet. Then I would get up and tell my ma that it was him who wet the bed. The two of us would stand at the foot of my ma's bed arguing who it was, and she would say: 'Keep quiet or the neighbours will hear you.' Then she would get up and change our sheets, saying, 'It's just as well there's a rubber covering over the mattress.' Lana thought it was all very funny and would start giggling at the sight of me and Jim standing there arguing over who it was that had wet the bed.

In the summer our neighbours would carry chairs and sofas down into the little patches on the street that were meant to be their gardens, though there were never any fences round them and nothing ever grew in them. I can remember when Tommy made the most of his garden: he must have worked on it in the wee small hours, and when morning came everybody was in the street admiring it. It was full of roses of every hue and all sorts of flowers, and Tommy was standing at his window with his chest sticking out and a smile on his face. He said he was going to turn Carntyne into the new Hollywood. He was so proud of his new garden that he asked us kids not to play in it any more. Hardly a week had past before every flower lay down and died. He had stolen them out of a toff's garden and planted them in his own muddy patch.

The neighbours sat in these patches for hours talking to each other, and they would often comment on how I was my dad's living image, or that I was just like my mother. Sometimes they got out a half bottle and passed it round, and when it took effect they would start to sing. They put everything they had into these songs, standing there with one hand over their hearts and the other reaching out as though to touch someone who wasn't there. Other neighbours would be looking out of their windows, and they too would manage to get a song in. They would ask us kids to sing for them and give us whatever small change they had, and we'd all scramble to the sweet shop.

Poor guys would come round the back courts singing; some of them were crippled and one was blind. They would stand beneath the windows carrying an old hat, and the idea was to try to throw the money into it. Some people used to throw down a red-hot penny, and the poor guy would scream as he picked it up. When the blind man came round my maw would produce a pound and something in a little bottle; I don't know whether it was whisky or cough mixture.

Tommy often went round the backs singing, with his accordion. He told the neighbours that he didn't want their money, and asked for a couple of slices of bread instead.

As kids we were warned never to go near strangers, as they could murder us or beat us up. Ma, Maw and my uncles told me I would love it at Elbow Lane Primary School at Parkhead, but that first day, sitting in a class full of strangers, was really frightening, even though Ma was there with me to start with. As soon as she left I panicked and ran after her, crying to be taken home.

Ma took me and Jim to chapel each Sunday, after making sure we were spick-and-span, and she always gave us money to put in the poor plate. I was taught my prayers at home and at school. I learned about God and how he came to be, and how he made the whole Creation, and how Jesus died on the Cross. Like school, chapel and prayers were a frightening experience, sinister and intimidating. The silent chapel had an eerie atmosphere and the priest with his long robes and booming voice seemed a menacing figure, telling us that hell was for bad people and that to get to heaven we had to be good. The only thing I liked about chapel was singing hymns, when everyone seemed happier.

It was great when our aunts came to stay with us, especially my Auntie Ruby. She was my ma's cousin – Maw's sister's

11

daughter – and she was very attractive, with blonde hair. I loved it when she brought her son Brian with her. Brian, whom we called Broono, was my favourite cousin.

As soon as Aunt Ruby saw me her purse was out and she would give me some money. When I refused she always said, 'Our wee Johnnyboy will never take a penny,' and she would give it to my ma and tell her to give it to me for sweets. She would bounce me on her knee and stroke my hair, asking me if I would like to come and stay with her, knowing fine that I would be so excited that I could hardly get the words out.

I can remember Aunt Ruby asking my ma, 'When does Andy get out?' and I knew she was talking about my dad. On the night he came home we had a full house and there was a party. Everyone was drinking except my ma, who never drank. Jim and Lana and I got out of bed and went into the living room where everybody was singing and dancing. My dad had us all on his knees, cuddling and kissing us and emptying his silver on to our laps. He told us how he had missed us and that we were certainly growing up. Everyone told him that I was his living image. I must have been nearly five at the time, and this is my earliest recollection of my dad. Before the party got out of hand we were sent to bed, all excited at having our dad home.

Next day Dad took us out in his new car – there were only a couple of the neighbours in our street who had cars at that time. There was a new excitement when my dad was home, and a lot of strangers coming to our house; but my uncles were hardly to be seen, and the house took on a new atmosphere. He made us come home much earlier than we were used to. When I asked if I could stay with my uncles for a couple of days he'd shout that this was my home, and nowhere else. When I went out to play he would say, 'Don't you wander from the back court!' One day he looked out of the window and saw me sitting on a little wall just staring at the ground.

'I thought you were wanting to go out and play?' he shouted. I looked at my ma, not knowing what to say, and she said, 'He was playing.' But my dad said, 'He's just sitting on that fucking wall staring at the ground.' My maw butted in and

12

told him to stop swearing and shouting at me, and asked him how he expected me to play in the back court which was full of broken bottles and puddles. He didn't like it and he told Maw that he was my father and that I'd play where and when he told me. I'd have to learn to obey.

My dad told me and Jim on many occasions not to go climbing with our best shoes on or to go jumping into puddles. His commandments were:

Never talk to strangers.
Never wander away from home.
Always be in on time for supper.
Never be out late when it's dark.
Never climb buildings.
Never throw stones at windows or vehicles.
Never get into cars with strange men.
If anybody hits you, hit them back; if they're too big to fight with, hit them with the first heavy object available, and aim for the head.
Never talk to the police, and should they stop you for anything, tell him immediately.
Never steal or take anything that doesn't belong to you and, most important, always *be good*.

He told me all this much more often than he told Jim. He was asking us to change our ways, and to us it seemed wrong because it restricted our fun. But most fathers were very strict with their sons.

If he saw me climbing he would go crazy and say that I was ruining my shoes, and that would be me in for a couple of days: if my pals came to the house asking if I could come out to play, he would slam the door in their faces. I felt quite confused. He gave Lana and Jim everything: it seemed that I would get nothing until I learned to obey.

He would send me to the shops without a list. I'd forget half the things he'd told me to get and when I came back from the shops he'd start shouting. I'd tell him I couldn't remember them all and he'd say, 'You didn't forget the fucking sweeties, did you? – and then I'd be sent to bed. My ma and Maw told

13

him that he should have given me a list in the first place, and ask why he had sent me to bed. 'Because he's fucking hopeless, that's why,' he shouted.

I'd lie in bed and the sun would be splitting the trees. As soon as Dad went out my ma and Maw would tell me to get up and I would watch television. They told me not to bother about him and that things would get better. But then he'd come in unexpectedly and catch me out of bed and he'd point at me and say 'Bed! And don't get out of it until I tell you!' Then he'd start shouting at my ma and Maw.

Ma would tell me to try to avoid him and not go climbing when he was about, as it would only mean him putting me to bed again. But he always found some excuse to put me to bed. He told me to clean my room. I cleaned it till it was sparkling and asked him if I could go out to play and he said, 'Wait till I inspect your room.' Then he shouted me into my room where, standing with an empty ginger beer bottle in his hand, he said, 'What's this, then? I thought you said you'd cleaned up here?' I started to tell him that it was only an empty bottle and that I would sell it to the ice-cream van, but he cut me off, shouting, 'Don't you fucking answer me back!'

My ma said, 'You would think that Johnnyboy wasn't your son the way you speak to him – that's your own flesh and blood.' He drew me a look with his bottom lip curled down, showing his teeth, and said to no one in particular that if I couldn't do what I was told then I would get treated this way. He also said that this was how his father had treated him when he was a kid.

He came into my bedroom and said, 'You'd better behave yourself, boy, because if you don't you'll rot in that bed of yours.' I couldn't understand it because I hadn't done anything. He said, 'Are you listening to what I'm saying to you?' I wouldn't look at him but I looked at the floor and said, 'Aye'. He shouted, 'Aye, what?' I looked at the window trying to think what to do or say, and again he shouted, 'You fucking look at me when I'm talking to you!' When I did look at him he grabbed me and pulled me about like a rag doll, and said, 'Don't you ever fucking look at me like that!' My maw

14

told him that he was sick. I was sent to bed again.

When his friends came to the house they'd do a lot of talking and drinking. Someone would ask where I was and he would say to my brother or sister, 'Go and tell my boy to come in here.' I'd walk in with nothing on but a vest, and he'd bounce me on his knee and tell his pals that he loved me and that I was his favourite even though he might not show it. He told them I was as stubborn as a mule and started laughing and stroking my hair. Then he would pull some money from his pocket and tell me to go out and play with Dannyboy. His pals would give me some money too. Before I went out my ma would inspect me and whisper in my ear to mind and be in early and not to climb or do anything that would antagonise him. Dannyboy and my pals would be glad to see me again, and I them.

One evening he told me to go to the chip shop. He gave me ten minutes. I could never have got there and back in that time, so when I saw a corporation truck turning the corner I jumped on its back. It started gathering speed, and we sped past the chippy. I banged on the side of the van, hoping they would hear me, but they didn't stop until we got into the city centre, miles away from home. I didn't know what to do or how I was going to explain to my dad why I was so late.

I got home to Carntyne eventually on foot and went to the chippy and got my order. I met one of the neighbours who told me my dad was out looking for me. When I knocked on the door my ma answered, and she sighed when she saw me. She told me they thought something had happened to me, and asked me what had kept me. I told her that some big boys had chased me and tried to steal my money. When my dad came in he was about to go for me, but Ma told him what had happened. He went mad. He went into his room and put on his hat – and he had something in the waistband of his trousers. He wasn't angry any more – at least not at me. He asked me if I could recognise them again, and I told him that I could. He told me to go downstairs and wait in the car for him. On the way out I heard my ma say something like, 'Don't, Andy, you'll end up in the gaol.' I heard him shouting that no one would fuck any of his family about and then he came out of the door and we headed for the car.

Once in the car he said, 'If the police ask you any questions at any time, tell them nothing.' He kept saying this as we drove to the chippy. He saw a bunch of guys standing at the corner and slowed down, asking me if I could recognise them. I told him no. We drove around for a while, and I kept saying I couldn't see them. We went back home. My ma and Maw were relieved to know that nothing had happened.

In school my teacher took to shouting at me to pay attention when she was speaking to me and when I wouldn't look at her she jabbed her pointing stick in my chest. She would prod me quite often with this stick of hers. My dad got to hear about about it and he asked me if it was true. I told him it was. He took me to school, and he walked into the class with me and his two Alsatian dogs. He told the teacher that if she ever put a hand on me again he would put her into hospital. My dad was a very smart dresser and looked like the film star Lee Marvin. The teacher must have taken him seriously because she never laid a hand on me after that – but she hated me, and showed it. When she spoke to the class she would never look at me. It was as if I wasn't there any more. I got so fed up that I started playing truant. We called this 'dogging' school. Me and my pals would go into the shops in the city centre and look at all the sweets on the shelves. We'd go in a group but pretend we didn't know each other. One of us would walk straight up and say, 'How much are those sweets?' pointing a finger at a jar of sweets up on the top shelf. When the owner looked behind him to see which sweets he was referring to, someone else would reach over the display counter and lift a bar of chocolate. By the time the owner looked round we'd all pretend to be looking at the prices of things. Once we got outside the shop we'd all laugh at how easy it was. This was a new experience. I knew to be caught would mean getting sent to a home but I didn't care – I remembered Maw telling me that I would be better off in a home than under the same roof as my dad.

My ma became suspicious and asked if I was 'dogging' school. I didn't like to hurt her by telling her the truth, so I told her lies. She found out in the end but she didn't tell my dad, as she knew he would beat me. But one day, when I came home from school, I noticed something was wrong. Everyone was too quiet. My dad said, 'What did you get taught at school today?' Maw was sitting on one of the armchairs, her head hanging down; my ma was raking the coal fire, as though she didn't want to see me getting hit. My dad was standing in front of me waiting for an answer: I noticed that his bottom teeth were showing. I kept looking from Ma to Maw, but he told me to never mind looking at them as they weren't going to answer his question. I told him I was being taught maths at school.

'You're a fucking liar!' he shouted. 'You weren't at school!'

I never even saw it coming – I only remember Ma picking me off the floor and screaming at him. He was trying to drag me out of her arms, and she was trying to hold on. The neighbours were shouting through the letter-box, asking if everything was all right. Maw was shouting, 'If I could see out of one eye, Andy Steele, I would tear the throat out of you!' All the while Ma was sheltering me with her own body, and she ended up with as many bruises as me.

He kept me in my bed for weeks, telling Jim and Lana not to go near my room as I was an animal and was on punishment. Even though he terrified them they managed to sneak in and give me sweets and biscuits. I looked out of my window and talked to Dannyboy and my pals.

My dad would come in and search me and my room, making sure *no one* had given me anything. Once, when he was searching my mattress, he felt it was wet. He smelt his hand, and when he realised it was urine he grabbed me by the hair and rubbed my face in the mattress. I couldn't even shout to my ma or Maw because my face was being rubbed hard into the mattress. He had all his weight on me and said, 'I should have smothered you at birth, you bastard.'

As a result, I developed a squint in one eye – my maw and aunts said it was caused by shock. I stopped eating and would

17

only take nibbles here and there. My ma and Maw, and even my aunts and uncles, tried to bribe me to eat. But I couldn't; all I wanted was to get away from my dad.

I believed in God, and it was an awful shock to me when I made my first communion to be told I would be given part of the body of Christ to eat. When the priest put the Holy Communion into my mouth I was terrified. It stuck to the roof of my mouth – I tried to budge it with my tongue, but it would not move. I panicked and spat it out into my hand and hid it under my seat. I never told my family about this.

My eating became poorer and poorer. When Ma told me that she was making my favourite meals, I'd say, 'I just want bread and jam.' She put a shilling on the table and told me that if I ate my dinner – even half of it – she would give it to me. She'd put a spoon heaped with mince to my mouth and she'd call me her 'wee darling' and her 'wee honeybunch'; I'd open my mouth and Ma would say 'See how my wee Johnnyboy does things for me' and she would be all smiles.

Ma arranged for me to go and stay with Aunt Ruby for a week or two. I loved my Auntie Ruby – she would have taken me home to stay with her for good, but even she was terrified of my dad. He was all against me going to stay with her for even a day, saying that I had a house of my own. My ma said that a wee holiday would do me the world of good. In the end he agreed, and everybody was happy. Ma washed and pressed my clothes, and gave me a couple of pounds for my pocket money.

Aunt Ruby collected me in a taxi, and we chatted all the way to her house. I asked about Broono and if he had a tent – hoping that if he did we could camp out at night. Broono and I were both about six. He had red hair and was fairly well-built for his age.

The close was in darkness and Auntie Ruby was scared in case there were rats. So I went in first with a big stick and banged the walls so that they would scatter and run into their holes. When we reached her door we heard screaming. She quickly put the key in the door, and as we entered I saw that Broono was standing in the sink and my Uncle Hugh was pouring bottles of cold water over him. His backside, like my own, was covered in bruises. Uncle Hugh didn't even look round to see who had come in. He was threatening Broono, saying, 'Don't you ever go on a roof again.' Each time he poured the cold water over Broono's head, Broono would raise his shoulders and shiver, as though he were having a fit. My aunt looked at me and shook her head in a sad sort of way, as if to say, 'I'm trying to get you away from all this, son.' Broono was almost blue with the cold when she lifted him out of the sink and dried him, arguing with Uncle Hugh.

'I've brought Johnnyboy to stay with us for a couple of weeks,' she told him, and I could see his face light up. But before we could say anything his dad had told him to get to bed, and he went off without a word. I hardly looked at Uncle Hugh, but I told my aunt that I was tired and asked her if I could go to bed. She knew I couldn't wait till I was in beside Broono. She told me to wait till I was fed, but I told her I wasn't hungry. She gave me a wink and said I could go off, and that she would feed Broono and me in our bed.

It was great for Broono and me to tell each other all the different tricks we were up to. We would sit up all night talking about how we would beat up our dads when we were grown up and send them to their beds, or run away together to London. Broono showed me his bruises and I showed him mine. Both of us were beaten for nothing. What we were doing was natural – climbing and jumping in puddles. What else could we do? When I asked my Auntie Ruby if Broono could come out and play she told me to ask his dad. He said, 'You can go out, Johnnyboy, but that bastard stays in his bed.'

The funny thing about Broono was that he could eat massive meals, and was always looking for more. I was still off my food and gave most of mine to Broono. When he had finished his meal and most of mine he would ask me to watch the door, then he would bolt for the cooker and check every pot. I killed myself laughing when he opened the oven and took out a chicken and tried to rip the legs off it. When Uncle Hugh walked in Broono hid the chicken behind his back. Uncle Hugh told him to put his shoes on and go down to the shops.

I said that if he gave me the money, I would go for him, but he said it was too dark – apart from getting lost there were murderers about. He didn't want anything to happen to me, but couldn't care less about Broono. Broono and I knew that if he was caught with the chicken he would be murdered there and then. Poor Broono had broken out in a sweat.

Just then there was a knocking on the outside door. Uncle Hugh told me to answer it. I told him that I was scared to, as I recognised the knock as my dad's. I hoped that he would answer it and give Broono time to get the chicken back in the oven. He went to the door, and who should walk in but my dad.

'I missed you son,' he said. I was so relieved I almost fainted. At times like that I loved him and felt so happy that I could cry. One kind word would touch my heart. Nine times out of ten I would cry and sometimes he cried too and told me he was sorry for giving me all those beatings and sending me to my bed.

'Do you think I like doing this to you?' he would ask.

I asked Auntie Ruby if Broono could come and stay with me. She patted my head and told me not to worry about it as she and my ma had it all worked out to take a wee holiday together. When I got home my ma said there was a bit of colour back in my face, but before long she was telling Maw how pale I was. And it would be 'Bed! Bed! Bed!'

2 FIRST FLIGHT

I started running away from home when I was very young – probably six or seven. I would get up when everyone was asleep, go into the pantry and make some sandwiches. The first time I did this it was about one o'clock in the morning. I looked out of the window and saw that it was foggy. I only knew it would be better out there than in here with my dad, in that bed of mine.

Since my dad had come home, Maw and Lana were sleeping in the living room. I stood by the door looking at their faces lit up by the moonlight. It hurt me to see Maw sleeping so peacefully because I knew that when they discovered I was gone that peaceful look would turn to worry. I was about to go into the scullery and climb down the drainpipe when Maw called my name in a sort of whisper. I tiptoed over to her. Lana was fast asleep, her long hair spread across Maw's shoulder.

'Tell me where you're going, son, and don't have me and your ma worried about you,' Maw said.

I told her I was just up for a piece and jam. She reached out and felt my clothes and said she had heard me putting them on. She made me close the living-room door and go and sit beside her.

'I know you're running away, son,' she said, 'but where do you intend to go? Out there at night on your own would be too dangerous for a wee boy like you. Your ma will be worried sick and would die if anything ever happened to you – and so

21

would I. I know your dad is giving you a hard time, son, but you'll only make things worse by running.'

Then I remembered something. I said, 'But Maw, he's told me to get out of his house before and never to come back and that I wasn't wanted here as long as he lived here.'

Her hand was stroking mine. 'I know that, son, but he doesn't really mean what he says and I know for a fact that if anything ever happened to you he would go mad. Just give him a chance. I would never tell you a lie. You're too young to explain it to. There are times I hate him for doing what he does to you. I can forgive him because I understand, but the bad thing is that you don't. He loves you, Johnnyboy – you might find that hard to believe, but it's true. I've even heard him crying after he's hit you. He probably sees too much of himself in you.'

I couldn't really understand what Maw was trying to say. I knew I had to get away from my dad. I told her that I was going to run away and pleaded with her not to tell. She said she wouldn't. The poor old soul was crying her eyes out and her whole body was trembling. She said, 'If you're going to run away, go to your Auntie Annie's in Bridgeton. You'll be safe there, son, and at least we'll know where you are. But God knows, Johnnyboy, it will only be a matter of time before he gets to you, and I dread to think of the beatings he'll give you.'

In those days I could think of nothing but beatings. To be a kid and get beaten by your father might not seem much, but panic sets in when you hear your ma screaming for mercy as though it were her that was getting a beating, 'Don't! Don't! Please don't – you'll kill him!'

Maw gave me a pound and asked me to wait till morning before I left. I was off at the crack of dawn – down the drainpipe outside the scullery window, across the back yard and through a close into the main road. It was dark and I had to walk carefully so as not to lose my footing. I had one hand on the wall for balance and was making my way towards the steps in the street, when I felt something like a bundle of rags beneath my feet. As I put my weight on it I knew something was wrong and then someone grabbed my leg. I thought it must be my dad. I was so terrified I couldn't scream or run – I had lost all my strength. He started to pull himself up by the long woollen scarf that Maw had given me, dragging me down at the same time. I thought I was going to be murdered, until I got a glimpse of his face, covered in black hair, and old and horrible-looking. I panicked and struggled – I didn't want to die at the hands of a tramp. The next thing I knew I was running back towards my close. In fact I was in such a panic that I ran straight past it. I didn't know if he was following me or not – I just kept on running. I passed men and women going to work. One or two shouted at me as I sped past them: 'Hey, son, what's the matter?' I wouldn't even look round, never mind answer.

I was a few streets away before I stopped running. The houses were different from ours – they were big sandstone buildings, mostly condemned, and lots of the windows had corrugated tin on them. The streets were ill-lit and haunted-looking. This part of Carntyne was 'original', and these houses had been built long before ours. Rats were scurrying about the streets as if they owned them. Nearby was the cleansing department, where the rubbish from the middens went, and it was moving with rats, some as big as cats. The houses had outside toilets, and at night people took candles as there were no lights in them. Some of my pals who lived there told me that they never used the outside toilets at night – they would pee in the sink, and if they needed to shit they did it in an old newspaper and threw it out of their window. Huge puddles caused by burst drains filled most back courts – they stank of urine and the smell was awful until you got used to it. I thought about Maw and Ma and the rest of my family lying in their beds nice and warm. I wanted to go back, but I couldn't. I was freezing; my legs were very cold because I was wearing short trousers. I realised that I no longer had my scarf.

I got a bus into the city centre at about nine o'clock and wandered about the shops looking at the toys. I knew that by now my dad would have discovered that I had run away and everyone would be out searching for me. All day I roamed the town, and when my legs got tired I sat on the pavement or on steps outside shops, only to be told to move along. It started to rain and I was colder than ever. I wondered where to go. I didn't want to go to my aunties, as I knew they would take me home. That's where I really wanted to be, but I couldn't bear the thought of my dad being there. I blacked out in a doorway and came to in a shop. Some women had me sitting in a chair, and one of them was holding my head up. At first I didn't know where I was. The sight of these strange faces made me panic. I tried to get up, but they held me down, telling me not to be afraid. A young woman asked me if I was with anyone. I told her my ma was outside in another shop. One of the women said I was the colour of death and must surely have pneumonia. They helped me to the door, and the younger woman released her hold on me just as the shop door opened. I ran, looking back once to see if they were chasing me, but they weren't.

It must have been about ten o'clock when I got a bus back to Carntyne. I got off near the cleansing department and walked the rest of the way. As I was passing the chippy I met one of my pals who told me that everyone was out looking for me. I asked him not to tell anyone he had seen me. The women who worked in the chippy knew me, so I gave my pal sixpence and he bought me a poke of chips. I ate half of them and put the rest up my jumper. I left my pal and made my way towards the dog-track. There was enough room for someone my size to crawl in under the back gate.

Once beyond the gate I was inside a corrugated iron corridor over a hundred yards long. It was pitch-black, and I stood there for about an hour without moving, listening and wondering if I should go somewhere else. I'd never really been scared of the dark, but I didn't know what darkness was till I found myself standing there. I was terrified.

I moved a couple of feet at a time, then stopped and listened, and when I didn't hear anything I moved a couple of feet again until I got myself to the empty car park, where hundreds of rabbits were running in every direction. It was much lighter out here with no roof over my head. At the far end of the car park were the massive steel main gates and about thirty yards beyond the gates was our house. I was freezing cold, it was raining, and my teeth were chattering. I took the chips out of my jumper but they were cold and I threw them away. I pulled my jumper down over my knees and rocked to and fro on the grass, trying to keep myself warm.

There was a lot of shouting in the street just beyond the gates. I stopped rocking and stood up, trying to make out what was being said. 'Haw, Johnnyboy!' the neighbours and my family were shouting. 'Haw, Johnnyboy!' It sounded like an echo. Some added that it was all right for me to come out, and that I wouldn't have a finger laid on me. I was biting my nails and staring at the gates, wondering what to do, when I heard a noise from behind me. I froze like a stone. I could hear footsteps. My senses told me to run, but fear kept me there. I couldn't turn round to see who it was. The only things I could move were my eyes, which were going from side to side, trying to look behind my head. Then I saw a man out of the corner of my eye. He walked on past me towards the big steel gates, never looking back. I was still standing there when the two big gates slid open and everyone came through with torches shouting, 'Haw, Johnnyboy!' I turned and ran back the way I had come in, down the long dark corridor and up to the back gate. I lay on the ground, too weak and dazed to yell, listening to my name being called over and over again. I had peed my trousers and could feel the heat next to my skin. I crawled under the gate just to keep moving. My urine had now turned freezing cold. If I could have done another pee I would have done it in my trousers for the sake of a little warmth. It's one thing being out in the cold in dry clothes but another thing when they're soaking wet. It leaves you with a feeling of hating the whole world.

I made my way up the railway embankment and sat there. I saw some men carrying bags of coal on their backs and I hid until they went by. All was quiet – there was no more shouting. I wondered where they were. I wondered whether Broono would look after me and hide me in his gang hut, and wished he was there to keep me company. I thought every noise was

25

a murderer on the prowl; every weird shadow I saw resembled something ugly, moving towards me; every drop of rain that ran down the back of my neck was like a bucket of water, and every time the cold wind blew against me it was as if it was trying to blow me back home. I wished I was dead, except that would mean never seeing my ma and Maw again. I wished that I was in a home instead – at least 'he' wouldn't get me, and my ma and Maw would come and see me every day. Then I thought of not being able to play with Dannyboy and my pals. I found myself wishing I was my dad; I would come and get me and tell me I was sorry and never hit me again... Wishful thinking is a great thing, and reality a terrible thing.

I was walking along an almost deserted road. I hid when I heard the occasional car approaching, but none of them stopped. There were tramps everywhere, some sleeping on newspapers, others sitting together talking. I heard footsteps on the other side of the road. It was so misty I couldn't see, but I recognised the noise of high-heeled shoes, and I ran across the road in the direction I imagined the woman to be. The money in my pocket was jingling, making a lot of noise. When I reached the other side I stopped and listened, looking all about me. Then I heard her shouting, 'Help! Murder!' I started walking forwards, calling out that I was lost and scared, until I saw her. She was a young woman, staring at me and looking about to see if I was alone. When she asked me my name I said, 'Johnnyboy'. She came towards me and put her arms round me, shaking and clinging to me as if I was her guardian angel – though if anyone had come towards us, like one of those tramps, I would have been the first to run. She told me everyone was out searching for me, including the police. She came from Carntyne and wanted to take me home: I agreed, though for every little step I took forwards I wanted to take ten backwards. She asked me where I had been and as I told her she kept interrupting with 'Oh my God!' and 'Holy Mother of God!' She said she would take me home and ask my dad not to hit me. We passed the chippy and I was beginning to panic as we hadn't far to go. I thought about running away, but I was too exhausted. My legs were wobbling and she offered to carry me. I told her I would walk.

When we were almost in my street she tightened her grip on my hand – she must have been reading my mind. Outside our close was a Black Maria with two policemen in it, and they stared at us as we rounded the corner. I was terrified and tried to run. I thought they were going to take me away to jail as they got out of their car and came towards us. The woman was holding on to me with both hands so that I couldn't get away, and the police radioed to say that they had found me. One policeman took me upstairs while the other stayed with the woman. I wanted her to come with me to stop me from being beaten. The policeman who took me upstairs told me I was going to get the hiding of my life from my dad, and that I deserved it. He searched me on the landing, using his torch to see with. I heard my maw shouting, 'Quick, open the door – Johnnyboy is coming up the stairs!' The policeman asked me where I had got the money from, but when he heard my maw shouting he put the money back in my pocket and told me to keep walking. The door opened and I saw my Uncle Billy standing there: behind him I could see only Maw, crying and asking if I was all right. Uncle Billy was glad to see me, and I was glad to see him. He beckoned me and the policeman in, and Maw held on to me and hugged me. When she realised my clothes were damp she told me to strip off there and then. Uncle Billy went out of the room and I could hear taps running – the thought of a nice warm bath made me feel better. Maw asked the policeman to go so that they could get me fed and bathed and into bed, but he said that he had to find out where I'd been. In the end he agreed to come back in the morning.

Maw had wrapped her long woollen cardigan round me, and sat me near the fire to keep warm. 'God must have answered my prayers,' she said. She told me that I wouldn't be beaten, that they'd just be glad to know I was alive and well. Uncle Billy came back as I was telling her where I'd been and what I'd been doing, and shouted at me that I had almost worried my ma to death and that I could think myself lucky that he wasn't taking the skin off my arse. Maw said that I'd suffered enough and raising his voice would only make me worse. He looked at my hair and hands and feet and said I was filthy. Then he removed Maw's cardigan and picked me up like a rag doll – which was frightening, as he had never even shouted at me before, never mind grabbed me violently. I was on the verge of crying and probably would have had he not thrown me into a cold bath. A strange noise came from my throat. Maw shouted at Billy to leave the wean alone, and he said he wasn't putting a hand on me. Maw was shouting at me but I couldn't answer – the noises were still coming from the back of my throat. My body jerked in the water as I tried to get out, but Billy held me in. Maw fell over something in the living room as she tried to find out what Billy was doing to me. I could hear her calling for help and cursing Billy. Once I stopped twitching Billy let go of me and left the bathroom, telling me to get scrubbed from head to foot. I sat there just staring and feeling numb. I couldn't grasp what was happening – I only knew it was something terrible and that I couldn't get away. My whole body was in pain. I couldn't even call out for help. When I tried to shout, my mouth opened but not a word would come out. Everything looked hazy. The wallpaper wasn't the same colour as before, nor was my body – everything was a different colour, I was terrified. I tried to get up but I couldn't. I tried to scream but I couldn't. My mind was screaming for everyone I knew – 'Ma! Da! Billy! Maw! Jim! Lana! Uncle John! Dannyboy! Tommy! Auntie Ruby! Broono!' – on and on, calling out their names. I heard people shouting goodnight to each other in the street – it was probably the search party back home again – and then footsteps on the stairs. The outside door opened and I heard my ma's voice saying something about giving me a good scrubbing with disinfectant. I could just make out her face and her long black hair hanging down. Her eyes looked strange, and her head was shaking from side to side. Her hand came into the water and she let out a murderous scream as she dragged me from the bath. She wouldn't let me go when the others came in, and she carried on screaming the building down. Someone was shouting for a doctor; others were telling her to wrap me in blankets and keep my limbs moving, and my legs and arms were being rubbed hard by lots of hands.

Ma kept lifting up my head and looking at my eyes. I could hear her calling my name and saying, 'Answer me, son!' but I couldn't answer. I was sorry for running away and causing all this worry, and asked her to ask my dad and Billy to give me one more chance: I'd be good and never run away again. I said all this without uttering one word. The house was full of people looking at me. Blankets were wrapped around me in front of the fire, with my ma kneeling down beside me. I heard Ma say to someone that when Andy Steele got to know about this there would be murder.

There was fighting that night amongst Ma's brothers because of what Billy had done to me. As for my dad, I didn't see him that night, nor for a long time after it.

3 GROWING PAINS

My dad had gone back to the army. The house was full once more, with Uncle Billy sleeping in my bed with me and Jim, and sometimes Uncle Atty as well whenever he was home on leave. Uncle Billy and his wife had split up and his children had been put away in an orphans' home. His youngest son was adopted by my Uncle Tam, but it was to be many years before I saw my cousin Peter again and in a place I'd never have believed possible.

I never took a dislike to my Uncle Billy. He wasn't the sort of man you could hate; I knew he loved me, and he'd shown it on many occasions. He said he was going to catch whoever wet the bed and make him wash the dishes for a week. He claimed he'd been unable to get a girlfriend since he started sleeping in our bed – every time he began to chat them up they would start twitching their noses. He mimicked the actions of a girl wondering what the smell was, and pretended he was talking to the girl; 'Smell? Wait a minute, honey, if you want to talk about smells, did you never hear about the time your father shit his trousers when he was called up to join the army?' His hand would go up as if he was trying to stop the girl from hitting him with her handbag, and he said, 'Don't take my word for it, honey, phone the cleansing department and ask for Clatty Charlie and his crew, they got the Victoria Cross for disposing of his trousers.' He started twitching his nose, then he looked at my ma and said, 'Come to think of it, I should get the Victoria Cross for sleeping in that bed with Johnnyboy and Jim!'

I was happy at that time, not only when I was having fun, but when I was going to the shops and helping Ma to do the cleaning and the washing; even when I went to bed, since I knew that I would be out of it as soon as my eyes opened. Ma would come into my bedroom in the morning and lift me out, tickling me and making me laugh. She'd carry me into the living room, where the coal fire was burning away. I'd stand in front of it while she put my clothes on, then she would turn me round to inspect me, and if there was a little bit of fluff on my trousers she would pick it off. She'd say, 'Who do you love the best in the world, son?' and I'd say, 'You, Ma!' Then Maw would say in a sad voice, 'Oh, what about me, son?' I would look at Ma and then at Maw, trying to figure out whom I loved the best. I'd say, 'I love the two of you the best in the world,' and Ma would hug me and Maw would kiss me too. Then Ma would hold me by the hands and Maw would have my feet and they would swing from side to side, and I'd be laughing and shouting, 'Swing me higher, up to the ceiling!'

In Carntyne there were a lot of very poor people, and quite a few would be evicted for not paying rents or bills. 'Sheriff's officers' who worked for the authorities would charge in to where these people lived and take the furniture. If they thought they couldn't sell it they would throw it into the garden or the back court: sometimes they even broke it up in the house and threw it out of the window. The family being evicted felt so humiliated that you'd see them in the street weeping and holding their children, staring up at their windows. It was horrible to watch. Most of the neighbours would be looking out of their windows or standing in the street, shouting at the sheriff's officers. Some of the men would have hammers and sticks and even iron bars, but despite the chants of 'Animals, animals', the sheriff's officers went about their work as if they couldn't hear. When the police arrived the men would hide their tools. Sometimes a neighbour would get word that the sheriff's officers were coming to evict them, and they would hide their valuables in other people's houses, moving furniture at night so that when the officers came there'd be nothing left for them to sell. Men would say to us kids, 'That van there belongs to the sheriff's officers' and tell us to smash its windows. The people who were being evicted would shout about their 'rights', and occasionally some old man would yell, 'Why are you doing this to me? I fought in the war for people like you, and I've got my medals to prove it!'

I remember visiting my dad when he was in the 'army', sometimes hundreds of miles away. Me, Lana, Ma and Jim were taken through a huge gate by men with hats on and uniforms. Ma told us that our dad would be glad to see us again and that he'd have sweets for us. We were led away by the men with hats and taken to a room. There were rows of windows with wire mesh on them, and people on either side talking to each other through the mesh. We followed Ma into a little box about the size of a telephone booth, and there was my dad on the other side of it looking at us. Ma had us stand on a little ledge and he tried to kiss us but couldn't because of the glass, and when he put his face to the window we would try to touch it. Dad asked us how we were keeping and if we missed him, and we all said yes. He and Ma whispered to each other and we'd sit there watching them. I could see tears in my dad's eyes, and Ma would look sad. I asked my dad when he was coming home and he told us soon and that he would buy us anything we wanted. He told us to help Ma with her housework and to be in early at nights. When my dad was talking to us he would put his mouth to the wire mesh and we would put our ears up to it. During one visit we saw my Uncle Dinny on the same side as my dad and we all spoke for a few minutes. Some of my dad's friends whom I'd seen at home, waved to us as we were leaving, and on the way out one of the men with a hat on gave us lots of sweets, telling us they were from my dad.

For some reason me, Lana, Jim and Ma left our house and went to live in another house in Carntyne, a dozen or so streets away. I think there had been a fight between Ma's brothers. Maw and some of my uncles stayed behind in the old house and I went to visit them almost every day. My Uncle Bobby Campbell stayed in Rigby Street with Aunt Nelly and my cousins, who were all older than me and Jim. Uncle Bobby was kind to us, and he would let me and Jim stay out quite late. One day his son Tommy, who was called 'T.C.', chased me with his friends through streets and closes. They shouted at me to stop, but I kept running and jumping over walls and squeezing through railings. I could hear them all laughing and shouting at one another. I thought they were chasing me because I had slipped out of the house and had been out for ages, so I just kept running. T.C. finally caught me. He was a good few years older then me. I was struggling and kicking, trying to get away, but he held me tight and told me to calm down and not to be afraid as no one was going to hit me. He told me my ma had a nice surprise for me, but I didn't believe him and said he was just saying it to get me to come in.

When we reached their door, I could tell that something was going on. T.C. took me in and told my ma that he had had to chase me all over Carntyne. Ma said it was just as well that he had caught me or I wouldn't get to see the big surprise she had for me. I was really excited. I didn't know what to expect. Ma pulled me over, and there beside her was a tiny baby. She told me it was my wee brother and that his name was Joseph. Everyone began to laugh at the expression on my face. Someone gave me some money – I think it was half a crown – and told me to give it to the baby – a gift to a new-born baby is traditional throughout Scotland and is meant to bring it good fortune. Ma let me hold my baby brother for a couple of minutes. I asked her if I could go and tell all my pals. She let me out but made me promise to be in early as I was to have a bath before going to school.

I don't know how long I stayed with the Campbells, but eventually we moved back to our old house. When Christmas Eve came me and Jim were up most of the night talking and listening for Santa Claus coming down the chimney. Next morning our toys and games would be at the foot of the bed all wrapped up in colourful paper. We tore the parcels open, amazed at what we had: cowboy suits, guns, rifles, football strips, little motor cars, clothes and lots of sweets – everything you could dream of.

Jim and I dressed up as cowboys and Lana put on her nurse's uniform and bandaged us up when we pretended to be wounded. The neighbours came in to celebrate, drinking and singing. Maw got drunk very easily and she'd always say, 'Where's my wee Johnnyboy?' I'd touch her hand and be lifted on to her knee, and she'd start singing and telling me how happy it made her to know that I was happy. I'd be passed from knee to knee and everyone would say how I looked much healthier and less nervous.

My dad came back home from the army and, like the first time, he gave us kids everything. His friends came to the house and he carried me among them saying, 'This is Johnnyboy – he's my favourite.' He gave me money and said he'd take us to the pictures or the zoo.

But before long I noticed the old atmosphere creeping back. My dad and his friends would gather in one of the rooms to talk. My uncles would stay away, or not come as often as before. When I asked my dad if I could go out to play, he snapped, 'Yes, but don't you be wandering or climbing, do you hear?' Before I could answer Maw or Ma had said, 'Don't talk to him like that, Andy, you'll frighten him.' He turned to them and said, 'How the fuck can I be frightening him? I'm only telling him not to wander or climb any walls!'

I stared at the floor, my eyes full of tears. My dad noticed this and started shouting, 'What the fuck's the matter with you? Every time I talk to you you start crying.'

Ma said, 'It's no wonder he's crying – every time you speak to him you raise your voice.'

He said I was crying for nothing; he put his finger to my lips and said, 'Button it – stop your fucking crying or I'll give you something to cry about!'

I could feel the fear coming back. I wanted to get away from him. Sitting in my room I could hear Ma crying and saying that she couldn't take any more of his picking on me for the least little thing, and Maw saying, 'That poor wee soul is going to end up having a nervous breakdown and never recover.'

34

They argued for some time before Ma came in and sat down beside me. She hugged me and told me not to be frightened, that I could go out to play and that my dad said I was to be in by seven. Maw gave me sixpence for sweets and I went out to play.

Everything I did seemed wrong to my dad, and yet everybody else was doing the same things. One time a pal of my dad's came to the window and laughed at the antics of his own son. My dad called down to me saying, 'Go on, Johnnyboy, let him see how good a climber you are,' but after his friend had left, he said to me, 'What have I fucking warned you about climbing with your new shoes on?'

I didn't know if I was coming or going. I started fidgeting and biting my nails. Dad would grab me by his thumb and forefinger and shake me back and forward by my jumper, saying, 'You had better learn to behave yourself because I'm getting fucking sick and tired of warning you. Any more of your nonsense and you'll be in a home! Do you understand what I'm saying to you – or is it just going in one ear and out the other?' Sometimes he'd get me when I was alone and say, 'You bastard, I should have smothered you at birth – look at you!'

He'd come into my room when everyone else was in the living room, and threaten me. I'd be scared to shout to Ma and Maw, and he'd be scared in case they heard me crying. Sometimes Ma or Maw would hear me and come in, but he'd slip into the other room as if he had been there all the time. Ma would want to know what had made me cry, at which he'd appear at the door and say, 'What the fuck's he crying for now?' I'd be too scared to say anything.

Then Ma would say 'Has he been in here tormenting you, son?' Sometimes I'd nod my head, and she would crack up and say 'I'm leaving with my kids. I'm not taking any more of this – he's only a kid and you're treating your flesh and blood like an animal.

My dad said that I was going off my head and should see a doctor.

Ma shouted, 'It's you who's off his head and you're trying to knock my son off his head, but I won't allow it – you'll go to the gaol first.' Ma would say to me, in front of him, 'The next time he hits you don't be afraid to shout to me.' I would hear them arguing and Ma shouting, 'I don't know why I married you.'

But he would always find a way of getting me on my own, when he would growl, 'You see the trouble you've caused? You bastard. Before you split the family up I'll make sure you're in a fucking home.' When no one was about he would call me a 'hawk-eyed bastard'; say it was impossible that I belonged to him, and that I'd be wise to stay out of his way. Ma said my dad's trouble was that he'd done too long in gaol.

My teacher kept coming up to my desk and moving my pencil from my left to my right hand. But it didn't feel right, and it always ended up in my left hand. She'd be back again, and once more the pencil was moved from my left hand to my right. I was the only one in the class who wrote with his left hand, she said. I knew she didn't like me, and often found some excuse to nag or hit me, but now it was because I was writing with a hand I wasn't supposed to write with. She took to calling from her desk when she got fed up with coming up to me: 'Get that pencil in your other hand, Steele.'

I couldn't understand what I was doing wrong. What did it matter which hand I wrote with? Even in the middle of my work I was interrupted with, 'Get that pencil in your right hand!' I began to hate school and being the odd man out in class. Writing with what to me was my 'right' hand was looked upon as a handicap. Whenever Ma and Maw asked me how I was getting on at school I was afraid to tell them I was left-handed; I merely said I didn't like it, and would ask them to keep me off and let me do all the housework for them. But no way would they keep me off – they told me I needed to go to school for my learning. I noted that Jim and Lana and my ma all wrote with their right hands. I just sat in class, not day-dreaming, as teacher thought, but worrying. It was a bad experience for me and my only way of showing it was by dogging school, which got me into even more trouble. My school reports were terrible, as was my writing, and dogging school didn't help my learning. As a result I was way behind the rest of the class.

When I look back on it all I can honestly say that the best thing I did was to play truant: that was bad in itself, but it was easier than writing with my right hand. Once I was belted by my teacher for, she said, defying her and writing with my left hand. I hated school and that teacher. When I told Ma that she was picking on me, and Ma came to see my teacher, she said I was a nice boy, stroked my hair and called me John, but she hated me. Everyone else was called by their first names but she just referred to me as 'Steele', and when she called my name the whole class would turn round. She had been snide to me ever since my dad threatened her. He would sometimes say, 'Remember, if that teacher tries to take you down in front of the class, you've got my permission to break a chair over her head, and if you can't do that get on the first bus home and I'll put her into hospital.' I wouldn't have dreamt of talking back to her, never mind hit her over the head with a chair. I just dogged school instead.

Whenever I did so I would be scared to go home, because I knew that what I was doing was wrong. If I thought my family knew that I had been playing truant I'd go home and listen at the door. Sometimes I'd hear my dad say, 'Just wait till he comes home – the bastard's not been at school, and he's been getting pocket money.' That would be enough for me – I'd be away like a shot.

If my dad was in when the school board or the police came to the door about me, he would rant and rave that he was going to take the skin off my arse with his belt. But before he got the chance Ma would say, 'You're too hard on him – I'll see him.' She would take me into my room. She'd pretend to be angry, and shout and hit the slipper on the wall, making believe she was hitting me. I'd howl as if it were me she was hitting, and when she heard my dad coming she'd stop hitting the wall and shout at me, 'Let that be a lesson to you – now

37

get into your bed.' He'd stand at the bedroom door saying she hadn't hit me hard enough.

Dogging school became a real habit with me and my pals. We'd meet at Parkhead Post Office, which was across the road from school, and break into shops that closed at lunchtime. The older boys said that this was the best time to do them as the shopkeepers had left the cash in the till, never imagining that anyone would break into their shops during the dinner hour. We'd go round the back and one of the smallest among us would squeeze through the bars and pass the money out. I was often used for this. We'd buy sweets and cigarettes, and the older boys would offer to teach us how to smoke. I'd smoke, but I couldn't inhale and it made me feel dizzy. People would stare at us, shaking their heads, and some told us to put the cigarettes out.

We'd go into the big stores like Lewis's or Woolworth's: the older boys would shoplift, and have us young ones watch for the store detectives. Occasionally we'd be chased – jumping over the counters was the best escape because the store detectives couldn't jump over them after us. In our panic to get away we'd run into people and knock them down. Sometimes some of us were caught and we'd be kept at the police station till our parents came for us. We'd sometimes give the police false names, hoping that after they'd booked us they'd let us go – and sometimes they did. If I gave them my real name they always asked me if I was Andy Steele's son, and I'd be pointed out by the sergeant to the other policemen. Sometimes they told me that my dad was a fucking animal and that I'd end up in prison, too.

I was always terrified when my dad came to take me home. He'd walk into the police station with that angry look on his face, and I'd go out biting my nails and looking at everyone except my dad. As soon as he saw me he'd say, 'Has anyone in here laid a finger on you? Don't you be frightened to say if they've hit you or hassled you.' The police would say that none of them had touched me. Da was ready to start shouting at the police if he thought someone had hit me.

Once we had left the police station he would say that I was

going to pay for what I'd done. On one particular occasion I was in the back of the car, his pal was driving and my dad was sitting in the passenger seat. Every so often he'd turn around and hit me hard across the face with the back of his hand.

'Do you know what's going to happen to you?' he growled. I knew it was the belt across the bare arse. His friend turned and said to him: 'For God's sake Andy, don't hit the kid like that.' When we got home he told Jim and Lana that the first one to find his belt would get a shilling. They pretended to look for it while Ma shouted, 'You're not lifting that belt to my boy.' Dad found the belt himself and removed my trousers with some difficulty, as I was trying to hold them on and screaming. He lashed me until I was black and blue, bleeding in the legs, back and belly. Ma tried to jump on his back but he shook her off, then hit her as well. Eventually Ma grabbed me and carried me down to the street, screaming for someone to get the police. Some neighbours took us into their home. Ma kept crying and hugging me and saying that I'd be better off in a home before he killed me. One of the neighbours told us my dad had left the house and gone away in his car.

Back home, Ma placed me on her bed and looked at the welts on my body, while I lay there in a daze. I could only move very slowly because of the pain. My cousins asked me to come and stay with them next door. Ma said she would send me to my Aunt Ruby's for a while. But *he* came back and told Ma that if she went for the police she'd regret it.

I was terrified when I heard my dad was back. I cowered in a corner and begged Ma to keep me away from him. She told the others to pack our bags as we were leaving. She left the room to get some of our stuff together, and when she came back she took me by the hand into the living room. I panicked when I saw my dad, but Ma told me I would never be hit again and that I was to come in and close the door.

I heard someone crying and when I plucked up the courage to look I saw my dad sitting there with tears streaming down his face and his arms out towards me. My dad kept saying, to no one in particular, 'What have I done to my son?' He asked me to go to him. I looked at Ma and she gave me a nod. He turned to her and said, 'Margaret, I've lost my son. He won't forgive me – my own son can't even look at me.' He begged me to forgive him. I couldn't hold back for long, and before I knew it I was in his arms and the three of us were crying and telling each other that we loved each other the best in the world – and I knew we meant it. My dad told me that he was terrified I'd get put away and he didn't like me getting into trouble with the police; he hit me for my own good, but didn't mean to be cruel. He asked us if we still wanted to leave – we had every reason for doing so, but he'd rather we stayed. I can't really explain why it touched me to see my dad crying and saying how sorry he was for all he had done. When you think you hate and are terrified of someone, and then find yourself loving him, it's a new kind of love that you thought couldn't possibly exist.

I had to get kept off school till the bruises went away. My dad would look at my body, and say that the cuts must have been caused by the buckle of the belt. He kept saying that I was his favourite child, and that he loved me and didn't mean to hurt me.

My uncles used to send me to bed for more serious things than my dad – for breaking someone's windows, or dogging school and stealing. Sometimes I lay in bed for days on end, or even a week or more. Whenever I was put to bed my dad or my uncles would hide my clothes so that I couldn't run away. I'd get Lana or Jim to look for my clothes. If they'd been hidden next door at Uncle John's, one of my cousins would slip them along to me. I would sneak out the front door while Lana and Jim were in the living room, or I'd hang from the window ledge and drop down into the garden. If Lana and Jim couldn't find my clothes they'd give me someone else's, and I'd run off in one uncle's trousers with the legs rolled up and another's shirt.

I'd wander about the streets after I'd run away. Some gardens had rhubarb in them and when I was hungry I'd steal some and stick it up my jumper. I always loved it when darkness fell. As a kid I'd heard stories about ghosts and monsters lurking about at night. Ma used to send me or Jim to the midden to empty the rubbish bin, and if it was dark I'd be scared to go into the back court, so I'd empty the bin on the bottom landing rather than go to the midden. The first time I did this the neighbours wondered who had dumped the rubbish outside their doors. Ma asked me why I'd done it, and I said I was frightened to go into the back court by myself. One of my uncles remarked that I wasn't frightened when I ran away from home and wandered about in the dark.

When I got tired and cold I'd go round the closes looking for door mats and make myself a bed in some field or on a spare bit of ground. But like all kids who run away from home I'd get scared and lonely, and would head for home or be glad that I'd been caught. If I was going to give myself up I'd slip up the stairs in the wee small hours and sit on the top-flat landing where I could hear my family going in and out. I'd wait till I could hear Ma's voice on the landing and then I'd start coughing so that she would hear me and come and get me. Ma would prevent anyone else from hitting me, but she would skelp me herself and say that I was causing her a lot of worry by running away. She'd show me her hands and say, 'Look, Johnnyboy, that's nerves, son.' Her hands would be shaking like leaves in a storm. Maw told me that I'd end up losing Ma if anything happened to me, and beg me not to run away again.

I went on dogging school and stealing, and I started pickpocketing with my pals. Ma got to know about this and she and my uncles went to the older guys' houses and told them to stay away from me. My uncles threatened their dads, saying that if their sons didn't stop taking me stealing they'd break their legs.

One day my dad was laying a new carpet in our living room when he found a summons which stated that I was to appear at the juvenile court for theft. He went crazy, waving the summons about and shouting, 'You told me this animal was behaving himself!' Ma never told him if I got into trouble, as she knew he would show me no mercy, but this time it was different. He tried to strangle me. His face was all screwed up, there were noises coming from him, and he kept pressing and shaking me like a rag doll. I remember Ma banging on the ceiling with a brush pole, hoping to alert the neighbours. Da kept his hand round my throat and dragged me into the scullery. I can remember seeing other people's hands around my dad's arms, trying to pull him away from me. He must've let me go, because I fell on to the floor. I could hear screaming and banging on the scullery door. He grabbed me again and I heard him say, 'This is what I should've done to you at birth, bastard!' He opened the oven door and was trying to force me in. He got my head and shoulders into the oven and was trying to close the door even though my legs and my back were hanging out. As I passed out I felt hands grabbing me and pulling me out of the oven.

When I came to I was in bed. Ma was lying beside me, staring at the ceiling. Maw was sitting on a chair, and some of my uncles and aunts were there. Ma looked round at me when she realised I was conscious and said in a sad voice, 'What are we going to do, son?' Everyone in the room went out without speaking. When we were alone Ma told me we'd have to get away from my dad, and that he would never step over our door again as long as she lived.

One day Uncle Atty came home, but without his uniform on. He was at home with Maw and me when there was knocking on the door. It was dark, so when I answered the door I took Major the dog with me. Three men were standing there in white coats. They asked me who was in the house and I told them. They pushed past me and looked in each room till they found Maw and Atty in the living room. Major was barking and growling at the three strangers. Atty stood up and the three men jumped on him, kicking and punching and dragging him out of the door. Maw kept moving her head about, listening to the thudding sounds coming from Atty's body; she threw ornaments in what she thought was the direction of the fight, calling them bastards and animals for kicking her son. In her panic she walked about with her arms outstretched, knocking down lamps and ornaments, feeling for Atty and the strangers but she was nowhere near them. I could see the fear in her face when she bumped into walls and stood there helplessly, calling the three strangers every name imaginable. They eventually got Uncle Atty out of the house, and I picked up the lamps and ornaments and put them back.

It was only later that I realised that Uncle Atty was in a mental hospital. I have been told that while he was in the army a gun backfired on him, which was why he needed psychiatric care. He was sometimes given shock treatment. His attitude to us never changed – when he came home from the hospital on weekend visits he would spend all his money on us kids and was forever buying us sponge cakes and bottles of ginger.

Ma had another baby – a little girl named Brenda, who was born on 9 March 1963. I gave her some money, placing it in her tiny hand and wishing her luck and a happy life. So there were now five of us – and still I was the only one who was getting into trouble. My dad was over the moon when Brenda was born. It was the first time he'd been present at a birth.

My dad would come and go, and Uncle Atty would come and go. One day Uncle Atty came home from the hospital on a weekend visit. He told Maw that he had lit a coal fire in the bedroom. At this my other uncles ran into the bedroom and Uncle Tam put his hand up the chimney and pulled down explosives and detonators – one of which went off in his hand. Atty hadn't a clue that there'd be anything like that up the chimney, and neither had Ma or Maw.

Whenever I was in the house alone I'd move all the furniture about, like a miniature architect. Maw said I wasn't to do it again as it was far too heavy for me to lift on my own and I would strain my heart, but I went on moving it around.

Some Sundays we'd go to Uncle Alex's house for dinner. This was an important event for Ma and Maw and my uncles and aunts, but I simply looked forward to playing with my cousins Alex and Christine. Aunt Chrissie would make a huge meal but it was agreed that I need only eat a little. My Uncle Alex had done a prison sentence during the War – fourteen days in Barlinnie Gaol for not closing his black-out curtains properly.

One year, just a couple of days after Christmas, I got out of bed very early. My toy gun had fallen down the inside of one of the armchairs in the living room. Everyone was asleep: Ma, Maw, Lana and wee Joseph were sleeping in the living room, me and Jim in the bedroom and my Uncle Tam and his wife in the other bedroom. It was quite dark, but I didn't put the light switch on in case I woke someone up. I tilted the chair back and felt underneath. I could feel my toy gun behind the canvas-like covering. I got a bread knife and slashed the canvas, then I tilted the chair on its back and put my arm in, but I couldn't find it. I struck a match and put it through the rip in the canvas, hoping I would be able to see my gun. The next thing I knew the chair was on fire. I was terrified and didn't know what to do. I looked at Ma and Maw lying asleep in bed but I couldn't move. The flames were running up the wall and licking the ceiling. There were decorations hanging everywhere and they were starting to burn.

Finally Jim ran in and got everyone out of bed. Christmas balloons were bursting with the heat, and the ceiling had caught fire. Uncle Tam ran naked into the living room and managed to get the armchair down the stairs and into the back court. By the time the fire brigade arrived everybody was out in the street trying to figure out what had happened.

The firemen asked me to explain and I told them that I had been looking for my toy gun. I thought I'd get a terrible beating, but instead I got a telling off. Ma said that I was suffering from shock and to hit me wouldn't be right. It was a couple of days before we got back into our house.

I was nine years old when I made my first court appearance. I'd already been in front of a children's panel, where social workers decided what was to be done with children in trouble. They sat round a large table and from time to time they'd look at me; some of them would smile, while others looked over the top of their glasses in a way that scared me. I was so frightened that I found it hard to answer their questions and looked at the ground while Ma nudged me under the table with her foot. I couldn't understand what they were talking about.

This time, I was charged with theft. Ma inspected me before we went into court. She took her head-scarf off and spat on it and rubbed my face and combed my hair until she was sure I was spick and span. She told me not to worry too much, as she would ask the judge to give me a warning and tell him I was a good boy, if I promised that I would behave myself, and that I'd never do it again. I kept praying that I wouldn't be sent to a home.

Courts can terrify kids – they certainly did me. They have a strange atmosphere, and everything is very quiet: it was great to hear someone coughing or rustling a piece of paper. I kept feeling I was going to faint. Men in black gowns were sitting round a table, reading. Occasionally they'd whisper and look over to me and I'd quickly look away. Every so often a door opened and someone walked into the court and whispered something to someone. When the judge came in we were told to stand, and when he was seated we were allowed to sit.

I was given two years probation. When we left the court I was so excited that I skipped all the way home. Maw told me God must have answered her prayers, but everyone said that the next time I got into trouble I'd be put away. Uncle John told me that he had been put in a home when he was a little boy, and that the monks who worked there beat him up for the least little thing. What he told me was enough to make me never want to get into trouble again.

Though I went on getting into trouble and stealing and dogging school, I never wanted to do these things. I was so mixed up and emotionally upset that I would wish I was dead. Whenever someone asked me what my problem was, I'd tell them I didn't know. I'd think about the courtroom and wish that they had sent me away to a home, even if it was for ever. I hated the world, and I'd be off again, wandering the streets on my own, more lost than anything else.

Ma got a letter from the Education Board saying that I was to be transferred to a special school that catered for backward children and cripples. To me this made no difference as it was still school, but it made a difference to my dad. He told me I was an embarrassment to him, and that the dog was more welcome in his house than I was. I started to cry, but was told to 'button it'. He pulled my clothes off, threw me on to the bed and closed the curtains, shutting out the daylight and leaving me alone in the dark. I could hear him playing with Lana, calling her his little darling. There were times I lay in my bed after my dad had given me a beating and I would think of him and me being happy some day and playing football together and him loving me and me loving him. – I would picture this and I'd get a strange feeling that would have me crying with joy.

4 GARTHAMLOCK

When I was nine we moved house to a place called Garthamlock, on the outskirts of Glasgow – a housing estate completed in the early 1960s. The buildings were three storeys high and each house had a veranda. We had three bedrooms, a bathroom, a scullery, a living room and a very long hall. The first thing that I noticed was the number of our close, which was 999. Ma said she thought it would bring us bad luck.

I found new pals there almost immediately, and we went bird-hunting and looking for foxes. Garthamlock was great – it was something new, and I hardly gave a thought to Carntyne. There were a lot of fields nearby, and some farms. I'd never seen a farm before, except when I went to visit my dad in prison, and I'd watch the cattle and play in the haystacks. I even got a job helping the farmer.

The Brown Family lived on the floor below. They had three sons and a daughter, Katrina, my first girlfriend. Next door was the Smith family. There were four girls, and one was as wild as a boy. Jean would play football with us and come climbing, and she could fight like a boy. Then there were the Fergusons, the Smalls and the Gallachers, and I liked them all.

The quarry near our house had cliffs as high as seventy feet, which we kids often went climbing over. Some of the older guys would leap off the cliff face into the murky water below, while us younger ones hooted with laughter. To us they seemed like heroes. One of them, John Henry, was about fourteen years old, but he had a beard and looked twice his age. Everyone liked John – especially our mas, who could depend on him to find us young ones and bring us home for our dinner. He knew all our haunts and dens, and he'd search and give chase. He couldn't catch us all; we'd scatter in every direction, but John would have others hiding in the long grass and they'd pursue half a dozen fleeing youngsters. They'd tickle us till our sides almost burst with laughter, and throw us up in the air as though we were balls.

In Carntyne I used to wear glasses. I hated them and would throw them away, but I always got a new pair. I was made to wear them in the house, but as soon as I went out I put them in my pocket. I had what the doctors called a 'lazy' eye. When I was nine I went to hospital to have it straightened. Miss Wright came to visit me in hospital and the other kids were amazed to learn that she was my probation officer; they'd never heard of such a thing. Ma liked her very much and she would tell me to be thankful that I had Miss Wright as my probation officer. She was forever buying me presents and asking me to behave myself and stick in at school. I don't know how many times I let her down without meaning to.

In the summer I went camping with my pals. We used to sleep in the back court in a tent – the back courts there were safer and cleaner than those in Carntyne, and the gardens were all looked after – and the Stevensons took us camping once to Loch Ness and showed me how to use a fishing rod. I'd never been so happy in my life. Jackie and George Stevenson and I would roam everywhere and have great fun. We'd write each other notes to give to our girlfriends and build pigeon huts or rabbit pens – everything but steal.

One day I was playing with my girlfriend Katrina, and she bet I couldn't climb a huge thin tree in our neighbour's garden. I grabbed the opportunity to show her that I was as good a climber as any, so up I went, and Katrina followed up behind me. We were having a good laugh, but before long the owner of the tree appeared below us in a fit of rage. Terrified and crying, we both came down, snapping twigs in the process, which seemed to madden him even more. When my feet touched the ground he pounced on me, putting my arm up my back so that I screamed with pain, and marched me up the path. As we entered the close my Uncle Billy appeared, raging at the man for hurting me. Billy attacked him and they went crashing into the hallway. The neighbour needed stitches as a result of a wound that he received in the fight.

Each week I went to visit Uncle Atty in the Gartloch Mental Hospital nearby. I loved him very much and I begged Ma to let him live with us. I was too young to understand that hospital was the only place for Atty.

One summer day I set off with Broono to visit Uncle Atty. Atty took us for a walk through the woods and showed us where the birds' nests were. When we got back to the hospital grounds he told us to wait while he went to get us our bus fare home. As soon as he had disappeared Broono, who was a scrap collector, climbed up on to a building and threw down some copper tubing, which he said he'd sell to the scrap man. He hid the copper from Atty. Atty said he couldn't get us our bus fare, but that we could borrow his pal's bike, and we promised to bring it back in good condition.

We rode home together, with Broono on the bar, hugging his copper tubing with one arm and holding on fast with the other. Suddenly a car came up behind us pumping its horn, and almost ran us over. We knew it was trouble and Broono jumped clear and bolted across the fields, still clutching his copper tubing. The bike toppled and I fell with it, hurting myself. A man grabbed me and pulled me into the car.

'You stole my bike!' he shouted at me, poking at me with his finger, and he drove me back to the hospital.

There he put me in a locked ward with some mental patients to wait for the police. Some of the patients began to touch me on the arms and face as if to make sure I was real. I'd been in wards before but I'd never experienced anything like this. The patients were all shapes and some had crazy, staring eyes: they were dangerous to themselves, if not to others, which was why they were in the locked ward. One was laughing out the side of his mouth which was distorted. No sooner had the nurse chased them away than they came back, laughing and staring and asking for cigarettes – two loonies were arguing over a cigarette butt, fighting like kids. The windows and doors were locked and barred – maybe they were going to keep me here for ever?

Male nurses were handing out medication to the patients, some of whom refused to take theirs and had to be coaxed or forced. All of them wore ill-fitting clothes and huge slippers that were clearly too big for their feet. One of them pretended to play a guitar: he kept his eye on me, as if to say, 'They're not fooling me – I know you're not a patient!'

Eventually the police arrived. They towered above me with their little black books out, taking my name and address and questioning me about the theft of a nurse's bike! A nurse told me if I didn't admit to the theft, and tell the police who the other boy was, I'd be kept in the hospital. When I told the truth they said, 'Try again sonny'. So I told a lie and they never questioned it.

As we went up the close, they made me point out my cousin to them. Poor Broono turned chalk white when the two big policemen caught hold of him and took him up to our house. Broono was in a state of shock – he would get a terrible beating from his dad when he went home. I wanted to tell them that Uncle Atty must have stolen the bike and given it to us. When the police left I told my ma the truth, but we didn't tell the court as we wanted to protect Uncle Atty. In court Broono and I pleaded guilty to the theft of a bike we never stole. I was given a six-months deferred sentence. Uncle Atty was never told of the incident, and I was warned never to take anything from him again unless I was sure it was his.

While we were waiting to go into court a man came out calling the judge an old bastard. A fight broke out, with the public cheering the guy, and some shouting curses at the police. Broono and I took the opportunity to jump up and down on a policeman's hat until our mas shouted for us to get off.

I still had to go to the special school. I hated it, and wanted to go to the same school as my pals. Every morning a grey van would pick me up. It was known throughout the city, and it was embarrassing to be seen in it. The pupils at that school were like outcasts, and were treated as such. Looking out of the van windows, I felt like a prisoner. I couldn't help but skip school because of the hate I had for it. There were kids there with callipers and wheelchairs, and others who acted as if they were really crazy and could hardly speak. But it was the school and most of the teachers I hated, not the kids. My pal James Morrison had been sent there because he was thought to be backward in his education. The kids in callipers and wheelchairs and the mongols got a hard time from the other kids, and James and I would defend them and get into fights for them. I still dogged school, and I was given a truant card that had to be signed every day by the teacher to let my parents know I was at school. Often I got someone else to sign it, copying the teacher's signature, till I learned to do it myself.

One day Danny Brown and I ran away when we learned that the school-board inspector had told our parents we hadn't been at school all week. We hitched lifts and skipped on to the back of lorries when they stopped at traffic lights, not knowing where they were going, and stole from fruit shops when we were hungry. We knew the police would be looking for us, so every time we saw a police car we ran in panic, leaping hedges if they were small enough and even hiding under parked cars. We ended up in a place called Bo'ness, twenty-odd miles outside Glasgow.

People gave us strange looks – we were filthy after sleeping in a field in cardboard boxes. A police car pulled up and called me over. I turned and ran, almost knocking down an old man who hit me with his walking-stick in return. The police said we looked like two miners, and they seemed quite amused about it.

In the police station we told them why we had run away. They said they had run away from home when they were our age and that they regretted it. They didn't lock us up in a cell but let us sit about the bar, and one of them played cards with Danny. I couldn't play so one of the police showed me the cells. One was full of lost-and-found items, dozens of bikes all crammed in. That night Ma came to take us home, and it was lectures all the way.

One day Dad said to me, 'Right, you're going to the shops to buy a couple of newspapers.' I was about to open the door when his hand fell on my shoulder and he pressed my face to the glass in the window frame. 'It's fucking raining,' he shouted. 'Are you mad, wanting to go out there without a fucking coat on?' Before I could answer he picked me up by my jumper and threw me on to my bed. He said that if I wanted to get out of bed I would have to apologise to him.

I could hear Ma calling him an animal; Lana was frightened and crying, Jim was sitting with his lips glued together, and Maw was walking into walls in her panic and rage. She said, pointing at a wall and thinking my dad was in that direction, 'You're making Johnnyboy's life a misery, all you do is pick on him and send him to his bed.' To which he replied, 'You've no say here – I married your daughter, not your family.' He came quietly into my room and said, 'See what you've caused? You're not wanted here, I don't want you!'

I wouldn't say I was sorry so I lay in bed for over a week. It was scorching hot and I looked out of my window at my friends enjoying themselves.

Sometimes the police would take me aside and ask me questions about my dad and where he was, or question me about break-ins in the area. When I told my dad this he'd go mad and write to MPs and the Chief Constable about my being harassed by police because of his criminal activities. My dad told me to get their numbers if possible and he'd take the necessary steps. Once I was taken to see the Assistant Chief Constable about being harassed after my dad had complained to him. I was taken to his office where he listened and *lectured* me.

I enjoyed stealing in the same way as my pals enjoyed football: it was becoming just like a sport. One day I tried to break open the back door of the dairy, which had closed for the afternoon. A lot of my pals were playing football at the back of the shop. They thought I was crazy and warned me that I'd get caught, but this didn't deter me. They played on as I started forcing the door with a steel chisel.

It was difficult to graft the door with everyone around me chasing a ball – every time the ball hit the door I got a fright. I was doing quite well when a car sped round the corner. Instinctively I turned and threw the chisel aside. The car screeched to a halt and two plain-clothes policemen leapt out, grabbed hold of me and demanded to know what I was up to. They checked the damaged door and then they took me into the car with them. All my pals were looking in through the car window at me.

'It wisnae me, mister,' were my first words. They asked me who I was, and when I told them they said they might have known. They seemed more concerned about Ma than about me or the shop. 'Don't you think your poor ma has had enough trouble with you and your dad?' one of them asked. I think it was for this reason that they let me go. I never did tell Ma. How could I have done?

Walking towards my pals who were standing nearby waiting to see what would happen to me, life felt better. It was a feeling I had had before, but not often: it can only be described as being given a new awareness. I no longer hated the game of football; in fact, I started playing when the police left. But I don't know, the feeling never lasted long enough and I would be at it again soon.

5 CRIME, PUNISHMENT AND PALS

One night, when I must have been twelve, I was approached by John Henry and another of the older boys, John, who palled around with my brother Jim. They asked me to go in through a small window for them and open the front door of a house and let them in. I was frightened at first because we weren't sure if someone was in the house, but they needed me because I was so small and skinny and they promised me money and cigarettes. They lifted me up to the window ledge and helped me through.

Once inside I was terrified. I could hear the two Johns hissing through the window for me to hurry: I'd nothing to fear, they said, for if anyone was in there, they'd kick the door in and beat them up. I opened the room door slowly and it creaked and groaned, like in a creepy movie. The silence in the house was terrible and I was haunted by the fear of someone grabbing me. I was so scared that I wet my pants; I could feel the hot urine running down my leg. I wished I'd never come in here and prayed to God to get me out. They were knocking on the window for me to hurry and open the door. Once I was in the hall and couldn't hear them at the window it was even worse. A car tooted outside, and I fell over something. I thought I must have run into someone in the dark, and lay there in a stupor, too scared to cry or even move.

'Hurry up, Johnnyboy!' I heard John Stuart saying through a window. His family were very friendly with mine; if his ma knew he'd sent me in here she'd beat the living daylights out of him. I got up and moved towards the front door. My fingers trembled for the lock and at first failed to find it; then the two Johns came in and ransacked the house, while I stood by and watched.

As soon as they had finished they took me with them to a fence who bought almost anything from crooks. So that the fence wouldn't see or recognise them it was decided that I would sell him a fur coat while they waited in the back court. I was to ask for a hundred pounds. When the fence came to the door I was standing there almost covered by a huge imitation fur coat. He was a small man with a foreign name – it was rumoured he was a Jew whose whole family had been slaughtered by the German SS.

'I give you five shillings,' he said as he gave the coat a thorough going-over. I told him I was to accept no less than a hundred pounds. He laughed and closed the door in my face, repeating, 'Five shillings.' I told the two Johns, who eventually went to the door themselves, arguing over a price and even threatening to beat the fence up for trying to cheat them. But five shillings it was. I was given a shilling, with which I bought two cigarettes.

One of the Garthamlock beat cops was nicknamed 'Nero' by the older boys in the area – he was forever chasing us kids and he would often arrest us for breaches of the peace or loitering. He came to the house and arrested me for the break-in. He said all the Steeles were thieves, and that I was a thief and would be locked away in due course.

Nero disliked me and harrassed me for things I knew nothing about. He asked me to plead guilty to things I'd never done, saying it would go better for me in court if he could tell the judge that I had been co-operative. When I refused he'd slap and kick me. On this occasion he took me to his office – John Henry was already there – and said I'd best plead guilty as they knew everything, even about the old fence. I denied knowing what he was talking about, and Nero cuffed me around the ears and warned me not to lie.

John Stuart was eventually caught as well. An identification parade was set up and the fence was there to pick us out. We were charged with house-breaking, and I was remanded by the court for approved school, social and background reports. Ma was in court and waved to me before I was taken away to the dungeons below. Once in my cell I cried my eyes out.

Later that afternoon the remands were taken from the court to Larchgrove remand home for boys. They took us there in a big black bus known as the meat wagon. It was full of kids, the oldest of whom was fifteen and the youngest eight. I'd taken my first ride in the meat wagon when I was ten and I remembered it well . . . I'd heard a lot about Larchgrove. Some of the older boys were talking about it and how they had been there plenty of times and weren't scared to go back. I was amazed at these kids and was dying to ask them about the place, but I was scared to talk with the two turnkeys sitting next to me. The meat wagon had three wooden benches in it, two up the side and one along the top, and we were all squashed in together. I fell off my seat when the meat wagon turned a corner and everybody laughed at me, even the two turnkeys.

There weren't any windows in the meat wagon, so we couldn't see where we were. Eventually we stopped and the turnkeys opened the door. I noticed that the meat wagon had reversed up against two other open doors, and that men in grey jackets were waiting for us to come out. They marched us into a square and made us strip off all our clothes and put on institutional clothing instead. I was given a pair of brown cord shorts that came down to my knees, a khaki shirt that was too big, a pair of grey socks and sandals. We were told not to talk. A kid standing next to me was crying and kept saying that he wanted to go home. I was about to start crying myself until I saw him being slapped about by one of the turnkeys, who shouted at him that he wasn't the hard case he thought he was. He said, 'I've got to laugh when I see you horrible lot coming in here for the first time and listen to you crying for your mas.'

One of the older guys who was standing next to me whispered to me that I ought to ask the turnkey for my 'coco' ticket. I didn't know what a coco ticket was, but I did what he said. The turnkey slapped me about the head and told me not to be smart, and everyone laughed.

We were marched away up a flight of stairs into a room with two long wooden tables, and told to sit on wooden benches and wait for our tea. I could hear other boys coming up the stairs, and saw them pass our dining room going to their own. They were all dressed like we were and they looked in as they passed to see if they knew any of the new arrivals. When tea was served I didn't eat anything but watched the other boys scoffing their food down. When they realised I didn't want mine they all fought over it. We were allowed to talk here, and we all asked each other what we were in for: it was usually shoplifting or stealing cars or house-breaking, pickpocketing or running away from home. We all whispered when it came to asking if anyone had any cigarettes.

After tea we were taken to our dormitories till six o'clock, when the turnkeys came back. Then we were taken into a gymnasium. Over a hundred boys were sitting about talking about everything and anything, boasting about how many times they'd been there or how much money they'd stolen. We were made to sit in rows and the turnkeys came round and started splattering white cream on our hair. It was nicknamed 'jungle juice', and we were told to rub it into our scalps. Then we were taken off for showers, and back to our dorms and bed. I couldn't believe it when a turnkey walked up to me and said, 'Put your bed down there beside the door.' Under his arm was a canvas affair about five feet long, with a metal frame and four very small legs. All the other beds looked like hospital beds and were made of steel. I thought the turnkey was joking, but he dropped the bed at my feet and walked away. We talked till lights out; a red light was left on all night so that the night watchman could see us and keep a count.

When I thought everybody was asleep I put my head under the blankets and cried my eyes out. For the first time in my life I asked myself why I was getting into trouble, but I didn't know why. When I stopped crying I lay in my bed thinking about Ma and Maw and the family and all the good times we had – never once did I think of the bad times.

I heard the night watchman come in and look about. As soon as he had left I got up and looked out to see where he had gone. I could see him walking down a long corridor waving his flashlight. He turned a corner and disappeared. I took a good look round the dorm and noticed that all the windows were made of cast iron and were so small that I couldn't get out of them even if I removed a pane of glass. The windows only opened a couple of inches. Other boys were up now; some were smoking, others were talking quietly, or had gone into other dorms to speak to their pals. Someone would always be watching for the night watchman: when he reappeared word would get passed through all the dorms in soft whispers. If the night watchman was drinking he would only appear occasionally and we would smoke or try to escape or have pillow fights. Sometimes during the night you could hear other kids being brought in by the police.

The part of the building I was in was called the 'new' wing, and was for the youngest offenders. The men who ran Larchgrove were social workers. They were called turnkeys by all the boys, but face-to-face with one we'd call him 'Sir'. We'd hear them talking and whistling as they came up the corridor, and when they reached the dorms they'd shout at us to get up and pull the blankets off. That first morning I was terrified when I discovered I had wet my camp bed. The floor all around me was soaking and the urine had spread along the highly polished floor. My pyjamas were soaking and clung to me when I stood up. A turnkey came over to my bed and felt it and shouted, 'Here's one.' I was going to deny it when I heard other turnkeys shouting, 'Here's another' and 'Here's another', till eventually there were about a dozen of us. The turnkeys told us to carry our sheets with us into the shower room. After showering in lukewarm water we were marched back to our dorms to make our beds and clean the floor. We were then lined up by our beds and the turnkeys came round for the morning inspection. A new friend, Hal, showed me how my bed had to be made.

After inspection we were all marched in silence and in single file to the gymnasium, where we were counted; then we were marched to the dining rooms. If anyone was caught talking the turnkeys would shout, 'Shut up, thing!' – and if whoever was talking didn't shut up we had to stand where we were till there was silence. At times like this it was almost impossible to keep absolutely quiet. Some boys would be letting out nervous laughs, while others talked out of the sides of their mouths to their pals. And then it would be, 'Shut up, you horrible lot!' The turnkeys would march up and down, looking each boy in the eye as they did so. If they caught someone talking they'd drag him out of the line and into the head turnkey's office, where he would get a leather belt across his backside; we could all hear the smack of the belt, and the boy howling for his parents. It put fear into everyone. The boy would come out holding his backside and the turnkeys would march up and down, staring at us and asking if anyone else wanted the same. Nobody was stupid enough to say yes.

After breakfast we were marched back to the gymnasium. New arrivals were taken down a long, highly polished corridor and into the sick bay, where an Irish matron examined us, checking for lice and rashes and asking lots of questions. Other people then asked us our names, addresses, dates of births, how many were in our families; after which we were taken to our classes.

The teachers were all turnkeys, and they too asked all sorts of questions. All the classrooms had huge windows that didn't open, and the doors were locked. If anyone needed the toilet he was let out and watched over by a turnkey. Hal and I would sit together whenever we could and talk about escaping and going to London. Like most villains, Hal was another mammy's boy.

All I wanted to do was escape and go home. Almost every week boys would try to escape. Some would, without warning, pick up their wooden desks, throw them through the window, and try to follow after them. I was in a classroom once when someone tried to throw his chair through the window and it bounced back, hitting the boy on the head. He got dragged away to the solitary cell.

At recreation we were allowed five little stones to play with.

We had to find them ourselves. We would put them in the palms of our hands and throw them up and try to catch them on the back of our hands, and then throw them back on to our palms. We played this game night and day, every day!

One evening I was sitting in the gymnasium talking to a boy about running away when a turnkey called my name and told me I had a visitor. I thought that I was going to cry with sheer joy, I was so happy. I ran back and told the boy I'd been talking to that I had a visitor – it made me feel more important than saying that my family had come to see me. When boys' names were called for their visitors everyone would be silent: there was no laughing or talking – each one of us hoped his name would be called.

And there Ma was, all dressed up to see me. I saw her taking sweets from her bag and placing them next to her. As I walked into the visiting-room one of the turnkeys shouted, 'Visitor for John Steele!' Ma put her hand up, and the turnkey motioned me towards her.

It was great to see Ma. I felt like throwing my arms around her and clinging to her, but there were too many people around and I knew the turnkeys would see me. She told me she was worrying herself to death about me – and was even more worried in case I ran away and got into more trouble. I told her I'd never get into trouble again if she got me out of there. Ma looked at my clothes and said I looked like a tinker. She made me eat the bars of chocolate she had brought, and gave me a bundle of comics to read. She asked what the turnkeys were like: I told her they were always shouting and slapping us, and she said that if they laid a hand on me the wrong way she would personally come up and wipe the floor with them. It made me laugh to imagine my wee ma fighting with all these big men.

When it was time to leave, Ma cuddled and kissed me and promised to come back soon. The turnkeys were all nice and spoke politely when our visitors were there, but I knew they'd change their attitudes as soon as the visitors left. I waved to Ma out the window until she was out of sight – and then I was brought down to earth again with, 'Right, you lot, strip off till we search you!'

Some older boys had been sent to Larchgrove for twenty-eight days by the courts. They were 'trusties', and were allowed to work in the garden or be sent on errands by the turnkeys, usually to buy cigarettes. Sometimes they would scrounge cigarettes for themselves from people in the streets and hide them in the linings of their trousers and share them with their pals; other times they ran away with the turnkeys' money.

Another new pal in my dorm was called Gak. He was very tall for his age, with red hair and freckles on his face, and anyone he didn't like he called a 'sneak'. He got blamed for things by the turnkeys because of his size – he'd often trip over his own feet, he was that clumsy, but in a funny sort of way. He had been here before, and at night, when I was lying in bed feeling sorry for myself, Gak would prance about the dorm and say, 'Don't let any of these sneaks get you down, boys. They don't worry me – nobody can ever worry you as long as you know he's nothing but a dirty sneak – and one thing the whole world hates is a sneak!' He'd go round all the beds asking us what we hated most in the world and we'd all say, 'A dirty sneak!'

'I'll bet anyone of yous a smoke that there's an old sneak sitting outside the dorm drinking whisky,' he'd say, his voice growing louder so that the night watchman could hear. As soon as the night watchman opened the door Gak would jump into bed and pretend to be asleep. On one occasion the watchman came into the dorm and shone his torch on our faces to see who was awake. I was under the blankets trying to hold my laugh in when he pulled the blankets down and shone his torch on my face. No matter how I tried, I couldn't stop laughing. He pulled me out of bed and accused me of shouting about him being drunk. He told me to stand by my bed until he told me to get into it again.

Just as he was going out the door Gak shouted, 'We all know you're a drunken old sneak.' The old watchman came running into the dorm like a madman. Gak was right – he had been drinking, and I could smell it on his breath. I wasn't laughing now. He went straight to another boy's bed and pulled him up and slapped him and made him stand beside his bed like me. Before he left he warned us that if anyone shouted again we'd all be standing beside our beds.

As the watchman was going down the corridor Gak rushed to the door and shouted after him, 'We don't mind you being a sneak, but don't try to frighten us!' – and then bolted for his bed before the watchman got back, puffing and panting and coughing up phlegm. As soon as he had got his breath back he came over to me, probably because I was the nearest, and started hitting me and demanding that I tell him who had shouted at him. I couldn't answer because I was crying, so he made us all get out of bed. When he went away we had pillow fights and carried on. We all forgot our worries in a strange sort of happiness that I find hard to explain. When the night watchman came back and saw the mess our dorm was in, blankets and pillows everywhere, he told us all to get into bed. As he was walking out the door, Gak shouted, 'Goodnight sneak!' but he kept walking and never said a thing.

When Ma and Lana talked about home I'd get a feeling in my belly knowing that I could be there instead of in a remand home. Lana laughed at my short trousers and my skinny legs and asked me when I was going to run away. Ma was angry and said to her that I wasn't going to. When Ma went to the toilet Lana told me she would get my clothes for me if I wanted to run away. She told me I was to whistle up to her window when the time came.

After the visit was over Ma said: 'Mind and behave yourself Johnnyboy and get out as soon as possible.' Lana was behind her and, reading her lips, I could make out that she was saying: 'Mind when you run away, I'll get your clothes.' I told them to tell everyone I was asking for them and we waved till they went out of sight.

There was an old turnkey who was nicknamed the Flipping Tit. He went about with an elastic band with a bit of leather on one end of it: he'd hold the bit of leather, stretch the elastic back and hit boys on the back of the ears with it and say to them, 'You flippin' tit' or 'Bird brain'. That was all he did – walk about with this elastic band of his, hitting boys with it. Everyone said he was crazy. The first time I got hit with his elastic band was when I was having a shower one morning. He came up behind me and hit me across the bare backside, saying, 'Get a move on, you flippin' tit,' and something about my wetting the bed. It stung where he hit, and he turned the water off and told me to get dried even though I was still covered in soap. As we walked past him to our dorms he said, 'Bird brains'.

One night I told my pals that I was going to run away. A small window pane in the shower room had been broken and was covered over with a bit of cardboard. I went under the shower and covered myself in soap, and while I was doing this my pal Homer threw my clothes out the window so that I wouldn't waste any time if I did manage to get out. As soon as one of the boys had managed to persuade the turnkey out of the shower room I ran out the shower, naked and covered from head to foot in soap. I jumped up on the window ledge, which was a good bit above my head, pulled the cardboard off and gave it to Homer. I put my legs out first while the others supported my body with their hands so that I wouldn't fall down as I wriggled and twisted, moving myself out very slowly. I was in agony, but I kept on wriggling till I got my backside out and then my back – I didn't know I was out till I hit the ground and heard Homer and the others shouting, 'Run, Johnnyboy.' Someone put the bit of cardboard back as I was pulling my clothes on.

At the other end of the garden was a sixteen-foot fence with spikes on top of it. I crept down below the dorm windows and headed for the fence, and I managed to climb over it without much difficulty. It wasn't till I was running across the road that I realised I had no shoes on.

My home was a mile or two away. I ran across the Edinburgh Road, through the Olivetti factory and the Queenslie housing estate till I came to the canal, which was only a couple of feet deep, and eight or ten feet wide. It was muddy and full of rats and bits of prams and old chairs.

63

It was pitch-black and I couldn't see any makeshift bridges across the canal. My feet were bleeding, and I was scared to wade in the water in case I poisoned my blood with the filth. I tore my shirt in two and wrapped the bits around my feet, making a crude pair of shoes, then I limped all the way to the real bridge next to the quarry. I was freezing, and I had to stop every so often to massage my feet. Once past the bridge I had a couple of hundred yards on waste ground before I could see my house. I lay in the grass for a while, waiting to see if the police would go to my house.

I could see Lana's bedroom light on and someone moving about, but I couldn't make out who it was. I could imagine everyone sitting watching the TV next to a warm fire, and I got that lonely feeling again sitting there in the cold with everyone looking for me. I thought about where everyone was. My dad was in gaol for firearms, my Uncle Bobby Campbell was doing time, Uncle Rab was in gaol, Uncle Atty was in the mental hospital only a mile away, Uncle Dinny was in gaol. And Dannyboy's Uncle Walter was serving twenty-one years for a bank robbery.

I made my way across the road and crawled through the hedge into the garden. I sat there for a while, straining my ears to hear Lana's voice. I threw some stones up to her window and eventually she came and pulled the curtain back. I stood up, hoping she would see me, but she closed the curtains again. So I threw some more till she came again, and this time she opened the window. Her face dropped when she saw it was me. We talked in whispers, and I asked her if she would get me some clothes. She threw them down to me along with some money, and asked me where I was going, but I couldn't tell her.

I went to the Ferrans' house, a couple of streets away, and tapped on Marie and Christine's bedroom window. When I said I was on the run, they told me to climb in and to be quiet about it so that their ma and dad wouldn't hear me. It's not that they would have thrown me out, but they would have tried to persuade me to go back or brought my ma round to get me, knowing that she would be worried about me.

Marie and Christine were the same age as me, and – unknown to their parents – they sheltered me all through my teens when I was on the run from homes. They made me something to eat and sat there wide-eyed as I told them about the remand home. Marie, who was the smartest of the three of us, said, 'I know they're cruel in there, but wouldn't it be better to give yourself up and get out as soon as possible and settle down?' She said that even though I was on the run I wasn't free. I knew this was true, but when I wasn't on the run I wasn't free either. All my young life was spent running away from something – bed, Carntyne, my dad, the world itself.

Christine said, 'Marie, stop trying to tell Johnnyboy to go back to that place – how would you like it if it were you?' The truth is that they were both right in what they were saying, but all I knew was that I was on the run again, and it didn't worry me. What did worry me was when I wasn't on the run. We talked for hours: I slept under one of their single beds, and we went on talking till we fell asleep.

Eventually I went home to Ma. They all stared at me as if they'd seen a ghost when I walked into the house. Ma was a nervous wreck not knowing where I was. She made me my supper and I told them about the turnkeys in Larchgrove hitting me for nothing. Ma was worried sick in case the police came and jailed her for hiding me in the house. She begged me to go back and said she would make sure they didn't hit me again. She said I couldn't run away all my life; I'd have to face the music sometime. Mr and Mrs Brown, our neighbours who lived down the stairs, tried to convince me to go back for my own good. I was terrified in case they took me back. One of the Browns' sons came up and held me to stop me from running away. I screamed that the turnkeys would hit me and put me in a cell, but Ma wouldn't believe there was a cell and said they couldn't lock wee boys away. I was taken down to Mr Brown's car, with his oldest son holding me.

When we got outside the remand home I made a bolt for it – the look of the place was enough to put the fear of death into me. I ran as fast as my legs could carry me, but Mr

Brown's son grabbed my jacket and stopped me. I begged him to let me go. Ma pressed the bell; I heard her say that they weren't to hit me, and they told Ma they didn't do that there. I was taken up and down various corridors, and after I had changed my clothes, they opened a big heavy door with a huge key. The turnkeys shouted at me, pulling me about and calling me names, and threw me into a small cell with a bit of wood on the floor as a bed. That was all there was. The window was low, with tiny little frames of glass in it, and so thick that it was impossible to see through it. One of the panes of glass was missing. There was a lot of writing on the walls that must have been done by kids who had been here before me. The turnkey who had been lured into the dorm the night I ran away came up to me and held the huge cell key under my nose, digging it in and making me stand on my toes. He cursed me and said that nobody ran away from him and got away with it. He hit me with his knee between my legs, and when I bent down he hit me on the head with the key. I could no longer feel the pain between my legs, but my head was aching and I could hear a noise like a siren. I felt more blows on my body, but made no attempt to ward them off. I held my head, wondering what the noise was that seemed to come from inside it. I was terrified in case it didn't go away.

When the noise stopped, I realised I was on my own in the cell. I sat on the floor and felt the lump on my head, and I started crying. I ran at the door, banging it and begging to be let out, but nobody answered. It was horrible being there alone, and I wished that my dad had killed me when he threatened to. I remembered Ma's words about their not hitting me or putting a wee boy in a cell, and I thought they must hate me to bring me back here and I hated them all in return. But then I heard someone knock on the door and ask if I was all right. Before I could answer, some comics and sweets were slid under the door, and my visitors said they'd be back in the morning. I felt sorry for thinking the way I had about Ma and everyone else.

Next morning I was taken down to the head turnkey's office. He was a bald-headed man, sitting behind a desk and holding a leather strap. He looked me up and down and said something about my being taught a lesson for running away from his home and causing him problems. He removed his jacket and told me to bend over. I couldn't move – I just stood there hoping he would take pity on me. He dragged me towards his desk and bent me over it. As he hit me with his belt I tried to put my hands on my backside to cushion the blows, and eventually he got a turnkey to hold me while he belted me. My body jerked with each blow of his belt. I didn't count how many times he hit me, but when he had finished he told the turnkey to get me out of his sight.

I walked up the corridor crying and holding my arse. Some of the boys passed me and asked me how many I got, but before I could answer the turnkey told them to get on with their work. I was put back in the cell again and the turnkey slammed the door.

I couldn't sit down, so I lay on my belly and thought about Ma, Maw and almost everybody I knew, and how I'd show them the bruises on my arse and let them feel the lump on my head and tell them to get me out of there. When I heard people talking in the corridors I felt a bit better, knowing that someone was there. To pass the time, I looked at the names on the walls and on the back of the door and on the wooden bed. I kept some bread to feed the birds, and I stood and watched them for hours. I left most of my food, and the turnkeys said that was why I was so skinny. They'd let me out for a wash and to go to the toilet, but a turnkey was always with me. I'd always take as long as I could – I'd wash my hands and face three or four times and sit in the toilet for ages, till the turnkey told me to get out. Occasionally there would be a good turnkey who wouldn't shout and closed the cell door quietly. I loved it when the door opened – it didn't matter who was there or why, just as long as it opened.

All this took place on the first of my many visits to Larchgrove Remand Home. A few years later, after a week or two at Larchgrove on remand for the house-breaking charge with the two Johns, I was taken to the Glasgow Sheriff's Court. This was unusual, as I was a juvenile and should have appeared in the juvenile court. Rather than sentence me in public, the judge had me taken into a little room, into which only lawyers, the fiscal, the baillies and the turnkeys were allowed. I was on social inquiry and background reports, which meant that I could get anything from a warning to being sent to an approved school. My ma was standing behind me, and I could feel her hand on my shoulder. The old man in his fancy attire told me I would be sent to an approved school for one to three years.

I felt my legs shaking under me, then a turnkey's hand gripped my shoulder and pulled me away. He took me through the court room and down to the cells. These cells are very small, with a small, stinking urinal bowl attached to the wall – someone had shat in it, which made it worse. After I stopped crying I told John and John Henry that I was to be sent away to an approved school. They passed me some cigarettes down the cells by swinging a jacket from cell to cell, till it finally reached me. On the cell doors there was a latch big enough for an arm to get through. John Henry was to be sent to Borstal, John Stuart to a senior approved school. Most on my landing had been sentenced and were waiting to be moved out to various establishments. They joked about their misfortunes. There was a lot of shouting, and cell doors were opening and slamming every few minutes. Eventually my cell door opened: 'Steele?' 'That's me, sir,' I said, and held out my hands for the handcuffs.

Larchgrove was as busy as ever. Some boys were cleaning the corridors, the smell of polish and brass was strong, and somewhere a turnkey was shouting orders in an exaggerated tone. In the head turnkey's office I was told that I was going away to another home where it was hoped that I'd be taught a lesson I'd never forget. On the desk in front of me – the same desk that I had been bent over to have my backside beaten – a warder was writing furiously, occasionally stopping to ask me questions. The little room was gleaming clean.

A turnkey entered, throwing me a glance that stung – it was the one who had beaten me up after my ma took me back to

Larchgrove when I ran away. He slammed something down on the desk and exchanged a few words with the head turnkey. On his way out he said, 'Good riddance, Steele.' The head turnkey glanced up at me, as if daring me to answer back. I looked down at the floor and wondered whether I would be able to escape from the new home I was going to.

The silence was broken by two strange-looking monks entering the office. Both were tall, and their long black cloaks gave them a creepy look. The head promptly got up from his desk and shook their hands. It was obvious they all had met before. After a few minutes they turned their attention to me, and the two monks looked me over thoroughly.

Before we left, I was made to dress in my own clothes – it felt good to get out of my scabby corduroy shorts and into the long trousers that Ma had bought me for my court appearance – and the matron took me into her sick bay and looked through my hair for lice. On my way out some boys said goodbye as they were scrubbing floors and, as ever, a turnkey nearby shouted for silence and more work. I knew I was leaving some pals behind, and I wasn't sure if I'd see them again.

The two monks took a firm hold of me as we walked out of the main door and into a black motor car. They put me in the back seat on my own and warned me not to try to run away as the back doors only opened from the outside. Then they lit up cigarettes and chatted to each other.

I was on my way to an approved school in Edinburgh, and soon we were passing fields and a part of the country I'd only seen in postcards and books and films. I could see haystacks in the distance like blocks of flats, and the smell of the country was fresh and clean. This is what I'd always longed for; wide open spaces, streams and forests and hills where I could roam without having to glance over my shoulder to see if I was being followed. I tried to remember the route we were taking, as I had no intention of staying at my new home.

The two monks told me about the school that was to be my home for one to three years, and they didn't paint a very pleasant picture of it. They asked me about my crime, but the taller of the two was more interested in my sins. How many times had I been to confession, he wanted to know. I was too scared to tell him the truth, and said I'd lost count. They told me God would be ashamed of me for running away from the remand home, and that the only way I could make up was by prayer. I had heard stories about the monks who ran these schools – religious fanatics they were called, and it was rumoured that they believed if someone did wrong it was because of the devil inside him, and they'd try to beat him out physically.

Soon we were near Edinburgh and heading for Tranent, just outside the city. I saw a man in a kilt, with a huge beard and bandy legs. He was having difficulty in getting a herd of sheep over the road, and to my surprise he turned and waved to the driver of our car. There ahead of us was a huge, brown, haunted-looking mansion. The car turned up a country road, with the school wall on one side and fields on the other. I had butterflies in my tummy now, not knowing what lay ahead.

The drive looked like a path cut out of the jungle, with trees and bushes and grass everywhere and birds chirping happily away. We drove up the school drive and stopped in the exercise yard. To my left and straight ahead were huge buildings, five storeys high and with many windows; to my right were smaller buildings and fields; behind me was a football and cricket field and a house among scattered trees. Monks were walking about the yard and field, and some of them waved to those in the car.

I was taken into an office and made to stand there until I was summoned into another office. Someone was at a typewriter – I hated their noise, for the only times I heard them were in courts, police stations and gaols. My first mistake was to call one of the Brothers 'mister', and the slap almost knocked me from my feet.

'Where's your manners, boy?' the brute yelled to me, his nose barely an inch from my own. I had been through all this before, but I couldn't accept it. 'Where's my manners?' I thought. 'Where's my ma, where's my home?' He was waiting for an answer. I braced myself for another belt in the face. At

70

times like this I cut off mentally without really meaning to, and while he was looking for my manners I was listening to Ma's warnings. If only I'd listened to Ma I'd never be here now with all these strangers. Even though the Brother was thumping me on the head, I never felt a thing. My head jerked from side to side with each blow, and they only stopped when an old man in a smart suit pulled me away. He stood me behind him, sheltering me from further punishment, and I felt safe for the time being. He was a giant of a man and, though his face was very red, his nose was even redder, like a strawberry – so earning him the nickname of Mr Strawb. I sensed that he'd do me no harm and after a few angry words with the Brother he led me away by the hand into his office and offered me a chair next to his own. His hands were very large, and he rested his chin on them while he looked me over. He told me about the school and how long I'd be there. Then came the dreaded question: 'Do you wet the bed, son?' 'No, sir!' came the reply. As he raised his eyebrows I lowered my eyelids – if he knew I was lying, he never said a word about it. From what he'd told me about the pee-the-bed-dorm I didn't want to go there. Called the Killicrankie, it was by far the largest dorm in the school; unlike the others, it had neither soft beds nor carpets, and one was woken every hour to go to the toilet. I was very glad when he told me he was my housemaster, and even more glad when he told me I'd be going into Ben Nevis dormitory. He asked me about my family life and I told him, leaving out all the beatings I'd had from my dad; he asked me if my dad ever hit me and I told him no, and again his eyebrows went up. 'Do you love your dad?' he asked, and I answered, 'Very much.'

He even poured me a cup of tea and offered me a biscuit, which I refused. 'Where's you manners?' he called, with a big smile upon his red face. I could only laugh and accept. He asked me about my Padden uncles. Again his eyebrows shot up – 'John Padden?' he asked, his face now serious. I was going to deny having an Uncle John in case he had done something bad to Mr Strawb, but I found myself saying yes. At once he was up on his feet and coming towards me. 'Does the rascal still box?' he asked, taking up a boxer's stance, with his feet apart and his big hands rolled up into balls like he was going to knock the world off its axis. He started shadow-boxing and making hissing noises down his nose, and I laughed heartily at him. 'I taught your Uncle John how to box in this very school when he was just about your age,' he said proudly, and it turned out that he had been Uncle John's housemaster, too.

Mr Strawb then spent the best part of an hour talking to me as though he was talking to his own child. I wished I could have him talk to me more – just to sit there with him would have helped. I didn't know what lay behind his office building and the fear of the unknown had a firm grip on me. This giant of a man was reaching out to help me, but I couldn't communicate, I couldn't even let him know how much I wanted to. But maybe he knew anyway.

I was led away by one of the Brothers along some corridors to a bath-house with rows of showers; it smelled of disinfectant so strong that it burned my nostrils at each breath. Hundreds of cockroaches were scurrying for cover. I was told not to pay any attention to them: the Brother assured me that they wouldn't eat me, and he stamped his foot down on one of the creatures, making a horrible crunching noise that echoed throughout the huge empty bath-house. He made me strip off my clothes and handed me soap and a pair of black pants. I stood naked under the cold shower, and I could feel his eyes on me all the while. His stare was frightening, but it was good to hear him talk to me, if only to tell me I looked like a skinned rabbit. Then I felt a stinging on my back and went crashing to the ground. When I picked myself up off the floor the Brother was waving the black pants in front of my face. It was hard to know what was happening – I had soap in my eyes, and felt dizzy from my fall.

'You'll wear your pants when showering at all times,' he warned.

When he turned off the water I was still covered in soap, but he made no attempt to turn it back on. I changed from

my wet soapy pants into a pair of blue cord shorts that came
to my knees, much like knickerbockers. I was led back through
the corridors and into the office I had left earlier.

As I stood by the window I could hear voices, hundreds of
them, and footballs being kicked amidst the sound of laughter.
I must have been spotted from the yard, because boys swarmed
over to peek through the glass at me, and I could hear them
call to others that there was a 'new boy' in. I could see faces
pressed hard against the windows, each anxious to know who
I was and where I came from. Not many of them had heard
of Garthamlock, and they classed me as a country boy. There
was much shoving and arguing at the window, and then
someone yelled my name. It was my pal Tony Tanburrini from
Larchgrove – and there was Gak! They were as excited as I
was. I was waving at them when I was thumped on the back
of the head and dragged away from the window, and I heard
Gak shout, 'Leave him alone, you dirty sneak!' I wondered
how long they had been there, and I couldn't wait till I found
out. I knew Gak would be in for stealing – he was a compulsive
thief, and it was said that he even stole from himself.

The Brother who took me to my dormitory spoke pleasantly
to me and helped me make my bed. My dormitory had about
eight beds in it – they were nice and soft, and the floor was
carpeted. All in all it was very cosy. The Brother told me that
I'd do well here at St Joseph's. Like most people I met, he was
anxious to fatten me up. Maw had always told me that one
could never fatten a thoroughbred, and this made him laugh.
Folks always commented on how thin and pale-looking I was –
it made me wish there were more thoroughbreds about.

The Brother then took me down some flights of stairs and
along some corridors, talking all the while. We entered a huge
hall where boys were standing while a body count was carried
out. Each boy had been allocated a house – mine was 'De la
Salle'. We were then lined up in our house order and given
numbers.

The hall was full, with maybe as many as a hundred boys
between the ages of twelve and sixteen. There were more, but
they were separated from us, housed in two fancy cottages

reserved for boys who had been of good behaviour. Some of the boys who lived in them actually believed they were different from us. There was a good deal of talking, but that stopped abruptly when a Brother raised his hands high in the air and clapped them twice. I noticed that the Brothers tucked their hands into the bottom of their wide cloak sleeves, Chinese style. When we were ready they marched us out in single file, across the yard and into the dinner hall. Mass was always said before meals, and only after it was finished were we allowed to be seated and wait our turn to go up to the hot-plate and collect our food. The cooks were ordinary women from nearby, and they were very pleasant and polite with everyone.

Whenever there was any extra food the Brothers would tease the boys by telling them that the best row would be allowed second helpings. Boys would sit in their chairs, arms folded and backs straight with their chests out and staring ahead scared even to blink. Some kids were bullied into sitting in these positions by older boys desperate for food. 'This row!' a Brother would roar, and about twenty or more boys would scatter and head for the hot-plate, fighting and pulling. Some even marched smartly at a fair speed, and it was one of those: 'I'm not in a great hurry' marches. 'This row!' the noise of chairs being pushed back was deafening and sudden. It was just like a sport. 'This row!'

After dinner we were taken out for exercise in the field, where about fifty footballs were kicked around. Some boys were playing chases, some smoking out of sight of Brothers and informers. I met Gak and Tony and some others I knew from the remand home, and I was talking to them when a boy came up to me with a bunch of his pals and asked me if I wanted to make it! Make it? I didn't know what he was talking about, till Gak told me he wanted to fight. This was the custom when a new boy came in to the school, but I didn't want to fight this guy for no reason at all and told him so. He called me a coward, but I still refused. People were gathering round us: some mocked me for not wanting to fight, others encouraged me by telling me the guy was a coward and that I had nothing to fear. The bully was obviously upset at being mocked

74

and he called me every name he could think of, but I refused to fight till he called my ma names. This is an old trick that is often used as a last straw: it usually works, and it certainly did with me. As we began to fight, the others stood round us in a ring, chanting. It was great to see the terror in the other boy's face and to hear him yell as I bit him hard.

Then a voice of authority was calling and blowing a whistle, and when the teacher got me off him I was shocked to hear the bully say that I had started it and attacked him for no reason. 'Is that so, lad?' the teacher asked. As I told my side of the story the bully called me a liar and showed him his bite mark. The teacher took out a little black book and told me I was booked for assault. I was put into a small circle, twelve inches in diameter, that had been painted on the exercise yard, and told to stand there for the remainder of the period. No one was allowed to speak to me while I was there. I saw the bully standing alone by the toilet doors, making stupid faces at me. I had to duck when footballs came my way: being in the circle was embarrassing and humiliating, but no doubt that was its purpose. All this time the Brothers paraded up and down, eager to catch someone doing something wrong so they could book them and make them lose marks. One needed points to get home on leave, and they had to be earned.

When we reached the classroom everyone was seated except me. An elderly woman teacher told me to stand till she spoke to me. For some reason she left the classroom, saying she'd be back soon, and telling one of the boys to keep an eye on us. We heard her high-heeled shoes clatter away down the corridor. Once she had disappeared round the corner everyone started talking and asking me if I had any cigarettes hidden on me. Being caught smoking meant severe beatings and loss of leave for a week. I had no cigarettes and said so. Tony said he knew where he could get some. Everyone was silent, looking from me to Tony, wondering what was about to happen. It was strange to be standing there, the focus of attention. No doubt each pair of eyes seeking me out was finding what they saw in themselves. There were faces I liked, and faces I didn't like and faces I wouldn't want to have. The desks were old and painted, as were the hard wooden chairs, but that didn't really matter – the things that mattered couldn't be spoken about. I wanted to cry out for my ma, but I had a feeling that this wouldn't be acceptable here, that it would be considered childish. Yet running away was only another form of crying out for help – I felt I didn't belong here with these boys (maybe they thought the same) and I wanted to run away home.

Tony said he knew where I could get some cigarettes, and that he would watch out if I went in and stole them from a room nearby. Everyone was whispering, and I could tell there was more to this than just stealing cigarettes. Tony opened the class door quietly, peeked outside and motioned me to follow. As I did so I looked round and there they were – about ten heads, all peeking out the door of our classroom. Otherwise the highly polished corridor was entirely empty. Tony stopped and listened outside a door, and before I knew it I was inside the room and the door had closed behind me. There was an eerie silence; I thought I'd be murdered if I were caught. There was a bed and a wardrobe, and on top of a fire surround were hundreds of loose cigarettes and enough money to get me home – but I was stuck to the spot with fear.

Someone opened the door behind me, but I didn't cry out or take flight. I felt at ease, that I wanted to talk to someone, even the man whose room I was in. There were many things I wanted to know about my life – what it was coming to, and why.

'Hurry up, Johnnyboy!' It was Tony at the door. I picked up as many cigarettes as I could, and a pound's worth of silver coins, and headed back to the classroom. Tony was already there, and everyone was excited at what I had just done. I handed out cigarettes to those who smoked. Tony lit up: he had both feet on his desk but after he'd extinguished his cigarette he waved his jumper in the air to clear the smoke. Only then did I learn why I'd been so crazy to steal from that room – it was the head Brother's room. I could see that they now saw me as a crazy guy whom they'd like to know more about.

The old woman teacher came back, and seemed none the

wiser about my bit of devilry. She had a dour-looking face and her attitude wasn't much better. She showed me my place in the class, close to her desk. I had to walk carefully in case she heard the money jingling in my pocket.

After school it was into the dinner hall for our tea. By now the whole school was talking about what I had done, some of the boys in my class were showing the cigarettes to those who didn't believe them. Even the bully whom I'd fought gave a nod in my direction. Jamie, who was sitting beside me, advised me to eat as much as I could so as not to draw attention to myself. He was in my class and became a good pal, and we both ran away some time later.

In the recreation building there was a snooker table, two table-tennis tables, a sweet shop and a cardboard bank where we cashed our cheques – we were all paid a shilling a week, and given a little cheque to cash at the bank. We'd go straight to the sweet shop to spend our money. A pal of mine, Tam, was given a job as one of the tellers, but the Brothers removed him when they discovered he had a talent for robbing banks.

I dreaded going to sleep that night in case I wet the bed and was discovered. One of the Brothers came round switching off the lights, and he spoke to me for a few minutes before saying goodnight to everyone. I was warm and comfortable in my bed; my pyjamas smelled fresh, and although they were too large for me they were a better fit than those provided at Larchgrove.

I don't know what time it was when the night watchman woke me up, but I could hear him cursing me. My pyjamas were clinging to me, and even my mattress was soaking wet. A Brother was mopping up the puddle beneath my bed. He led me away through the darkened corridor by the hand. Still soaking wet and smelling of urine, I was scared out of my wits by what he looked like: his long black cloak made me think of a murderer on the prowl. He spoke to me only once, and that was to tell me that he knew I was a pee-the-bed from the moment he saw me.

He took me to a little room full of sheets and other clothes, made me strip off my wet clothes and threw me a long, Wee

77

Willie Winkie-type nightgown that came down to my ankles. All the pee-the-beds were given such night shirts. I felt humiliated wearing it, and was glad that no one would see me walking along the corridor in it. He marched me back, and this time he took me to Killiecrankie, the pee-the-beds' dorm. I noticed a Brother going round the dorm, feeling under the blankets of each boy's bed in case anyone had wet his bed. It was rumoured that he was feeling for something else under the blankets, and with this in mind I tried to wake up whenever he approached my bed. I was shattered to find myself in Killiecrankie, but that night I was led away again and given a change of sheets and a nightgown. My mattress felt like a hard rubber dinghy.

When I woke next morning, I was asked if I was a pee-the-bed, to which I shamefully answered yes. This seemed to delight my new dormitory companions, and an argument broke out in which one boy accused another of being the worst pee-the-bed that ever lived! Another boy then claimed to pee his bed three or four times a night, and he was proud of it as well! My excuse for wetting the bed was that I had a cold.

Down in the recreation room we were counted and marched across the yard for breakfast. It was a dark morning and a bird was singing away on the rooftops; the dinner hall was all lit up and cosy-looking, with the food laid out on the tables – bowls of cornflakes and toast and tea-pots steaming away. I don't know why, but it is one of my fondest memories of St Joseph's. The clatter of spoons and knives was deafening, but it was a happy sound. The women in the cookhouse sang away happily above the din and the Brothers and teachers seemed more relaxed in the early morning.

Fights were a regular occurrence at the school, and Tony was involved in many of them. He used to go berserk, smashing windows and throwing chairs, and it was typical of him to be fighting that morning with some kid from Dundee who had called him a bastard. It took some time for the teachers and Brothers to quieten him down – he was kicking and squawking and swearing into the bargain. Tony's tantrums were known to us as flakeys.

In the mornings after breakfast we had to do our housework

and clean the dorms. The pee-the-beds had to wash and air their mattresses. We'd often play games when the Brothers weren't about – being caught meant being punished, but a little fun was worth a beating. Not all the Brothers participated in beatings – there were some who showed much love and affection to the boys, and would laugh if they caught them playing games when they were meant to be working. Once our homework was done a woman who worked in the laundry would come round the dorms with a huge can of assorted sweets, and every boy there was given one. We all loved her, and I never knew her to raise her voice. I loved it when she came around, and felt safe and protected by her presence.

6 STILL RUNNING

The atmosphere had changed again. I wanted home – but I'd have to wait so many weeks, eight they said, and even then I could only get home if my behaviour was good. They gave good chase when I ran away. I had no intention of stopping for anyone. I scampered over a four-foot wall and across the fields and headed for the bushes. I wasn't only being chased by the Brothers, but by the 'hound dogs' – 'trusty' boys who had been ordered to fetch us back. Much depended on whom they were chasing – if they liked the boy they helped him. I stumbled and fell as I ran, occasionally scratching my bare legs in the nettles. In the distance I could see the mining village of Prestonpans, famous for its battles. To the left of me was another Glasgow boy on the run: his name was Peter, and he had a speech problem which made him speak out of his nose. The shouting was getting louder, and I headed for bushes and lay there, getting my breath back.

When I looked through the hedge I saw that the hounds had Peter. He was crying and begging them to let him go. They were laughing and cheering and had him by the arms and legs and were throwing him high in the air. I knew that I'd be given the belt and put in the circle if I was caught. I had on me the money I'd stolen from the head Brother's bedroom, and I thought it best to dump it in case I should get caught with it. I was just about to do so when a hand fell on my shoulder. It was Ginzo my 'hound dog', and he was laughing. He said he had no intention of taking me in and told me I was heading the wrong way and was bound to get caught. He gave me some tips as well as some cigarettes. He advised me to stay in the bush in case someone spotted me from the bing – a huge pile of mining waste from which the Brothers could spot runaways. I could hear Peter screaming as they dragged him back to the school. There were creepy-crawlies all over me – every time I brushed them off some more took their place – and my legs were stinging and scraped. Once again I was at peace and, for the time being, in the bush.

I didn't know much about history, but there was much talk at the school about the village of Prestonpans and its history going way back. When I finally crept out of the bush it was dark. Prestonpans seemed a warm little place and for all the trouble there years ago, it certainly was peaceful now. I wished I had on a pair of long trousers – my knickerbocker-type corduroy shorts were odd-looking and old-fashioned and attracted people's attention. I was small and thin and pale, and looked younger than my thirteen years, and if folk saw me out at night they might well suspect that something was wrong.

Every time a car came my way I dived for cover, sometimes leaping over hedgerows into people's gardens, waiting to see if it was all clear before I emerged. Even the closing of a door or a window had me scampering for cover. But, like all runaways, I was caught in the end, and was given a good hiding with a belt.

I remember the Brother taking off his wristwatch and rolling up his sleeves, as though he was going to destroy me. Afterwards I was given a lecture on right and wrong and Christianity and the devil. No one mentioned the money or the cigarettes I had stolen. I was told to pray for forgiveness for running away, but Mr Strawb said I should ask for guidance instead.

Everyone stared at me over dinner that evening. Some boys asked me how many strokes of the belt I had got. Others acted as though I had leprosy, but once the teachers were out of sight they asked me all about it.

As the weeks wore on I became more friendly with Tony

and Gak, and with a newcomer called Tommy – and it was with him that I decided to escape again. Tommy came from Glasgow too: he was in the same dorm as me, though he only peed the bed so that he could get into my dorm. We were both looked upon as pests, out to cause trouble, by many of the Brothers and teachers.

One Saturday we both went into the toilets and changed quickly into some civilian clothes which we had managed to get hold of. We ran till we reached a small wall, scaled it and lay listening in a field on the other side.

Feeling free was a traumatic experience: I loved being on the run, and when they caught me – as I knew they would – I'd run away again and head for home. Funny that I should head for home, having spent so many years running away from there!

Once again I felt at peace with myself. But as we lay there talking in low whispers, deciding which way to go, one of the teachers crept up on us. It was too late for us to run by the time I spotted him, and he dragged Tommy and me back to the recreation room like two rag dolls. Then he took us away to be punished with the leather belt.

By the time I left the office, my backside black and blue, I had made up my mind to run away again. There was no stopping me, I hated the place more than ever.

'When are you going to come to your senses, Steele?' the head Brother had asked, poking my chest with a stiff forefinger and spraying saliva in my face. But I felt that I had come to my senses by running away. All my life I wanted to go home, even when I ran away from it.

Not long afterwards, when the big bus drove into the yard to take boys on leave for the weekend, I was shattered because I wasn't allowed home to Ma and Maw and the family. I could hear the boys singing happily as the bus pulled out: some of the teachers reminded me that I could have been on it if I'd behaved myself and not kept trying to escape.

Those who weren't going home were taken in an old-fashioned bus with no back window in it to the picture house in the nearby town. On the way we'd all sing and stamp our feet and even the Brothers and teachers joined in. Tony, Gak and I sat in the back smoking the butt of a cigarette and blowing the smoke out of the window. One of us would hide low behind the seat while the other two kept watch. As the big bus stopped we all rushed forward with excitement. During the short walk to the picture house boys would stop and pretend to be tying their shoe laces while they hunted for cigarette butts on the ground.

One day a couple of dozen of us were taken to Edinburgh's Commonwealth swimming-pool. People stared at us as we marched down the street, Gak calling every passer-by a sneak in his strong Glasgow accent. In the pool we were watched closely by the teachers in case we ran away. Gak told us that a dirty sneak from another country was in the changing room and that he had a camera and a wallet in the little tin locker where he kept his clothes. He led the way to the changing room and wrenched the guy's locker door open. The wallet was full of foreign currency but there was one ten-shilling note which Tommy took and passed to Tony. Gak said he would sell the camera to some old sneak in the street for a few pounds. But then its owner appeared and started shouting, which brought the teachers running and we were searched for the money. They made us all strip off our pants hoping to find it, and it fell out of Tommy's bum.

Mr Strawb was concerned by my behaviour and said he would do what he could to help me. Whenever he spoke kindly to me it made me cry, and on the odd occasion he cried himself. It hurt me to know I'd let him down by running away. He watched out for my being picked upon by certain teachers, and had a couple of run-ins with them as a result. He also told some of the stricter ones to leave off me.

We were told we were going berry-picking in Montrose, and that we'd be there for about six weeks. Some who had been there the year before said it was great, so we were all looking forward to it . There seemed to be nothing but fields for miles around. Our accommodation was in two army-type barracks with rows upon rows of beds. The smaller hut had the cottage boys in it, and the bigger one held the rest. There was no hot water at the camp.

Twenty yards or so away from the huts was a giant and crooked tree. It was called the smokers' tree – one could almost walk up to the top using the branches as steps, and no one could see up from below because of the leaves. There could be as many as forty boys at one time in it, all smoking; from a distance a large cloud of smoke could be seen hanging in the air.

The weather was beautiful and sunny when we marched to the berry fields to earn our wages. A lot of stealing went on. Baskets of berries would suddenly disappear, and when this happened it was called 'niggaring'. Some kid would shout at the top of his voice, 'I've been niggared!', and the teachers and Brothers would rush to him as if he was being murdered. A Brother was picking away singing to himself as if he hadn't a care in the world, when I spotted his big black bucket full of berries. I intended stealing them from him; he was stealing my youth, and besides I didn't like him. Down I went on my hands and knees and crept through the hedgerows. I could see the backs of his legs and his basket about a foot away. As I stretched out my arm to lift the basket he turned and saw me. He pulled me through the hedge, screaming 'Thief!' at the top of his voice.

We were paid by weight for the berries we picked, and boys often peed in their berry baskets to make them heavier, while others put bricks in them. I did this once. I filled my bucket with stones and then covered them with berries. I had to drag the bucket along to be weighed, as it was too heavy to carry. The man at the weighing machine tipped it over with his foot, spilling its contents on to the ground. He knew there was more than berries in it. Before long my ears were throbbing, and I could hear Gak calling, 'Leave him alone, ya dirty old sneak!' I ran back to the rows with my tail between my legs. When I looked around I saw Gak and the others throwing berries at the man and hiding behind the hedgerows as he searched for the culprits.

I was much happier in the camp than at the school. There was more to do and there were wide open spaces to be explored, but still a watchful eye was kept on me and my pals. As happy as I was, I was even happier running away, and so it wasn't long before I was scurrying across a field in a bid for freedom.

7 BREAKING OUT AND IN

Back at school, we were watched more than ever now that it was known that my pals and I would try to run away wherever we were. One evening about a dozen of us were taken roller-skating in Edinburgh. I had never been skating in my life, and I couldn't even stand with my skates on without falling down. Since our shoes had been locked away, we had no option but to run away bare-footed or with our skates on. We didn't get very far in our roller-skates. Once outside the rink I fell flat on my face, but got up again and ran a few paces, sparks flying from the bottom of the skates. We had no chance of getting away.

One night I went to chapel to pray before bed. Tony came in, followed by Gak and Tommy and Rusty and my new pal Nicky, who was also in Killiecrankie – like me, he had tried to pretend he never wet the bed, but was soon found out. Tommy said he had some cigarettes but no light. A candle burned all night high up behind the altar, and I let Tommy stand on my shoulders to reach it. Gak kept watch, but I was too slow when a Brother appeared. Everyone pretended they were praying, but when I opened my eyes Tommy was still clinging to the candle-holder, puffing his cigarette.

Mr Strawb spoke to Ma about my behaviour and wanted to know if there was anything that could be done to stop me running away and getting into trouble. 'Does he have any hobbies?' he asked, but Ma couldn't come up with anything. Mr Strawb's big strawberry nose looked brighter than ever against his silver hair, and he winked as he spoke to me. Suddenly Ma remembered that I used to keep pigeons. At once he was up on his feet and pacing the office floor, a finger to his lips. 'I've the very thing for him,' he said.

True to his word, he got me a pigeon hut and some pigeons. I was overjoyed and I thanked him with all my heart, while he looked on in amusement and gave me a big friendly wink; and Ma left much happier to know that someone was caring for me. Some of the other boys and even some of the teachers and Brothers resented my having a pigeon hut or 'dookit' and pigeons. Plokey, a teacher I particularly disliked, told me I didn't deserve a dookit for all the trouble I'd caused society and the school, and said that if it was up to him he'd take it off me. He used young boys as spies to tell what I was up to, and rewarded them with sweets and a false smile. He got great pleasure out of this. What a sleekit man he was, with eyes everywhere: whenever he thought I was up to something he'd walk about with his lips pouted out so that they touched the bottom of his nose, his hand behind his back and his head going from side to side. He often came sniffing around the dookit to search it and torment me, so that I'd end up crying and running to Mr Strawb. Whenever Plokey wanted me to come to him, he'd screw his little face up and beckon to me with his finger and he was always giving unnecessary slaps to our ears and the back of our heads.

On one occasion Gak, Tommy, Rusty, Tony and I ran away through the fields till we reached a haystack, where we decided to hide until it was dark. There were many scarecrows in the fields around and we managed to grab one and take it back to our hideout in the haystack, where we sat it on a bale of hay and pretended it was one of the Brothers. Gak said it was a dirty sneak for frightening the birds; he kicked it high in the air and rolled about the long wheat with it – occasionally we'd see his lanky legs come up through the wheat, and bits of the scarecrow too. We lay all night in the haystack, staring at the stars high above us and spoke in low tones of their mystery. Gak thought that whoever was responsible for putting the stars out of reach was the greatest sneak who ever lived.

In the wee small hours we decided we'd head for the town of Tranent and try to get some cigarettes, so off we went across the fields under cover of the clouds. We helped ourselves to clothes off some washing lines. I stole a jumper, which looked almost like a coat on me but kept me warm. Gak was wearing the scarecrow's hat to hide his red hair, which so often gave him away.

We kept walking till we reached Portobello, a few miles from the school, where we crept about looking for a place to break into so that we could get our fares home. Occasionally we stopped to pick up cigarette butts, and smoked them joyfully.

We eyed up a few shops and decided the easiest one to break into was the launderette, so we broke in through the roof. Once inside we found bags of money, all in silver coins. It was so warm in there that we didn't want to go, but we had to move along. On the way to nowhere we saw a caravan site, probably for gipsies, and a van for selling food. We were terrified to go near it because we'd heard stories about gipsies and what they did to those who did them wrong, but the goods in the van got the better of us.

Gak checked out the camp to see that no one was about, after which I managed to slide open a window in the side of the van and get inside. I passed out some cigarettes and money to the others and we fled. We had money and cigarettes, but we were cold and hungry. I found a bit of toffee which had been stamped into the ground by a thousand busy feet – but who cared?

We came to some half-built buildings, where we decided to stay till the trains started running to Glasgow. We looked around for a cosy spot and settled down to sleep, some old newspapers wrapped around us. I couldn't sleep and, to my surprise, I found myself wishing that I was back in Killiecrankie dorm. I was so uncomfortable that I got up and walked up and down, stamping my feet to get the circulation going. Tony wanted us to give ourselves up, because it was so cold, but the punishment to come made us hesitate. We gathered close together, this was okay for a little while, but in the end we decided to go back to the school. We boasted about how brave we'd be when we were being belted with the leather strap, but the truth of the matter was that we were all terrified.

As we neared the school, it looked eerie and haunted, and the Brothers wandering around in their long black cloaks made it seem even more creepy. We went into the school yard on tiptoe and made our way to the shoe room, where we broke in through a window and roamed about in the dark till we found our shoes. This done, we headed for the other side of the school and Mr Strawb's tailor shop, where he kept our clothing and school blazers and flannels. We broke in and helped ourselves. Gak behaved like a male model, posing in all the different clothes. It was great to be out of the cold. Rusty and I broke into the kitchen and stole a huge piece of cake which we scoffed in minutes; and then we scampered off again across the fields. We were heading home and feeling good: this was one morning I'll never forget.

We knew there'd be a hullabaloo in the school when they discovered what we'd done, and even more so when they learned about the launderette and the food van, but all that mattered now was that we were on our way home again, yahooing and leaping in the air as we ran through the fields. It's amazing what a little thieving can do to the morale: with money in our pockets, some food in our bellies and decent clothes on, we could've passed for ordinary schoolboys.

We jumped on a bus that took us to the station. The conductor came upstairs and told us to be quiet, and while Gak argued with him I pickpocketed some silver from the conductor's bag.

Once off the bus we had to be more careful: it was daylight, there were police about and it was possible that they were looking for us. Although we had enough money for our train fares we skipped on without paying. When the train started moving out for Glasgow we felt much happier. We roamed the compartments, broke into the buffet and stuffed our faces with sweets and cakes and ginger ale. After we had plundered the buffet, we discussed where we should go when we reached Glasgow, and it was decided we'd go to my home town. Once there, it was great to be home and walking through the streets again and talking to old friends. They were amazed to see me and my pals, and they offered to put us up and shelter us from the police.

My sister Lana came to see me when she learned where I was hiding, bringing my clothes and shoes. She told me that Ma was going crazy not knowing where I was. One thing for sure, I couldn't go to Ma: she'd hand me in to the authorities for, as she said, my own good.

All my pals in Garthamlock were in on the gang scene, fighting with rival gangs from nearby housing estates – Easterhouse, Queenslie and Ruchazie. My pals from the approved school weren't troubled by them because they were with me – and because my Garthamlock pals resented the police and felt obliged to help us. Gang fighting was one thing I couldn't get involved in – I was happier being on the run and stealing.

My pal John Stuart was also on the run – from St Andrew's, a senior boys' approved school. I saw him darting in and out of closes. He warned me to be careful as Nero was on the prowl and would try to catch us. There were about a dozen of us standing by the shops when Nero came slinking around the corner, like a machine trained to stop runaways. We all ran in different directions to confuse him, and the only person he caught was an innocent passer-by. No matter how inconspicuous I tried to be, it wasn't long before all my old pals knew I was on the run, and the neighbours too.

The next morning Rusty and I left for my pal Jamie's house in Bridgeton. Jamie, who was at my approved school, had a mynah bird called Ringo, which had been stolen from a pet shop and had only one leg. Sometimes when we were on the run we'd go to his house and his ma would call out, 'Get back to that approved school, yous pair!' and before long the mynah bird was also shouting, 'Get back to that approved school, yous pair!' Once the police came to look for us and Ringo shouted that we were back in the approved school, when in fact we were both hiding in the next room. Ringo used to get drunk and sing, swaying about on his one leg.

No one was at home when we got to Jamie's house, so we

roamed about looking for a shop to break into. It was getting late and dark; we were chased by the police but got away by dodging through back courts and closes, which were filthy with mud and broken glass. Police cars seemed to be in every street we passed – Bridgeton was a real rough area. It was pouring with rain and we were drenched to the skin when we saw a man coming towards us. He asked us if we were on the run, and said we could stay at his house if only for an hour or two. Once inside his cosy little house we were given towels to dry ourselves and he made tea while we heated ourselves at the fire. He started asking us questions – where we were from, who we were, and why we were on the run. When I told him we came from Garthamlock, he asked me if I knew the Steeles; when I told him that I was one of them he almost hit the roof, and his wife came rushing in from the scullery. They made us eat till we were full and then take a bath while our clothes were being washed. When I told him about the Brothers and teachers, he said I should tell my dad to blow the school off the face of the earth. He said he couldn't blame us for running away, but he couldn't have me staying there at his house without my parents' knowing. He wanted to take me home, but I said that I'd make my own way home in the morning.

When we went back to my home, no one was in, so I climbed in through a window. We had something to eat, and then my ma and sisters came up the stairs. They were shocked to see us sitting there. I expected her to start shouting, but she merely asked if we were hungry. While she was making some soup the police came to the door. I panicked and ran for the window, but Ma pleaded with me to give myself up. After we had had our soup we were taken away by the police.

As we drove back to the school, all I could think about was how to get away again. I knew I'd be punished for what I'd done, but somehow I cut myself off from the Brothers' threats and even the slaps about the head. My backside was raw from the leather strap and my body was covered with the other bruises that I got while trying to get away from them, but I didn't feel any pain when the belt made contact with my skin – it was as if I was in a trance. Once again I felt that I was being watched like something from another planet . 'Only an animal would do what you have done,' the Brothers told me, and there was no concealing their hatred. They treated me like an outcast and told the other boys not to go near me in case I got them into trouble. Before bed I was told to go to the chapel and pray for an hour for my sins. One of the Brothers knelt beside me, staring at the crucifix high on the wall; he paid no attention to me, but when he got up to go he patted me on the shoulder.

8 A LITTLE MISCHIEF

At one of our school meetings the head Brother said that he was sick of certain boys causing trouble and not co-operating, running away and breaking into places in the Edinburgh area and getting the school a bad reputation. Of course he was referring to me and my pals. Imagine our getting the school a bad name. The school was full of thieves, pickpockets, shoplifters, house-breakers and God knows what else, and he claimed it was boys like me who got his school a bad name by running away and breaking into shops near the school. The only way to get home was to break into a shop for the train or bus fare. He then said that the next time we wanted to run away we should ask him for our fares – and he'd give us half an hour's start before phoning the police! I thought a great deal about what he had said as I lay in Killiecrankie that night, wondering if he meant it. There was no harm in asking ... or was there?

When I told my pals what I'd done they said I was crazy, but it was the head Brother who was crazy. He beat me up so severely that my head was bleeding from a bang with some heavy object. He was in a mad frenzy, screaming at me for being such an evil wrong-doer, and he couldn't stop beating me. He told me he was going to get rid of me, and the quicker the better.

I ran away again with Jamie Mac from Bridgeton, and we made our way into Edinburgh. Outside the station were some shops which looked easy to break into. We picked a sort of

93

confectionery shop, and climbed up on to the roof, where we ripped off the slates. We dropped into pitch blackness and lay in a sort of attic, listening for any unusual noises. Then I walked along some wooden beams, before putting my feet through the plaster. Immediately the light of the shop filled the darkened attic. Below us I could see glass cases with cigarette lighters and pens in them – from that distance I felt rich. It was like looking into another world.

I suppose I was in another world from those good people who passed by the shop window below me. I was a child in a child's world with a child's mind and looking through the eyes of a child.

Most people think a thief's a thief till one of their own is caught, when it's, 'Oh, it's not like my child to do that – he's not a thief.' Only when it's someone else's kid is a child a thief. I was only in this shop because I wanted to get home to Ma and my family. It was up to me to persuade judges and procurators and police that I wasn't a thief! When I was charged at police stations or asked by a judge if I'd anything to say and answered, 'It wisnae me,' I was really trying to say 'I'm not the person you think I am.' Its only a common phrase, but nobody ever looked into the depth of it, and usually they answered: 'Is that all you have to say?'

When Jamie and me entered the train station we both acted in a serious manner so as not to look like wrong-doers. I looked anything but respectable – my pockets were full of stolen goods and I was filthy from smashing through the roof of the shop and white in places from the plaster – but I kept walking with my nose in the air and headed for the gents' toilet. We were in there for about half an hour, cleaning ourselves up and talking in whispers. We were so excited by our good fortune that we started dancing cowboy-style and singing. When Jamie eventually peeked out the door the whole station was in darkness – we'd missed the last train and were stranded. We decided to thumb a lift home instead. Two men stopped and said they'd take us all the way to Bridgeton. They wanted to know what we were doing out at that time of night.

'You're taking chances taking lifts from strange men,' one

of them told me. He went on to say that he'd thought for a moment that we were from St Joseph's. My heart was in my mouth.

'What's St Joseph's?' I asked, and he explained that it was a place for 'bad' boys. I was glad when we reached Bridgeton Cross. As we were getting out of the car the driver switched on a police radio – two policemen had helped us to get away!

At Jamie's house, Ringo the mynah bird was having a ball. 'Get back to that approved school' or 'Here's the polis,' he squawked half the night, hopping about on his one leg; and, as usual, we were caught and taken back to St Joseph's.

One day Ma came up with my dad's good friend Bobby Campbell, with whom we'd stayed in Carntyne. Uncle Bobby had just finished a nine-years sentence for robbery; they released him a year early because he'd had a massive heart attack. Bobby asked me if any of the Brothers or teachers were bothering me and he went so far as to pull up some of the Brothers and tell them not to mess me about. He was very smartly dressed in his three-piece suit and black Crombie; he looked like Humphrey Bogart.

Whenever Ma visited me, the Brothers and teachers couldn't have been nicer, and Ma was none the wiser.

'Are you sure you're not antagonising the teachers? They seem nice enough to me,' she'd say.

I know Ma had a lot of worries in those days. My dad was in one part of the country doing time, Jim was in an approved school outside Glasgow, and then there was me in Edinburgh. She was always there when needed, travelling all over the country to visit us. Every time I ran away the police would inform her, and she'd be worried sick about me. I've seen her lie on the couch with her face buried in her hands, sobbing and crying out that she couldn't take any more.

I was so mixed up that I couldn't concentrate at school – I could only think about running away. I was one of many dunces in the class – the only subject I was interested in was reading. I wasn't the only tearaway at the school, there were dozens of us, but I wanted, with all my heart, to be good in

95

the eyes of others. There was talk of my being transferred to a senior approved school because of my behaviour, but I just shrugged my shoulders, thinking I could always run away. Some of my pals thought me crazy but I didn't know who was crazy, me or them. I can only assume they thought this because I wouldn't – or couldn't – give in.

I was on the run and in Garthamlock when I learned that John Grimes was in Larchgrove. John and I had been good pals since my childhood – we had done a lot of stealing together and he was just like a brother to me. I got in touch with a pal and we decided to go down to the remand home in the middle of the night and break John out. I visited John with his ma and I had to be careful not to be recognised. We were really happy to see each other and told each other the gossip. When it came to talking about me breaking him out we talked in low whispers, but she could sense we were up to something and she started crying. She was a large woman of about seventeen stone, and very pleasant and cheery. One thing about Sue was that she believed all we told her about these places and the brutality, whereas a lot of women didn't. Sue would get angry at the thought of her son being beaten by the turnkeys. She told the turnkeys at Larchgrove that if they ever hit her son she'd wipe the floor with them. They never even bothered to argue when they saw the size of her – she called them all the wimps and freaks under the sun. John told his ma to keep quiet as they'd beat him up when the visit was over, but this only made her worse. I promised my pal that I'd break him out a few nights later.

This wasn't the first time I'd broken someone out of Larchgrove but on the night I went to get John it was snowing and blowing a blizzard. My pal stayed outside as I climbed the high steel fence. I felt a bit sentimental standing there looking at all the cast frames with dozens of tiny windows. It was dark in the grounds, but there were some soft lights in the dorms. I crept up to the windows and moved about below them in case some boy looked out and reported me to the authorities. I could hear boys talking to each other, and occasionally a cigarette butt would come out of a dorm

96

window. I heard a boy calling for his mammy. I looked at the dorm windows, hoping to recognise John. When I looked behind me I could see my footprints in the snow, so I had to back-track and brush them away with my jacket.

I finally found John – in fact I heard him before I saw him, talking with his pals in the dorm. When he saw me, he came to the window all excited, a big smile on his face. Soon other faces appeared alongside his, some laughing, some bewildered. John put his arm out the window and shook my hand. I could hear him telling the others that I was his pal, and they asked me for cigarettes, which they hid in their mattresses. I heard the night watchman telling the boys to pipe down.

I had a huge wooden post for bursting the cast frame on John's window. If you place a wooden post or iron bar between two small windows and force it downwards with all your weight, the cast may well snap – sometimes there are bad flaws in the casts and they go easily enough, sometimes they won't break at all. I put the post between the two broken window frames and pushed and heaved and twisted, but nothing happened. John had blankets at the window to smother the sound of shattering. But I couldn't budge it on my own. I tried to get the post through the window – with the weight of all the boys on it, the cast would surely have snapped – but it was too thick. John begged me to leave before I found myself joining him, and I climbed back over the fence after saying goodbye to John and his pals. Later I went and stole a few boxes of crisps and sweets and passed them in to John. It was the best I could do for him under the circumstances. There were times when he did similar things for me.

9 THE BEGGAR WITHIN

One night, near New Year's Eve, Ma came into my bedroom and told me that Uncle Bobby Campbell had died. The next morning I went round to Bobby's daughters' house. My Uncle Billy asked me if I would like to go into the room where Uncle Bobby lay to pay my last respects. He saw that I was frightened, so he offered to come with me. Uncle Bobby was covered in a white sheet. I saw Billy make the sign of the cross, so I did the same. Billy said that Bobby was a real gentleman, and one of the best. I prayed, and when I opened my eyes Uncle Billy was gone. I was alone with a dead man. I kissed him on the cheek and said goodbye.

I wasn't really into the pop scene, though I had been into country music. My pals thought this was strange, but my taste in music came from my dad and my uncles. I never did like dancing because I was too shy – I fancied waltzing and country dancing, but there was no way I could boast about this. I was classed as old-fashioned when it came to music.

I started dating a lassie called Jeanette, who was known to be the best-looking teenager in Garthamlock. My folks wanted to enter her in a beauty competition but she was too shy. She laughed when she heard about my taste in music.

Whenever I was on the run I went to Marie and Christine's. Jeanette often stayed there so I had great company, and I'd spend hours telling them stories about St Joseph's. They were flabbergasted. They always fed me well and hid me under one of the beds. I never thought about sex with them – I was too busy thinking about stealing to be interested.

Marie or Christine would shelter me for as long as possible, but whenever their parents saw me they'd plead with me to give myself up. But there was no way I wanted to go back to approved school or to that special school. Those schools were a laughing-stock. I can remember kids chasing the grey van and shouting that we were all loonies, and it's true that our school included people who were in very poor mental and physical condition. Whenever I was waiting for the grey bus to pick me up I would hide in case anyone saw me. All my pals knew about my going to the special school, but they never said anything to my face. And I felt left out when I heard my pals talk about the fun they had at their schools.

I found myself drifting away from my pals in Garthamlock – they didn't have anything in common with me, and they began to think me crazier than crazy. Some of my pals in their early teens were slashing and stabbing rival gang members. To me this was crazy, and I couldn't and didn't do it. I could never have slashed another person, or an animal for that matter. I passed my pals carrying knives and hatchets and looking for strangers to hack pieces out of, but I'd rather go stealing than fighting. I became, like most kids on the estate, a member of a gang. The oldest members were in their late twenties and the youngest about ten. Nero the policeman loved chasing the gangs away from the street corners – sometimes he'd come up on the pavements in his police car, scattering us in every direction. We had nowhere to go when he chased us away from the street corners, so kids went looking for trouble in nearby housing estates.

The Garthamlock boys would gather on one side of the quarry near Ma's house and the Easterhouse gangs on the other side. The Queenslie Rebels would be there as well, hundreds of people armed with every weapon imaginable. Older members of the gangs always started the battles. They would rush at each other, screaming obscenities and brandishing their weapons. The police seldom got involved because they were too outnumbered.

Some of my pals even had their gang names tattooed on their hands and arms. For many of them, fighting was part of growing up. There were often battles in the school grounds, and kids from other estates found it hard to get to school.

One of my pals, named Ped, had a wooden arm, which he used to defend himself in gang fights. He was a dangerous character, and had been known to knock people out with a swipe from his wooden arm. The authorities confiscated it on a few occasions. Some of the lassies in our gangs were even crazier than some of the guys. They'd slash and stab guys in rival gangs. One lassie I knew, whose name was Mary, split a guy's head open with a hatchet and thought nothing of it.

There was nothing on these housing estates for the kids. Sometimes a youth club opened, but not everyone could get into it. There were no cinemas, no pubs and no entertainment for anyone: they were just like the American Indian reservations. Whoever built them owes a helluva lot to society.

Being on the run in my home town wasn't as easy as I imagined, because apart from looking out for Nero and other policemen I had to be wary of some of the older boys. They often gave chase, dragged me home and handed me over. 'It's not just for your own good,' they'd tell me while I kicked and struggled to get away, 'but for your ma's sake.' One day about six of them caught me, and when they took me up the stairs to my ma's house I got one hell of a surprise. My dad appeared at the door in a rage – only it wasn't me he was raging at, but those who had dragged me home. He told them they'd probably got the police on their tails, and the last thing he wanted was those dirty filthy bastards at this door. He took me into the house and asked me if I wanted something to eat or if I wanted a bath – I expected him to go crazy. Maw felt my legs and arms and said how thin I was getting, and my dad agreed. After I'd eaten he made me tell him about how I was treated at the school and about the times I'd tried to get away. Before I could finish he said, 'If any of those fuckpigs ever lay a hand on you – put a heavy object over their heads.' He advised me to give myself up, for my own good – and Ma's. He said he'd personally take me back and tell them if they as much as laid one finger on me, he'd blow them out of their habits with a stick of gelignite.

Next morning I bathed and Ma pressed my clean clothes till they looked immaculate. Maw slipped me a pound note before I left. One of my dad's friends, George Drummond came with us. I met him later in Peterhead Prison, where he seemed to own everything that moved. He was a giant of a man and very powerfully built.

On the way to St Joseph's my dad and his friends cursed the Brothers and teachers, and asked me who gave me beatings. Ma kept nudging my leg, as if warning me to tell them no more. From the look on her face, she was worried about what might happen when we reached the school. So was I – but I hoped there would be a fight because it would give me an acceptable excuse for running away. I couldn't very well stay there if my Dad and his friends set upon the Brothers.

As we neared the school I became even more frightened, and wished that I hadn't volunteered to give myself up. George Drummond told me to point out the first bullying teacher and he'd put one on his Dan Flin. 'Dan Flin' is slang for the chin.

'A fucking stick of gelignite they'll be getting,' said my dad.

As we entered the gate, my belly turned. I took my folks up to the head Brother's office. He was sitting behind his desk, dressed in his black robes. My dad said he didn't want me to be punished as I had decided to give myself up, and that if I was going to be given the belt then he'd put me in the car and take me home – and put the Brother in hospital. It was agreed that I wouldn't be punished.

The head Brother said that I'd been in a lot of trouble and wouldn't co-operate with the authorities, who were trying their best for me – and that if I'd stay back from Gak, Tony, Tommy and the others I'd get along a lot better. He sent for my school report and said it was terrible, and that my behaviour was the worst he'd come across. He asked my dad what his business was, and he said he was a partner in a scrap yard. I was trying to hold in my laugh – I'd heard about all the safes he'd blown open. 'And who's this?' he said, looking towards George Drummond. 'This is his Uncle George,' my dad said, and George said he was a fruit merchant.

The Brother raised his eyebrows, turned to me and said, 'You have more going for you than any other kid in the school, with your father and uncle being in business.' I was very lucky to have family in business, he said, as there were guys in the school whose parents couldn't even afford to buy them a pair of trousers. He then said that if I promised to 'screw my nut' for six months I'd be allowed home for good – but I knew that there was no way I could stay out of trouble for six months. To others it would have seemed an offer that couldn't be refused, so it was best to agree. Ma was so pleased at the outcome of it all, and my dad gave me a 'I got you a good deal' wink of the eye.

'Six months good behaviour and I'll have him home to you, Mr Steele.' This was all the head Brother was asking for. He didn't want me in his school, and the quicker they got rid of me the better.

Before my folks left my dad turned to me and said, 'Just on the off chance that one of these fuckpigs should beat you up or be snide with you in any way, take this phone number: if you ring, we'll bring you home.' The head Brother said that as long as I behaved myself I wouldn't be needing it. But I did.

Not long after my dad's visit the head Brother called for me and angrily informed me that my dad and Big George were both in gaol for safe-blowing and explosives – and that my dad had been given six years. I was shocked to hear this – and realised then that their visit to the school had only made matters worse.

10 ST ANDREW'S REFORM SCHOOL

One day I was called to the head Brother's office and informed rudely that I was being sent to another approved school as I was a bad influence and would never learn. The same two Brothers who had brought me to St Joseph's from Larchgrove took me away to St Andrew's Approved School in a place called Rhu, near Helensburgh. It seemed a long way from home, but I'd get back somehow.

As we drove up the driveway I could see boys who looked much older than myself working away with wheelbarrows and shovels and picks. They stopped their work to look in my direction, obviously aware that I was a new boy. I couldn't believe it when I saw them smoking cigarettes in front of the teachers. I was fourteen now, and I wondered if they'd let me smoke too.

The teachers seemed more gentle than those at St Joseph's, and greeted me with a smile as they passed. I was the youngest, youngest-looking and probably the smallest boy there.

An Irish matron took me to the stores to get some clothing. She spent the better part of the morning telling me how frail-looking I was and feeling my arms and legs. She started cuddling me just like Ma used to – I later learned she was this way with other boys she liked. She reminded me of the kit woman at St Joseph's who gave us sweets and was so kind. People like this put smiles on unhappy faces.

I was taken to see the headmaster. He was known to the staff and boys as the 'wee man'. But when speaking to him we addressed him by his surname or as 'sir'. He told me he wanted to help me as much as he could, and that he meant that sincerely. My past record, he said, was pretty bad and he hoped that I wouldn't cause him the trouble I had caused at St Joseph's. He offered me a cigarette. I refused, saying I didn't smoke. A teacher offering a boy a cigarette was, to me, unheard of. I was frightened to take it in case he was only tricking me, to see if I smoked, but he insisted and gave me a packet to keep. 'Go on,' he said, smiling. 'Light it up, son.'

I felt awkward doing so, and at the same time really great. Something was happening to me – I was in another world with better people. I was changing, my outlook on life was different, the world wasn't such a bad place after all. These people didn't have the eerie look of the Brothers at St Joe's. They wore suits, not creepy-looking cloaks, and their attitude was different. In six weeks, they told me, I could be allowed my first home leave. It never occurred to me that I could have been home for good had I coped with the regime at St Joe's.

The school was much cosier than St Joseph's. My housemaster, although he wasn't as good as Mr Strawb, was okay with me; my house unit was called Douglas House, and it was fairly new and modern. I was told I would go to work, which included joinery, painting, bricklaying, plumbing, gardening and the mechanics shop. This was all new to me – I'd never worked in my life. I hated the thought of going to school, but work! Well, that was something I couldn't wait to tell Ma and Maw. I was to spend one week with each work party: it would take eight weeks to assess me, and then I'd go in front of a board with lots of teachers and others, where I would be discussed in full and then allocated a work party. Even though I was to go to work, I would still attend school so many times a week. My schoolteacher was known as 'D.C.', and he was forever being made a fool of by the boys.

My pal John Ferran was also at this school, but he was on the run when I arrived. On my first day a tall guy came rushing over to me shouting, 'Are you Johnnyboy Steele?' He turned out to be my cousin, Billy's boy Peter, whom I'd last seen in Carntyne. I was overwhelmed with joy to discover my long-lost cousin. I asked him to run away with me but he didn't want to know. Months later I took Peter home with me on a home leave, and it was great.

My housemaster showed me around my new home and my new dorm with its fine beds and curtains – the place was spotlessly clean, and the beds all tidied up. There was also a housemother who cleaned and cooked and was involved with the running of the school. I was given a kit number for my clothes, and a locker to keep my kit in. We also had lockers in the dorms where we kept our Sunday clothes.

Everybody was walking about, smoking and playing games – there was no one to follow me about, and no locked doors or even windows. I felt as though I had been rescued from disaster and hardship; St Joseph's and St Andrew's seemed worlds apart. The new leaf my ma always wanted me to turn seemed a possibility at last.

But then my housemaster told me that when I'd finished St Andrew's I would have to go back to the special school till I was aged sixteen. I was heartbroken. I hated that fucking school, and wanted to forget all about it. I said I didn't want to go back there, but my housemaster was adamant. He also said that I was a dunce and could do with some schooling. I told him I wasn't a dunce and he said 'Do you think you could sit behind this desk and do the work I'm doing?' I didn't know what he was doing behind that desk – but I knew what I was doing – I would be off at the first opportunity.

From time to time D.C. took us hill-walking and climbing, and it was on the first of these occasions that I ran away. I couldn't help myself – it seemed easier to go than stay. We were walking along a long quiet road near Arrochar when I told my pal Jim Malone that I was going to run away and asked him the best way out of there.

'Fuck knows,' he said – and he told me he was coming too. We came to a bend in the road, and once round it we bolted.

So there I was on the run again, and happy for all that. We kept on walking, staying clear of the road in case we were spotted by the police or someone who'd give us away. There were hills all round, and the farther we walked the more lost we felt. I knew that Ma would be shattered – I had written to her to say that I had settled in and would be good and get home soon.

God knows how many miles we covered in the bitter cold and darkness. In the distance we could see lights. We assumed it was a carnival, so we headed in its direction, hoping to be able to steal some money to get us home. However far we walked we didn't seem to get any closer – in fact we seemed to be getting further away. Finally it dawned on us that we had been following a ship!

The cold almost had me in tears and I decided that if I heard a car coming I wasn't going to run, even if it was the police. At last we came to a small cluster of houses, which looked very cosy. I noticed a big bar of chocolate near the steering wheel of a parked car. I went to look for a brick to smash the windscreen, but when I got back Jim told me that the keys were still in the ignition. That meant the car doors must be open, so we wasted no time getting in. It was very warm inside, and we ate the chocolate and searched the dashboard compartment. I was sitting at the driving wheel. I told Jim I could drive – I couldn't, but I thought I'd have a go. I was too small, so we had to put some things on the front seat to raise me up a bit, just enough to see out of the windscreen. Before I knew what was happening the car was belting down the road. I was terrified, and I thought we were going to be killed. Jim let out a scream: his feet were up on the dashboard and he was shouting for me to stop, but I didn't know how to. The last thing I remember was a bang, and feeling as if someone had beaten me up.

When I came to I was alone in the car. I got out fast, even though I was very dizzy, and staggered down the road. I noticed Jim running like hell. He was shaking like a leaf. We ran down a long dark road, and every now and then Jim would mutter, 'Never again!'

It was cold and wet and I was sick of running. Whenever we saw the lights of a car in the distance, they'd disappear as

106

the car turned a bend and then reappear, beaming across the sky till the car eventually passed. One oncoming car was a police jeep. Neither of us even bothered to run for cover. We were so cold and drenched that we were grateful to the big Highland police officer for stopping for us.

He rolled down his window and asked where we were going.

'Ir ye from St Andrew's approved school? Ir ye the laddies who've run awa?' he asked.

'Aye, mister, and we're freezing,' I told him.

He got out of the jeep and opened the back door for us to get in. He drove us back to the school, and we arrived there in the dead of night. We were left in the recreation room of Shandon House for an hour before our housemaster came for us.

'I hope you are cold and hungry – serves you right for running away,' he snapped.

I was eventually called to the wee man's office, and his face was scarlet with anger. He said the car had been a policeman's car; luckily for me, he was very friendly with the policeman and there'd be no charges. I was terrified but I managed to pluck up the courage to tell him that it was I who had stolen and crashed the car. 'Liar!' he shouted. He said I was too small, and that I was only taking the blame for Jim Malone. They held me down across a huge table, while I was severely punished with a leather belt. 'Tell the truth!' he was screaming at me. He then turned on Jim and accused him of getting me to take the blame for the car. 'That lad couldn't see out the bloody windscreen!' he screamed.

Everyone laughed when we told them that we'd stolen a policeman's car. Stunts like this made people think I was crazy.

11 HOME LEAVE

My brother Jim had been sent to St Mary's approved school for stealing, my dad was serving his six years, so Ma had them both to worry about as well. Before long my sister Lana had been sent away to a convent for not going to school. Poor Ma, she had a hard life – no wonder people said she would end up a nervous wreck. I'd heard a lot of women say they couldn't have gone through what Ma went through. She was always visiting one of us in some establishment. I can remember her saying, 'What kind of family will others be thinking I've raised?' while Maw tapped her fingers on her knee and bit her bottom lip, looking skyward with her sightless eyes.

When I finally got home on leave I cherished every moment of it. All around me my pals were fighting in rival gangs – Jim was involved, and had been charged with attempted murder while fighting in one of the big shopping stores in the town centre.

The three lassies, Marie and Christine and Jeanette, were my real friends. I was in love with Jeanette: young love was great for me, even though she wouldn't let me have sex with her. But my love of stealing and of running away was stronger than anything else I ever felt, and I couldn't stop. I couldn't tear myself away from it, much as they begged me to.

The sad thing about all the gang fighting was that innocent passers-by were always getting seriously injured. Only when the police came in force did the gangs disperse and flee. It was always a good idea for the boys to have their girls with them, so that when the police came they could link arms and walk away like courting couples. Most times the weapons would be given to the lassies, as the police wouldn't search them.

Nero harassed me whenever he could, along with most of the other boys who hung about street corners. There was another bunch of coppers who roamed about in a blue unmarked Commer van. They were known as the 'Untouchables', and had been specially formed to break up the gangs. They were ruthless and often brutal, and as soon as their van was spotted everybody fled. One day I was arrested by the Untouchables and taken home. They told Ma I was loitering and was to be kept in the house or I'd be lifted for being a known thief! Ma and Maw shouted at them to leave me alone as I wasn't causing any harm, and that I was home on leave from the approved school and behaving myself. Before they left they said I was to be off the streets before ten o'clock at night or they'd arrest me. It was the law, and was put into practice all over the country. It was known as the Powers Act.

I hated the thought of going back to St Andrew's on a voluntary basis, even though life was quite good for us. Sometimes we'd have a disco, and girls came in from the surrounding area by the busload. I remember getting all dressed up and combing my hair back, in the fashionable style. The older guys boasted about how many lassies they'd have before the night was out, and we were warned by the housemasters that there'd be no taking girls up to the dormitories. There were a few wisecracks from some of the boys. When the bus arrived we were all at the window, eyeing the girls up and down and yahooing with excitement.

It was great dancing with the lassies, and of course much smooching went on – some guys went behind doors and curtains, some slipped off with lassies to the dormitories where more than smooching took place. Before the night was over we had dates galore, and telephone numbers had been exchanged.

St Andrew's offered me a lot, but I didn't appreciate it at the time. We used to go canoeing and yachting, and did other

109

outdoor games. I could get along with most of the teachers. My housemaster lived with his wife and children in a house attached to our unit, and we got to know his family well and treated them with respect. His little son of four or five was a favourite amongst us boys and he'd wander about among us. I was only one of many who fell in love with the new house-mother in Douglas House. Every week one boy from each house would be allocated to help the housemother with clean-ing and washing dishes and setting tables and serving food – and soon Douglas House was full of volunteers. Miracles do happen ... I stopped wetting the bed when I went to St Andrew's.

Despite all the goodness of St Andrew's I went on running away – doing what I was best at. One day Ma came to visit me but I'd run away just before she got there. As a punishment I was made to wear short trousers.

There was quite a bit of boozing and pill-swallowing going on – everyone was into a bit of the wild life: this was the done thing among the young ones. I never took a pill and seldom had a drink – the taste of drink put me off easily enough. Some of my pals could pass for eighteen and get served in a pub, and to them this was an achievement. I couldn't get into pubs – unless I was breaking into them – since I was still very young-looking for my age.

The headmaster at St Andrew's said he was going to get rid of me and send me away to another school if I didn't stop running away. Individual teachers would speak to me about my behaviour and try to talk me out of my way of life. 'Don't waste your life living like this, son,' one of them kept telling me. But that wasn't to be.

One night when I was on the run, I was sitting in Marie's close talking to an older boy, Big Shug, and keeping an eye open for Nero. I asked Shug if he would watch for the police while I grafted one of the shops, but he didn't want to know. Then I saw an old pal of mine selling newspapers, so I thought I'd ask him for a loan of a few pounds. He said no, but when someone came over to buy a newspaper and he took some change from his pocket I lifted a pound note out of his hand

and walked away, telling him I needed it more than he did and that when I could I'd pay him back.

I had just got back to the close when Nero and his partner arrived with the police van. I was charged with assault and robbery. Nero's partner acted the good guy and promised me that he would save me from getting beaten up if I would admit to a couple of break-ins, just to clear their books. But I couldn't admit to anything. In court the following morning I was remanded in custody for two weeks social and inquiry reports. I was told I'd be going to Longriggend remand unit.

12 LONGRIGGEND

On the way to Longriggend I sat in the van and listened to guys talking openly about what they were in for, about the slashings and stabbings they'd done. Guys can be held in Longriggend if they are between the ages of fourteen and twenty-one, so there were older guys than me in the van, some with beards and moustaches. Everyone was handcuffed, and we were watched closely by the warders. Longriggend is near Airdrie, only twenty miles from Glasgow, and after a while someone in the van pointed it out in the distance. It used to be a hospital before they made it into a jail, and all around it was a twenty-foot wire fence.

The reception area smelled of floor polish and Brasso, and the place was spotless. Warders screamed at us to get lined up and listen for our names, and to answer 'sir'. They started calling out names, and one guy who failed to say 'sir' got beaten up in front of us all.

'You bastards will do as you're told in here – okay? There's no hard men in here – only us!' a wee fat warder with silver-rimmed glasses shouted.

They treated us like animals. You were either a 'cunt' or a 'bastard' to most of the warders. We were made to strip off, wrap towels around our waists and wait in line till we were called. When my name was called I hurried up to a warder who looked right into my eyes and said, 'Who the fuck did you assault? You don't look like you could burst a plastic bag!' This made them all laugh.

112

Before we went for a shower one of the warders read out the rules of the place. The rule that struck me most was that there was to be no talking during the recreation period! I was given a black army-type battledress which was sizes too big for me – I had to roll up the trouser legs and jacket sleeves and turn down the waistband. I felt ashamed to be seen wearing such clothes, though everyone else's clothes seemed too big, too. Everyone was given shaving brushes except me and then we were marched out of the reception and into the halls where, warders from different halls were waiting to pick us up.

All the other guys in C Hall were much older than me. At slop-out time I had to collect a chamber pot, which looked as though it had never been cleaned out. I wrapped my towel round it to hide it from the others. Everywhere I went I heard older guys comment on my size and say that it was a shame having a young kid like me in there.

'Wit ur ye in fur, wee man?' I was asked time and time again. Some of the guys knew my brother Jim, and gave me sweets and tobacco – which I wasn't allowed because of my age. If it wasn't for the kindness of the guys there, I don't know what I would have done.

I was made to hang my clothes outside my door as a security precaution. One of the warders told me that I wasn't to look out the window of my cell, or talk to anyone. I wasn't to smoke – 'And don't press that bell, unless you're fucking dying,' he growled. He also told me to be out of bed in the morning before they came in. My bed had to be made up into a bed block; I had to fold my PT clothes and towel and spread them out on the bed in a neat fashion, as shown in the diagrams. Half of the time the screw was shouting at me – which had some of the guys shouting at him, telling him to leave me alone, that I was only a kid. They called him a fucking big bam, which seemed to make him worse.

Other screws came up from the landing below to find out what all the noise was about, and they started kicking the doors and threatening to beat guys up. I got the blame from the warder, and the others started punching and kicking me. The cell was tiny, with steel-barred windows, and with all the

113

warders in it and me on the floor I felt as though I was in a matchbox. I felt their boots sink into me, but I never felt the pain. I felt afraid, but because I didn't cry they said that I was a would-be hard man and that they'd sort out the likes of me, and kept on kicking me. So I let the tears fall and they left, satisfied. One of them said he'd be in to see me in the morn. There was a mad look on his face which terrified me.

My light was kept on all night, and occasionally I could sense the warder peeping through the spy hole. I never slept, but I lay there until I was startled by the ringing of a bell and the kicking of doors.

'Get out of those beds, you lot!' a warder was shouting. I dived up and made my bed according to the chart, but the warder kicked it on to the floor, saying it wasn't good enough. We had to stay in our cells till the warder shouted, 'Outside your doors and stand to attention!' We had to have our pots in our hands, and once outside it was 'One pace forward', with urine spilling on to the shiny waxed floor as we headed for the toilets to slop out and wash and shave.

After slopping out, a warder handed me a letter to write to Ma, telling her where I was. I was warned not to write anything about the remand unit. 'I hope to fuck you're not one of those cunts who can't write,' he said.

It was difficult for me to walk since my trouser legs fell down over my shoes and made me slip on the floor. Once we'd slopped out, it was 'outside and face your doors! One pace forward, march!' and down the stairs till we reached a huge dining room which held more than a hundred guys. There were rows of long wooden tables, with as many as sixteen sitting at each; the tables were very old and the names of guys and their gang names had been carved into their woodwork. We couldn't go to any table we liked.

Everyone was dressed in the same coloured battledress; some of the guys had had their hair shaved off, either because they had bugs or because their faces didn't fit. Not only was everyone dressed the same, but it seemed as though we all did the same body movements at exactly the same time – it was as if we were all robots, programmed by the warders. I felt as

114

if I had left my own body and was looking down upon myself and the others sitting there. Once again that feeling in the back of my neck and a kind of high-pitched sound in my ears warned me that a black-out was coming on – except that I was scared to let it happen, and the fear of collapsing saved me. I rested my forehead on the table and felt its cold top against my skin.

We were given a bowl of watery porridge and a bit of cooked ham. I ate neither, but I drank the tea, which was horrible and a funny brown colour. It was said the warders put bromide into it to stop us from getting sexual urges. We weren't allowed to talk, and whenever guys whispered to each other the warders would scream, 'Shut the fuck up, cunt, or you'll get your balls blackened!'

At night we were taken down to the dining hall to watch TV. There was no talking or smoking allowed. 'Shut up, cunt! Face the front, cunt! Up the stairs, cunt!' Some guys couldn't take much, and they either attacked the warders or smashed up. Quite often they hanged themselves.

One of the warders used to steal pies from the hot-plate and hide them under his hat, and the grease would run down his head. This made all the other warders laugh their heads off, and he would then eat the pie in front of us all. He pulled this stunt at least once a week. Another warder had a piece of string and some poor kid would have to walk about the hall and pretend the warder's dog was tied to it. This also made the other warders laugh a good deal.

After breakfast I was taken to see a prison doctor. There were about twelve of us in a little room, stripped to the waist, waiting our turn to go in and see him. When it was my turn I was asked if I had any illnesses, or had ever been in a mental hospital or to a special school. I was then told to drop my trousers and the warder handed the doctor an electric lamp so that he could check if I had crabs. He then checked my head with the lamp. 'One for the lousy seat,' he said to the warder. I was taken into a little room and sat down on a chair. In less than a minute all my hair had been shorn off, right down to the scalp. I felt sick and naked and humiliated. I couldn't look

115

the others in the eye, but hung my head in shame. I felt I had no identity left.

When Ma came to visit, she nearly had a fit when she saw me. She was sitting across a table from me, and the first thing she wanted to know was who had done that to my head.

'You look like you've just been in a concentration camp,' she said. I had to ask Ma to keep her voice down, fearing the warders would hear her. 'The dirty liberty-taking bastards,' she kept saying. The first time I ever heard the word 'dehumanising' was when Ma used it that day. She said she was going to see her MP and some lawyers about it.

I was told I'd be going to school in D Hall along with the other teenagers. I was never so glad to hear this, since it meant I'd be in a classroom and away from all this witless persecution and fear. The governor of D Hall told me that I wouldn't be allowed a radio or photographs, that there was to be no physical contact in the visiting room, and that I must obey all the rules, including no talking. I'd be allowed one library book at a time, and I must never sit on my bed during the daytime. In reality they were running a detention centre. We were untried prisoners, and we were denied all privileges in order to make life more painful. As far as they were concerned we were all guilty.

'Looks like you're following in your dad's footsteps,' the governor said to me, shaking his head from side to side. I was warned that, should I try to run away, it would be my last attempt. I was then taken back to my cell and locked in.

I looked out of my window, and all I could see was other parts of the gaol, with its twenty-foot wire fence topped with razor wire. This bare existence was not life – not for me it wasn't. Occasionally the door opened, and 'Do you want to go for walkies, lad?' the warder asked. That's what they called our exercise period – like we were dogs they were talking to.

There was about a dozen boys in the classroom, and most of us had had our hair shaved off. Some of them swore blind that theirs had been cut off because they'd been cheeky to the warders. Both the teachers were warders, and one of them was a bully. His idea of giving us the strap was to hit us with the truncheon which all the warders carried in a specially made pocket in their trousers – the leather strap handle was on show at all times, so that they could get them out fast if required. He'd make us hold out our hands and hit us on our palms. He was hated by all the kids. The other warder never seemed to bother us, so we all looked forward to his taking the lessons.

In the gymnasium we were made to do exhausting press-ups and running, wearing our PT clothes and sand shoes of all shapes and sizes. After PT we were taken to a shower room with as many as fourteen showers in it. There was no privacy, and we were made to go in naked together – I used to try to hide my penis with my hands. The warders stood by and watched, giving us so many minutes to get showered and out.

Eventually I was returned by the court to St Andrew's. I was really glad to be away from Longriggend and all it stood for. The headmaster sent for me and went over his philosophy with me again, trying to get me to see the light. 'I don't give in so easily,' he told me.

One night I ran away with my pal Jim; we scampered away up a huge hill and on to the disused railway, often pausing for breath and to look over our shoulders. On the way home me and Jim laughed at our good fortune. When we parted I headed straight for Garthamlock and Marie's house, where I lay under the bed in the darkness and I listened to the merry banter of Jeanette, Christine and Marie.

Whenever I went to the toilet one of the lassies would make sure no one was about, and then I would slip down the dark hallway like a thief in the night. I would watch from Marie's window as the police walked by in the darkness – her close front was one of the main 'gang haunts' on the estate. In the wee small hours I always get sentimental. I fall head over heels in love with life and see nothing but good in everything. The lassies would wake me before they got up for school so that I could be away before their ma came to wake them up. I hated leaving the cosiness of their little room and their company.

Some people in Garthamlock would ask me to get certain

things for them, like televisions, and since I was known as one of the local thieves I'd oblige. I wasn't very business-minded, since I gave most of it away for nothing. I wasn't a kleptomaniac – I simply liked stealing and breaking into places; it was exciting. I was always good to whoever sheltered me from the law, and I'd never touch a penny belonging to them.

I was barred from one of the local shops, and whenever I tried to buy something there I was told to get out.

'You come in the back door when we're closed!' the manager said, so I had to go to another shop or get someone else to go in for me. Ma was embarrassed about going to the shops because I had broken into most of them.

One night Aldo and John Grimes and I decided to break into a social club. It was dark when we stumbled across it by accident. Once inside the building we stood rock still, listening for any noise. My heart was pounding in the eerie silence. We burst a wooden panel in the bar and crawled in to get at the cigarettes, drink and money. We were gathering them together when we heard a noise from outside – of men with jingling keys. Then we rushed to get out of the little hole we'd made. I was first out, but when I discovered the police were entering the club I fought to get back in just as my two pals were fighting to get out. All three of us were trapped in the bar, and they knew we were there because of the hole and the light shining through.

The police began shouting through to us, asking how many of us were in there. Then they shone their torches in our faces to startle us, and started pushing us around, asking our names and intimidating us. When we arrived at the police station they checked us out and discovered that I was on the run from St Andrew's. I cursed myself for not giving a false name – otherwise I might have been released along with John and Aldo.

They began to count the packets of cigarettes and the bottles of booze – one of the policemen was sitting behind a desk with the stolen goods in front of him. The three of us were made to stand in a line, side by side and to attention and as I stood there something strange happened to me: I saw myself

118

differently. Maybe I saw myself as others had seen me; it was like looking at a stranger and noticing more clearly than ever before what was happening to my life. The truth was in front of my eyes – I wanted to turn and run but there was nowhere to run to. I felt my face go cold and sweaty, and my back go cold and sticky, and then the room began to spin round and round. When I came to, I was sitting on a chair.

We were charged with the break-in and attempted theft. Aldo's and John's parents came to get them out, but I was held in custody to await my return to St Andrew's. I slept the night in a police cell. I was given a thin rubber mattress and two grey, dirty-looking blankets. Every few hours the cell door would open and a head pop round and ask me if I were all right.

One day D.C. took us hill-walking and got us lost. He couldn't work the compass properly and had us going round in circles, saying, 'It must be this way, boys.' A while later he'd say, 'Naw, it must be this way.' D.C. wasn't an idiot, but far too soft-hearted. My pal Jaz shouted 'Fuck up, ya big bam!', and everyone started winding the teacher up. As a matter of interest, *bam* according to the English dictionary means a Highland Gentleman, whereas in Glasgow slang, *bam* means an idiot. Anyone living outside Glasgow was called a *teuchter* and most of them were known by the Glaswegians as *sheep shaggers*. I've seen guys walk right up to outsiders and say: 'Hey, are you wan an a' they sheep shaggers?' This may seem like bullying, but it was more of a territorial thing than anything else. We chased sheep and cows through the mist, like they were another gang – one of the boys calling the sheep a bunch of fucking bams!

We spotted an isolated cottage in the distance. As we got nearer we realised it was a condemned building – which was disappointing, because we'd hoped to get inside and steal. One guy had actually claimed the money meter. Way ahead of the teacher we crashed in the door and windows, and were up on to the roof wrecking the building even more, while D.C. cursed us, waving his fists. We were like demolishers on the warpath.

Eventually D.C. managed to get us away, only to take us round in more circles until someone spotted a long thick rope hanging from a branch on a huge tree. Below the tree was a deep gully, and the rope swung straight over it on to the other side. 'Stop, you lot!' he shouted, but we ran to it regardless of his threats. There were as many as six of us on the rope at any one time, and even the teacher had a go. Some guy. Still he couldn't find his way. 'Right, boys, we'll just head for a road and try to get the police to get us home,' he said. He was panicking now and couldn't conceal it. It was Jaz who pointed us in the direction of home. The teacher knew Jaz was a highly intelligent kid, so we followed him all the way to St Andrew's. It was late and dark when we arrived, and we all steamed into a warm meal.

I was asked by my housemaster if I'd like to go along with some others to do forestry work. I was delighted and promised not to run away. In the van we were all singing merrily – our sacks were full of sandwiches and fruit juice and tea and cakes. Our job was to cut the weeds from around the young forest trees, which were no taller than six inches. We hacked away for a few hours and then we were called up for our tea break. We had to make do with water from a loch; I tried to fill the kettle without getting insects in it, but it was impossible, and we had to pick out the insects that were floating in the tea mugs. It was great working there. After work we were driven back to the school, and in the morning we were off to the forest again. But I only lasted a few days before I felt the urge to run away again.

During one of the big breaks when most of the boys were home on leave, I was asked by the deputy headmaster if I would like a job in the garden. He said it would occupy my mind for a while. He was a heavily built man with a fat face and a drink problem. He gave me and my pal Lev the job of unblocking the sewers for ten shillings a day. We pulled on our Wellington boots and overalls; the deputy showed us what sewers to unblock, and left us with the day to ourselves.

We got the huge steel manhole cover up, and were nearly knocked out by the stench. The hole was about twelve feet deep, with a steel ladder leading down. Once inside we stood on thick planks of wood which were quite slippery. There was shit floating everywhere, and even though we were disgusted we made a joke of it. Our voices echoed in the sewer, so I had a go at yodelling. We laughed at the thought of one of us falling in amongst the filth. Lev was a really happy-go-lucky guy, and when he spotted a table-tennis ball floating around in the filth he tried to bring it closer with a stick. One minute he was there and the next he was gone! And then this hand came out of the filth toward me. I couldn't move for laughing. He was covered in shit, and no way was I going near him. He was flapping around like a penguin, coughing and spluttering. That was the end of our plumbing escapade.

As I mentioned earlier, Little Owny, my housemaster's son, was forever wandering about among us. He was a lovely kid, but he was dying from leukemia. We often bought him presents and watched him play. He never went anywhere without getting attention from one and all. We were in the dining room when D.C. told us that he had died. Ginzo stood up and prayed for Little Owny and then we all began praying for his wee soul to go to heaven. Half of us were crying. Most of the boys in the school regarded prayers as nonsense and hardly said them, but on that day it was different.

After this my housemaster went to stay with his folks, so his house was empty for some time; and it was during this period that a dozen of us decided to break into the greenhouse in the garden. The old gardener, who was one of the teachers, had grown a prize tomato, and was often seen talking to it and polishing it up. There was much talk about this tomato amongst us – it seemed that everyone wanted to have it. One night I got up and woke the others, and we slipped out of the house dressed in our pyjamas. Crawling through the grounds like commandos on a raid, we couldn't keep from laughing at the old gardener discovering his prize tomato was gone. Once in the garden grounds we made sure the greenhouse was empty, as it was rumoured the gardener stayed with his plants to keep them company. We lay around and smoked for a while and then crept over to the greenhouse. One of the boys wanted to put a huge boulder through the glass windows, but there was no need as the door was open. We began filling our pillow slips with tomatoes and other vegetables. When at last we found the prize tomato everyone tried to take a bite out of it. This developed into a tomato fight, in which we pelted each other at random and plants were ripped down and kicked about.

Next morning I was taken to the headmaster's office and asked if I was one of those involved in the greenhouse break-in.

'Naw, sir, it wisnae me,' I said.

The headmaster was almost foaming with rage. 'What's your number?' he shouted. I told him my kit number was fifty-one. Before him was a huge bag full of pyjama trousers, and the head searched it until he found a pair marked fifty-one. He threw them at me. 'Are these yours?' he bawled. I admitted that they were. 'And you're sure you weren't in that garden?' I denied it. 'Then what do you say about this?' he said, pointing to the knees of my pyjama trousers, which were all green. The other teachers who were there chased me and held me over the table to be belted. I didn't think he was going to stop. Well, that's how we were all caught, by our pyjamas.

In the school assembly hall we were all fined and lost our leaves. When I looked to the back of the hall, where the staff were seated, I noticed the old gardener sitting there with tears in his eyes. After that I didn't get on with him at all.

I'd sit in Marie's close while on the run from St Andrew's, and Ma and Lana would try to talk me into going back to the school. Maw often told me that we would end up losing Ma to an early grave if I didn't stop worrying her. It didn't stop me, but it did worry me, for I loved Ma dearly and I never got a chance to show it. And my dad wrote to me from gaol, warning me that Ma couldn't cope with my behaviour. I tried to explain myself and told him that I just couldn't stop. He wasn't too pleased with my reply, but it was the truth.

I went to visit my dad when I was on leave. All I got from the moment I went in was lectures about my behaviour. Before I left he gave me a few Christmas cards to post for him, saying he didn't trust the authorities at the gaol to send them. He gave me a big hug and asked me to be good. I was just on my way when I was stopped by the police. They wanted to know what I was up to and where I was going. Some passers-by stopped to stare at what was going on, but they were told to move on. The police looked at my dad's mail and started laughing when they saw the addresses, and one said: 'That's where you're going to end up, gaol!' They then gave the mail back to me, and told me to get on my way. I had a look at the mail that my dad had asked me to post: Jimmy Boyle, HM Prison; Frank Wilson, HM Prison; Ben Conroy, HM Prison; the Kray Twins, HM Prison; etc.

One day, while in St Andrew's, I was sent for and told that a doctor wanted to have a talk with me. He was a psychiatrist, though what that meant I did not know. He was better known as the 'head shrinker', and that frightened me. I had heard much about these doctors – it was rumoured that they decided who was and who was not a 'loony'. The atmosphere in the little room was horrible and frightening. One question he asked me was, 'If I gave you a billiard ball and a knife, would you peel it for me?' My pals who had seen other psychiatrists before had warned me about this. The answer to give is, 'Yes, I'll peel it, if you'll eat it!' but instead I told him I didn't know if it was possible. A few days later one of the teachers told me that my trouble was that I had a 'split personality', whatever that was. This had no effect on me. They'd been telling me I was crazy for a long time.

Meanwhile the gang fights seemed to get worse. In the late

Sixties the singer Frankie Vaughan went to Easterhouse to talk to the gangs, trying to bring peace to the communities. He managed to bring some gang leaders together and get a peace pact in the surrounding area. Gang members handed in weapons of every kind, which were placed in huge dustbins. This was televised live to millions of viewers throughout the country, but how long the truce lasted is another matter. A lot of young guys handed in weapons so they could say that they had taken part – rumour has it that one boy got a good beating for putting his dad's brand new kitchen knife in, still in its packet!

If I went into other housing estates to break into their shops, I had to be careful not to be spotted. One night, John Grimes and Aldo and I broke into a row of shops and just across the road was a public house called The New Inn, so we had to be careful in case some drunks spotted us. The next thing we knew a gang had come upon us. They all had weapons, and they pulled out razors and steak knives when they saw us. They were older than us, which was a good thing because it lessened the chances of their using the weapons on us. After they had eyeballed us they asked us what we were doing in their territory, where we were from and what our names were. I thought my life would soon be over, there in the darkness behind the shops. Some of them laughed and told their cronies to leave us alone, but others weren't having it, and, saying things like, 'Cmon, ya bastards, we're the real McCoy!', they came closer, brandishing their tools till our backs were against the wall. I told them that we were only out stealing and weren't in a gang, and that we were from Garthamlock and on the run from the police. This helped us because, like most gang members, they hated the police. One of the guys who seemed to be the leader asked us our names, and I thought of giving them a false one, fearing that they may have had trouble with my brother Jim – in which case they might have taken revenge on us. On the other hand if they did know Jim and hadn't had any trouble with him, then it could help us, so I took the chance and told them my real name. Luckily it worked: some of them knew Jim, and I could tell by their attitude that they weren't at war with his gang. We all felt better then, and the weapons were put away.

Before they left to go back to the pub I asked them to help us get the bars off the shop windows. A couple did so, but the others left, saying it wasn't their scene. These guys came from Blackhill, which had a real bad reputation then. It was said that when insurance companies sent their men in to collect their debts, they needed a police escort. Blackhill was a slum area, but for all its faults a lot of the people there were staunch. If they saw someone stealing or fighting there was no running for the police. I'm not saying there weren't any police informers, but they were few and far between.

The law of the jungle was that there'd be no giving information to the police, and those who did became outcasts if they were found out. But that isn't altogether true, because there are guys who have 'grassed' on others and been accepted, either because they could handle themselves or because they were stupid and nothing else could be expected of them. I've known guys who couldn't stand up to police interrogation and they've spilled their guts and told them everything they wanted to know, even admitting to things they haven't done. I don't think myself any better than others, but I never did grass anyone – it wasn't in me to do so.

Home on leave I met and fell for a lassie called Barbara. She came from Queenslie, the housing estate on the other side of the canal from Garthamlock. Maw said she preferred Jeanette and missed her. At night I would walk Barbara home to her house. I had to slip in and out of her estate in case the Queenslie Rebels saw me. She was in an awkward position, too, going out with a guy from another estate, and sometimes she got hassled. If the bridge was clear Barbara and I would stand under it and smooch for a while. Her dad was Irish and Barbara said she would like me to go to Ireland with her and her parents – it was all sweet talk and part of our romance. On the way home I also had to be careful in case any other gangs were lying in the grass waiting to give someone the treatment.

Everyone thought Barbara a good-looking lassie – Ma called her Shirley Temple because of her blonde curly hair. Whenever I left home to go back to the approved school I'd take Barbara into my bedroom so that we could winch and cuddle. Ma said that if we wanted to winch we were to do so on the settee like she had to do when she was our age.

One day I was sent for again by the headmaster. He said that when I was finally released I would have to go back to the special school till I was sixteen years old. Although my housemaster had told me this when I first arrived at St Andrew's, the news shattered me – I hadn't expected it to happen. All that night I lay and thought about it. 'Fuck them!' was my attitude. Bounce, my housemaster, said he would rather I stayed on in the approved school till I was sixteen – he said I'd only end up playing truant and getting into more trouble – but there was no way I was volunteering to stay on at the approved school. I wanted out of there as fast as I could.

On the morning I was to be released I had to attend the assembly hall where an official announcement was to be made in front of the whole school. There were a few of us being released that morning, and each of us was asked to stand up so that the 'wee man' could say something about us. When my own turn came I was overwhelmed with emotion as I listened to the wee man speak of my past deeds.

'I never thought I'd see the day,' he said with a big smile. Olly, my work teacher, had given me a bonus on my last wage packet – the first bonus I ever had in there – and the wee man made a joke of it which had everyone laughing. He said that it was okay for me to go, and wished me good luck in the life ahead. There was thunderous applause and cheering as I walked out of the room. I think I would have made it if I hadn't had to go back to the special school: it was easier for me to go on dogging school and stealing than to go back there.

Some years later there was a big enquiry into the conditions

126

and treatment of kids in Larchgrove Remand Centre, and a few of the turnkeys were exposed for ill-treating the kids. They were sacked from their jobs. No one was charged because not enough witnesses came forward, but I know the brutality went on, as do countless others. In the mid seventies Nero himself was charged and convicted, along with other police, for house-breaking.

13 BORSTAL BOY

It was no surprise to many that I ended up inside yet again, and this time I was sent to Borstal. This was in March 1972, and I was sixteen years old. The charge was house-breaking.

I was kept in Barlinnie Prison for a few days before being taken to Borstal. I had been in Barlinnie before, but only passing through on the way to Longriggend. It's an eerie-looking place, with its Victorian buildings, and very busy, with many warders and prisoners walking about. I recognised some pals of my dad's, who winked in my direction. One of them slipped me some tobacco. Of course, a warder with big steel-capped boots and peaked cap asked me if I was Andy Steele's son, and when I said I was some other warders came over to have a look at me. They asked me where my dad was and how he was and I answered their questions as politely as I could, always remembering to say 'sir', for that's what's demanded in these places.

After giving the warders our particulars we were put into a little room where we were given a mug of weak tea and a bowl of what was commonly known as mystery stew. The pass men who worked in the reception area were mostly first offenders. Many reception workers and trusties are decent enough guys but some of them thought that they were warders, shouting at us and demanding this and that. The warders knew that these guys were pulling all sorts of strokes, stealing tobacco and cigarette lighters from us, but they turned a blind eye to this –

and when the warders beat and humiliated prisoners, the pass-men turned a blind eye themselves.

In the reception area there were 'dog boxes' for holding prisoners while they're getting undressed and changing into prison attire. Sometimes as many as four guys were kept in them for hours on end. The seat was only large enough for two, so prisoners took turns to sit and to stand. If you can imagine yourself in a box in which you cannot spread your arms without touching the sides, with no window, one dull light hanging overhead and the door locked from the outside by a steel bolt, then you'll know what I mean when I say it was very uncomfortable and degrading. Some guys couldn't stand it for long and would try kicking the door down; they'd end up getting a severe beating from the warders. It was horrible being in that little dog box listening to the squeals of some guy getting beaten up. The warders could be heard shouting and running, their heavy boots crashing on the floor and their keys jingling.

Each time a passman went by the doors, you could hear people asking him for water or a bit of tobacco, or to go to the toilet or pass a message to someone in another dog box. The passmen were often abused and threatened for doing the warders' dirty work. But they were well protected, and if they were assaulted the warders would take revenge. Some passmen were in for horrible crimes; child molesting, rape and the brutal killings of women and kids. I often thought that such guys would be given a hard time in gaol, but the 'trusties' and prison informers weren't a threat to the warders – though they were a threat to the cons.

Eventually the door of my dog box opened and I was called out by a warder in a white coat and told to follow him to the surgery, where a doctor was waiting to examine me. Everyone there was stripped to the waist, and there was much coughing and clearing of throats, just as there is outside a doctor's surgery.

Guys came out, pulling up their pants and trousers after being examined by the doctor. Those passed as 'clean' were taken away to their dog boxes; those considered 'unclean' were taken to a little room to be shaved and treated. When my turn came I found myself summoned into a small, brightly lit room. Medical warders in white coats wrote down my answers to the doctor's questions. As he examined my private parts the doctor asked if I'd ever been in a mental institution, had fits or blackouts, wet the bed, been to a special school or had any mental illnesses in the family. Then I was told to turn around, bend over and spread my cheeks. I hesitated for a moment and received a punch to the belly from one of the warders; the doctor never batted an eyelid. Then I was taken back to the dog box and locked in.

We were like a herd of cattle in those dog boxes. Prison regulations required that we weren't kept in them for more than fifteen minutes, but some of us were there for hours. I was glad when I heard my door bolt being drawn back and the warder there telling me to follow him and to bring my towel with me.

When the warders took us out of reception I was thankful for a breath of fresh air. Ahead of us was a long road, with five huge halls with hundreds of barred windows from which we could hear cons shouting. The road was very busy, with warders and cons coming and going: nobody seemed to talk – it was all shouting. Old winos were walking about picking up cigarette butts.

Each of the halls was four storeys high. The first thing one notices when entering is the length of them, and then the noise of doors banging, keys jingling and shouting. If a warder on the ground floor wanted another on the top floor he would shout, and the vastness of the hall carried his voice easily enough.

The steel gate closed loudly behind us. We were lined up in single file and told to stand there and keep quiet while the warders did some paperwork and filled in door cards for the prisoners. The door card is a sheet of cardboard giving one's name, prison number, date of birth and religion. Then we were taken up to the top floor and put into cells. I was in with two other Borstal boys, and we were to stay there until we were taken away a week later. The warders had put the fear of God into us by telling us that we'd be a sorry lot when the Borstal warders got through with us. There were many stories going round – about how we'd be marched military fashion from the jail van and about the beatings at reception.

Each of us was given a chamber pot – filthy, as usual – and a small plastic basin for washing in. We had to wash in one basin of water, and some of the guys had to shave in it too. We were allowed to shower and have a change of clothing only once a week. We had one single bed and a bunk bed in the cell – these were made of steel, and had lumpy coir mattresses. The cells were cold, and there was no heating. High up on the wall was the cell window from which we stood looking out at the rest of the gaol.

After we'd discussed Barlinnie and Borstal we thought we should have a sing-song, one at a time. When it was my turn to sing, my two companions looked at me strangely – I sang a Jim Reeves song. A warder heard me singing and shouted that I was a better singer than I was a thief. I got carried away and sung my heart out. Older cons in nearby cells called for more, and for a moment I forgot all else. Years later, while I was in long-term solitary confinement, singing helped me keep my sanity.

During the night we had to use the chamber pots, but we agreed that if one of us needed to shit we'd do so in a bit of paper and throw it out the window. This was very common in gaols – there was even a work party whose job it was to collect the 'shit bombs'. We used to hear them hitting the ground below us with a thud. Some guys would shout, 'Bombs away' or 'Cop yer whack for this!' when throwing them out of their cell windows, while others tied messages on to their bombs, reading something like 'Best wishes from the Phantom Bomber'. When one of us decided he had to have a shit, the other two would go under the bed covers so as not to cause any embarrassment and to hide from the smell.

Next morning everyone on my side of the landing had to empty their pots into the one slop-out sink. The place was stinking – there were eight of these sinks to cater for a couple of hundred prisoners. While slopping out we talked to the older cons. They told us about Borstal, and gave us good advice on how to handle ourselves. They all had done their Borstal training, or so they said, and we listened intently to old glories. 'Crime does not pay,' they warned us. I've no doubt they were told that when they were our age, yet look where they were now.

Sometimes we had a decent enough warder on our gallery and sometimes we had a dog who treated us like animals. One of the older guys heard a warder messing us about and he called up to him to leave us alone as we were only kids and not bothering anyone. 'Come down here and try fucking me about, ya bam!' he shouted, but the warder never took up the offer. We were fed in our cells at all times. We weren't allowed to go to the dining halls or mix with any others in the gaol because of our age. The food was cold by the time it reached us, and I hardly ate it.

I was grateful to get away from Barlinnie, though I wasn't too pleased about going to Borstal. In the van we listened to the warders and police talk about the regime there, so we knew what was expected of us – and what we could expect from the warders. When the van stopped outside the hall at Polmont my heart was beating fast. The warders were there to greet us. They weren't wearing uniforms, just plain trousers and jackets, but they still had those long chains hanging from their pockets on which they carried their keys. I think they had keys on their chains that were of no use to them, simply in order to rattle them.

'Quick march! Move!' – and they started shoving and pushing us into the reception area. This was to frighten us – and it worked. They punched and kicked and mocked us, and those who had long hair were called poofs and girls. It all happened so fast; 'Stand up straight! Get over here! What are you in for? Do you think you're a hard man? Get those shoulders back! Arms straight! Quick march! Left, right, left, right!' We didn't know what was going on – one warder told us to do one thing and another ordered us to do the opposite.

One of the kids had long frizzy sideburns, and he was pulled by them along the floor, screaming in agony. Like the rest of us, he never questioned their brutal treatment. We knew that they were a law unto themselves, and that they had been doing this sort of thing for years. No one wanted to be beaten up for protesting and then locked up in the cells. Once they realised that we had got their message they weren't so rough with us. We were given some clothing and shaving gear – and even though I hadn't a hair on my chin, I was forced to shave with the others.

We were taken to the Allocation Centre, where everyone spends a few months when they first enter Borstal. As soon as we entered I could see guys in immaculate gaol uniforms marching here and there in military fashion, the warders screaming, 'Left, right! Left, right!' We were pounced upon immediately by warders, who yelled at us to march. We didn't have a clue – at least I didn't – and I was slapped about the head for being out of step. When I turned to see who was hitting me I was slapped and punched from behind by another warder who shouted at me to face the front and keep my shoulders back. All the humiliation and brutality were deliberate: nothing was ever done to change the system because those responsible believe it works. It's the same idea Napoleon had when he was asked, 'Who will you get to guard the hard cases on Devils' Island?' and he replied, 'Even harder cases' – but the difference was that here in Borstal we were only kids.

On the galleries above us I could see prisoners marching back and forth, and some marching down stairs with their arms pressed into their sides. The place was spotless – it even smelled clean. In the mornings all were up sharp, with each bed made up into a bed block: the warders carried small sticks during inspection, and the bed block had to be the exact length of the stick or else... the cell floor must be highly polished, with not a speck of dust to be seen: anyone whose cell was not up to standard would be deprived of recreation. Inspections were carried out every day, and at night we were forced to stand in our pyjamas at the foot of our iron beds to await another inspection.

No one was allowed out of his cell until the warder shouted, 'Outside and face your doors!' In one swift movement we had to be outside our doors and about-turn and face them; we were all in our shorts, with pot in one hand and a towel neatly folded over the arm. If we weren't all outside at the same time the warder would make us go back in and do it all over again. Sometimes this went on for an hour till the warder felt we had it right. Every time we came out our doors, for no matter what, it was always 'Outside and face your doors!' – we couldn't walk out naturally. Just before lock-up we were asked if we needed the toilet – if so we had to march there, with a warder screaming, 'Left, right! Left, right! Left, right! Left!'

We were allowed no more than two minutes in the toilet, after which the warders would start shouting into the small cubicles with their half doors, 'Nip it and get out of there now!' I've seen kids being dragged off the toilet seat. Sometimes we weren't given the chance to clean ourselves – our pants would end up dirty, and we could only change them once a week. The warders found that funny. I was standing next to a guy on parade and he whispered that he was badly in need of the toilet. The warder caught him whispering and started shouting: then he punched the guy on the belly, kocking the wind from him and causing him to mess his pants.

We had to jump to attention whenever the governor came in and shout out our names and numbers. Then he walked about checking for dust. Many times I was deprived of recreation because my cell wasn't up to standard, and instead I was given a bucket and brush and made to scrub out the toilets. Some of those who carried out inspection were none too clean-looking themselves, but what could one say. . . .

The bottom floor was reserved for epileptics and other medical cases, and some of the suicide risks. I was on parade one day when a guy had a fit, wriggling violently on the floor in front of us all. The warders screamed at us to stand to attention and face the front. They took their time in getting the poor guy up off the floor, after which some medical warders took him to his cell.

Sitting alone in my cell one day, on the wooden chair they

provided, I felt overcome by panic, by a sort of claustrophobia in which the cell seemed the size of a phone booth. I dashed over to the window, and was glad to see everything the right size in the world beyond. The next thing I remember is being beaten up by the warders, who said I had attempted to escape by picking my lock with a plastic comb – and it's true, I did. I didn't know where I was going, except that somehow I was getting out of that cell. While I was down on my knees, slipping the comb in and sliding back the lock, I thought I heard footsteps on the landing outside. I paused for a moment, and then the door came crashing in on my face and nose, stunning me. I came out of my daze when I felt the warders' boots digging into me.

'Up!' They made me stand to attention while they interrogated me and slapped me about. I couldn't tell them about the panic attack – I was afraid, not so much of them but of the panicking itself: I didn't know what had happened to me.

'You were trying to escape!' they kept repeating. Even though I hated the bastards I was glad they were there, for I preferred their company to being alone at that particular time.

I was marched down a long corridor known as the 'mile'. They kept screaming, 'Left, right! Left, right! Left, right!' – and to confuse me one warder told me to swing my arms shoulder-high while the other said I was to swing them waist-high. The corridor smelt strongly of disinfectant, and was grey-looking and cold. There were doors on either side, but I could only guess at what lay behind them. We stopped at one, and I was marched into North Wing. People were moving about, some of them from the various schools I had been to. They called to me, but the warders told me not to answer. Other warders were waiting to take me down to the dungeons. They too began screaming out orders; the bastards from behind were kicking and those in front were pulling, trying to make me fall. Once we were underground they strip-searched me and put me through the usual humiliating procedure of bending over, as if they got some sort of satisfaction from it.

Left to my own devices, I tried to imagine myself back home with Ma and Maw. I'd read to Maw by the fireside and help

Ma with the dishes and do all the good things that she always wanted from me. Sometimes the world of imagination can be a better place to live in than reality. Singing was another good form of escape, so I sang all the songs that my dad used to play. I couldn't sit still for two minutes – I would get up and walk back and forth or round in a circle. Every now and then I'd hear the spy latch on my cell door go up and see an eye appear. Sometimes the latch would stay up for a while, as if I was under close scrutiny, and other times it would go down immediately. Sometimes I felt like masturbating during the day, but it could be embarrassing if I was caught. Sometimes I'd sit underneath the spy hole, so that if the warder looked through he wouldn't be able to see me. Kids who were caught by the warders were made fun of or mocked. At night time it was different, masturbating in bed felt more natural. But my mattress and bedding were kept outside the door all day and I wasn't allowed to sit on my bed – which was only a sheet of wood with hinges on it, attached to the wall.

I had to appear before the governor the morning after I'd tried to pick my lock, charged with attempting to escape. I was marched into his room wearing my 'best' battledress, which was kept for visits, governor's inspection and recreation. My heart was pounding in my chest as I listened to the charge being read out in an eerie silence. All the while the governor sat in his chair, looking me up and down as though he was looking for a spot of dirt on my clothes. The warder described how he had opened my door to find me on my hands and knees with a comb in my hand, but he never mentioned the beating I got, or how he kicked in the door, knocking me over to the other side of the cell, or about my nose being burst. I was found guilty of attempting to open my cell door and damaging government property – the comb – and I was ordered to be kept in the cells for a week: four days in the dungeons and three in the cells above. So back I went to the dungeons. I wasn't allowed any tobacco at all, and I was given one book to read, at night only. I was told not to write anything about my punishment in any of my letters.

While I was in the dungeons I was taken out every day to

scrub the 'mile' corridor with a brush the size of a nailbrush. No sooner had I scrubbed a bit of the floor than someone would walk over it. The warder who was guarding me seldom spoke except to tell me to fill my bucket with water and start scrubbing. My knees were sore from kneeling and my trousers were wet, but I couldn't rest if I wanted to. Whenever he felt like it, the warder would walk up to my pail of water and kick it over. After work I was taken to the gymnasium to do my circuit training under the careful watch of the PTI. I was quite wiry and strong for my size and build, so I managed to do what was required, but the PTI said I must have been cheating, so he made me do it all over again. I was soaking in sweat and my PT pants were clinging to me but I carried on lifting the different sets of weights. When the PTI was satisfied, I was taken back to the dungeons, where I was allowed a shower but no clean clothes and then locked up again. I paced up and down the floor of my bare cell, occasionally stopping to look at the names scraped into the wooden board and walls. Some names I recognised as those of my pals. I'd sit on the floor and sing my heart out – I thought I sounded good in the empty cell, which gave a kind of echo.

I think there were some 400 guys in Polmont Borstal, between the ages of sixteen and twenty-one, and I was one of the youngest there. Each of its five wings had a governor. But the worst wing was the Allocation Centre; this was where all the hard punishment took place. If some guy wasn't standing up straight on parade, it could cost him a punch in the gut and abuse from one of the sadistic warders. There was a room known as the 'sweat box', used for marching lessons. It was very hot in there, and the dust was always so thick that we all coughed and spluttered while marching on the spot, and this had the warders calling us all sorts of names from old women to morons. Some guys were pushed beyond the limit and collapsed. They were left there till everyone was finished. One warder always carried a bed-block stick under his armpit, like a sergeant-major. He was notorious for hitting guys with it and he seemed to enjoy his reputation. He would boast to the newer guys that he was the 'stick man'.

'Have you never heard of me?' he would growl, sticking out his barrel chest, his face all screwed up to look mean. If anyone ever attacked one of the warders they'd get a terrible beating. Everyone was aware of this, and that's exactly what the warders wanted as it put fear into a lot of guys.

At meal times, when we collected our trays, we had to shout, 'Thank you, Matron' – even if she wasn't there. One day I forgot and the warder who was standing at the hot-plate tripped me up, spilling my dinner over the floor. I was taken into the principal warder's room and shoved about and shouted at by two of them. After they had finished with me they made me apologise to Matron, even though she wasn't there, so I said out loud, 'Thank you, Matron,' cursing her under my breath as a fat bastard. I don't know why I said thank you, because I never even got the meal.

There was one warder in the Allocation Centre who was as strict and regimental and smartly dressed as they come – but he was also very fair, and whenever he was on duty the warders' attitudes changed and their bullying wasn't so obvious. If he thought a warder was out of order he'd put him in his place. They hated it, but he was the principal warder and their superior. If there was extra food on the hot-plate, instead of throwing it away, he would give it to those who wanted it. The warders weren't happy at this but they didn't show their true feelings. The senior warder came to work in a different suit every day, with shirt, tie and handkerchief to match, and he was known as 'the Baron'.

I hadn't been long in Borstal when my brother Jim hit the headlines. He and two other guys had got away scot-free after being charged with robbery and discharging a sawn-off shotgun over the head of a hotel-owner: they had been kept on remand a day too long under Scottish law. I read about Jim in the newspapers at recreation time, and was really glad to learn he had been freed. I remember the day when he was arrested – Ma went berserk and threatened to kill herself, saying she couldn't take any more – and now I could picture

138

her face at the news of Jim's release. One of those set free with Jim was a guy called Shadow, who had married Tommy Campbell's sister and was close to our family. Everyone was talking about the trial, and most of the guys were laughing because the police and court officials had been humiliated.

There were always fights in the Allocation Centre, and occasionally I kept watch for some guys who were having it out in the toilet or a cell. Nearly all the guys in there were members of a gang, and some of them continued their gang wars inside. Some guy would get a slight stab wound and never report it, as it would mean an inquiry.

One day I was told to show a new arrival how to make up his bed block, and I was quite shocked to see that he had only one arm. His artificial arm had been confiscated because it could be used as a weapon. He didn't seem too upset about it, but I don't know how he felt deep down inside. He said that the doctor had passed him as fit, and he wasn't even excused from PT – they made him do press-ups along with the rest of us. Some of the warders thought it funny to see this wee guy doing his one-arm press-ups, and they'd snigger behind his back.

We all had to go to school and sit an exam at the Allocation Centre, and those of us who needed more schooling were kept on for a while. There were three teachers, one for each classroom, but only one was well thought of – he was the only one who treated us like human beings. My first day at class wasn't a very good one. The teacher, who was also a warder, couldn't get us to have a conversation with him, so he took some chalk and wrote on the blackboard, 'Class is scared to talk to teacher' in big letters.

One guy was sitting by the window and looking out in a daydream, as we all do at times. The teacher walked quietly up to him and slapped him full force on the side of his face. The noise was deafening. It was touch and go if the guy was going to retaliate or not. He hesitated, the teacher hesitated and for a second he showed his hand: there was fear written over his face. I cursed the teacher under my breath and hoped that the guy would get up and kick his fucking face in. The teacher told the guy to pay attention. It certainly broke the silence.

The swimming-pool was a good thing, but the bad thing about it was the warder in charge of it. His job was to give us a hard time, especially when we were in the Allocation Centre. He'd make us all scrub before entering the pool. He was right to do so, but he went to extremes. When he was in the shower he would scrub his arse with a toothbrush and then clean his teeth with the same brush. This was to show us how tough he was; psychological intimidation, one might say. He was forever hitting guys with his huge pole, or making us all stand along one side of the pool because someone had done something he didn't like. He'd walk up and down and put the pole on someone's bare toes and lean on it so hard that the guy cried out in pain.

The one good thing that I can say about him was that he kept that pool spotless. The pool was his pride and joy – and one way to get back at him was to shit in it. This happened on a few occasions, and it was rumoured that he burst out crying and then took a mad turn, running into the changing room to check everyone's underpants to see if they were clean. In his office he had mirrors placed at certain angles so he could watch us. At times he'd try to provoke a fight with one of us, but I never saw anyone hit him back. If he caught someone larking about in the pool he would always call him 'cunt' – 'Right, cunt! Out of the pool!' – and all the while his wee rotten face would be screwed up in a threatening way.

One day Ma came up with some of the family, including my Uncle Atty, but he was kept outside because his name wasn't on the visit pass. I was sorry not to speak to him. Ma said that in a way she was glad he didn't get in just in case he caused a commotion or wanted to take me home with him. When the visit was over I went straight to the window and looked out and saw my wee Uncle Atty on the green. I knocked on the window to catch his attention; the warder told me to get away but Atty had looked up and began waving frantically so I

140

stood and waved back. The warder made no attempt to pull me away – he probably feared that he'd be seen – but warned me again to get away. That cost me a few nights scrubbing the toilets, but it was worth it. I spent them thinking about our Atty and that mental hospital. I often thought about going to visit him when I was out.

The weeks passed, and it was time for me to be allocated to one of the halls or to another Borstal in a different part of the country. Those sent to open Borstals were trusted not to run away, so it was unlikely I'd be going to one of those. Nor did I want to go to a wing in Polmont known as Carrick House, reserved for 'head bangers' and guys with other problems.

In the end I was sent to East Wing. The night before I was to move I hardly slept a wink, I was so glad to get away from the Allocation Centre. I was more bitter than I could remember, and felt a real hatred for the warders – not forgetting the matron whom we always had to thank for our food, even when she wasn't there! Maybe that was the whole idea of the short sharp lesson – to make one hate.

As it turned out, East Wing was more modern than any other place I'd been in, but the regime was as old as ever. I was taken to a cell in 'B' section. It contained a small sink, a small locker, a chair and a bed. The same rules applied here as in the Allocation Centre: cells to be spotlessly clean at all times, and the floor kept highly polished.

When I was taken along to see the governor of East Wing the first thing he said to me was, 'I know your father.' I can remember him saying to me – as many others had – that I'd end up in prison all my days: I wonder now why so many of them drummed that into my head, and whether it wasn't wishful thinking.

I took an instinctive dislike to the matron, who was sitting next to the governor. She was heavily made-up and wearing a short skirt, and trying to look much younger than she was – she must have been at least fifty. She seemed to be too much involved and I guessed she fancied herself as a warder. The governor explained the regime in East Wing and said that I could make it easy for myself by co-operating with them, which would get me out sooner, or I could go the other way and get out later.

Before long I became involved in a fight with a guy from Dundee. He fancied himself as 'Jack the Lad' and must have thought me an idiot, so he had a go at bullying me. I didn't want people to think that I could be bullied, so I challenged him to fight. He looked astonished and then tried to laugh it off. By then all the guys had gathered to watch, as they usually do. It was agreed that there'd be no knives used or any other weapons, and that the fight would take place in my cell. As I walked into my cell the guy leapt on my back and tried to strangle me, shouting that he was going to kill me. I staggered about the cell with him clinging to me. The pot went flying across the floor and I almost slid, but I managed to keep my footing. However hard I tried to shake him off my back, I couldn't. I tried biting him but I couldn't get my teeth near him, and I ran at the wall, using him as a ram. I caught a glimpse of faces peering in at us, and it maddened me to think that they were going to watch me lose the fight. I took a crazy turn and threw him over my shoulder on to my bed and started butting him with my head; when I saw the fear in his shifty eyes it gave me more strength, and I kicked and punched him till he said he had had enough.

He never bothered me after that, nor did I bother him. Everyone was talking about it, and some of the Glasgow guys said that if the 'outsiders' tried to give us Glaswegians trouble then we should do battle with them, but nothing came of it except paranoia and verbal abuse behind backs. A lot of the outsiders were decent guys – especially the guys from Paisley. They were much like Glaswegians and they were always in a large mob. Their gang was known as the Disciples, and one of its best-known and most respected members was a guy named Winnie. His father was friendly with mine, and after the incident he asked me if there was anything he could do to help. He talked about stabbing the guy, but I told him I wasn't into violence. Too many people get the wrong impression of us Glaswegians – they think we're all bad men and carry open razors and slash people just for the sake of it. The warders seemed more interested in kids who lived outside Glasgow. One day I was walking along the corridor with about a dozen other guys when the passmen came by with our dinner. There were a couple of trays of duff for our pudding, so we stole a slice each. Matron was watching without our knowing. I was the only one there from Glasgow, and she came straight up to me and said she was having me put on governor's report for stealing a slice of cake. I was locked in my cell till I could see the governor in the morning, after which I was sent to the dungeons for three days – all because of a slice of cake.

After I'd been in the wing for about a week I was allocated to a work party. This involved working with textiles, and I was asked if I could use a sewing-machine! I couldn't, and I didn't even know that guys used sewing-machines. I felt humiliated sitting at a sewing-machine, and I guess the others had too when they first arrived. The warder took me to his office and explained the rules to me. There was to be no talking during work and no skiving, and if one needed the toilet it wasn't to take longer than two minutes – any longer meant one was skiving, and one's wages would be cut. There was to be no smoking in the toilet, or else it was the dungeons for a spell. It's a wonder we were allowed to draw breath.

One day the governor asked me if I had ever done any bricklaying, and I told him I had been on the bricklaying party at St Andrew's. He asked me if I would like to help to build a new gaol for women, known as Cornton Vale. I told him I wouldn't like to help build any gaol and would rather tear them down. He wasn't amused, and told me I had a bad attitude.

I got a letter from Ma in which she told me that my Aunt Ruby had been murdered by my uncle. I cried all night for her. She was the first person to die who had meant something to me, and I thought of all the good times I had had with her and how she had sheltered me when I was on the run. I thought about Broono and my other cousins, and wondered what would happen to them. I asked for leave to go to the funeral but was refused – I was told it had to be someone in my own family. A few nights later I opened my eyes and saw my aunt standing near my bed. I got the fright of my life and hid under the blankets, too scared to press the bell. This was the first time in my life I had seen a ghost, but when I finally looked out from my blankets there was nothing there. I was sorry I had hidden, and prayed that her ghost would come back again. But she never did, and I never told anyone about it in case they thought I was crazy. A few months after my aunt's death her husband Hugh was serving life for her murder.

I was very quiet while I was in Borstal and never bothered much with anyone, though on a couple of occasions I was sent to the dungeons for petty offences. I was allowed home in April 1973, after serving eleven months. I said goodbye to my pals, some of whom I'd promised to keep in touch with when I got out. The warders drove us to the station and left us to catch the train into Glasgow. It was a great feeling to be free again. It was like finishing a life sentence. I said to myself the hard life was all over: regardless of what the bastards thought, I'd never be back in again.

14 MY WEE JOB

Ma and Maw were as excited as I was when I got home. Ma made a huge dinner for me while I sat and told Maw all about my Borstal training. Maw felt my arms and shoulders and said that I hadn't fattened out any – then she laughed, saying that I was a thoroughbred and couldn't be fattened. Ma made me promise to get a job and settle down and was forever preaching to me that I didn't want to spend my life in and out of gaols. She was right – I didn't.

I took Maw out for walks at night. We'd have a good talk and a good laugh, and if we passed anyone we knew we'd stop to say hello. There's something about the wee small hours that attracts me, and Maw was the same. I loved the peace and tranquillity. I remember asking Maw if there was any gipsy blood in me, but she just laughed and said I was a true blue-eyed Scot. It was great to be with my family again. If my dad had been home we'd have all been together for the first time in a long time. Jim had married while I was in Borstal, and it seemed that he would settle down to a quiet life with his wife and kid. He had moved away from Garthamlock, so at least he had a good start. Everyone knew that the police would hound him after he had got out of the Stepps Hotel robbery. My dad wrote to his MP and the Chief Constable about his fears of me and Jim being harassed by the police – I think he even wrote to the Prime Minister.

Jobs were plentiful then, but I hated work – I'd had enough of it in the textile party at Borstal. Ma kept pleading with me

145

to get a job, so I made an effort and looked up the adverts in the papers. I spoke to a man at the unemployment centre and was offered a job at the zoo! I thought he was kidding at first, and when I laughed he seemed upset. It might please him to know that I ended up in a zoo later on – in a human zoo known as the 'Cages' of Porterfield Prison.

In the end I found a job as a store boy at a grocery store – an aunt who had worked in one of the many Henry Healy shops saw her boss about me. She said I'd better not embarrass her by stealing anything from the shop. Ma and Maw were really chuffed; Ma wrote and told my dad in Perth Prison that I had myself a wee job, and I received a nice letter from him. All my aunts were talking about it, as were the neighbours, and Ma boasted to one and all saying, 'That's my Johnnyboy got himself a good job.' I went to see one of the Henry Healy managers, but two days later, I gave up. I just couldn't do it. I think it was because I was too shy, though the people who worked there were good, decent people.

My job was to carry boxes in from the vans to and from the fridge and freezer. The shop was in the city centre, a few yards from the bus terminus, so I could see all the Garthamlock people coming and going from their work and they could see me in my white coat. I wasn't allowed to serve the customers, but my first day there a wee woman came in while the others were upstairs having their tea break, and she approached me to serve her. I was going to shout one of the lassies down, but I didn't bother, and I asked her what she wanted. Whatever it was she wanted I couldn't find it, so I grabbed the first thing I could see, which was a huge lump of meat. I gave it to her for nothing and asked her to leave in case they discovered it. She had a job getting it into her shopping bag. I was trying to listen out for the lassies coming down from upstairs, and instead of getting out of the shop and away with the meat that she had got for nothing she asked me for some more. She pointed to this and that, so I grabbed handfuls of what she wanted and gave them to her. She thanked me, and as she left she said in a whisper, 'God bless you, son.'

When I came home from my first day's work Ma had a huge

meal laid on for me. All I got out of her was, 'How do you like your new job, son?' I couldn't tell her the truth because I didn't want to hurt her. She was so happy, and I lied to protect her. That night I went out stealing and breaking into shops. It was easier than working. Ma had the alarm clock set to get me up for my work in the morning and had my breakfast ready, and she gave me some cigarettes to take to work. I didn't have the courage to tell her I wouldn't be working much longer. I can remember clearly the look on her face when one of my aunts told her that I was no longer working and had only lasted two days. She looked humiliated and shattered. I wouldn't be surprised if she'd had a cry that night.

Ma told me to be in early at nights, saying she didn't want me wandering around the streets to get lifted by the police, but once she was asleep I slipped away and went out stealing. Whenever I saw a police car coming towards me I sprinted through a close and away – especially late at night, because if it suited them they could lift me for being a known thief.

There were wild parties at the weekends on the estate, and more often than not they ended in a fight. Some of my pals' mothers thought their sons were angels, never knowing that they had done more stabbings and slashings than Genghis Khan. Big Gerry from Garthamlock had a ma who thought him an angel. At home he'd speak politely and have me doing the same, and I had to pretend I was working whenever she asked, and deny I was ever in trouble with the law. Most of us told our mas lies to protect them and stop them worrying.

I never spent many Christmases with my family because I was either on the run or locked up, but I have fond memories of the ones that I did spend. Dad was usually in gaol, but his friends delivered presents from him. Ma always did her best to give us a good time, and Maw had a good excuse for getting drunk.

'It's Christmas,' she'd say to Ma, 'and this may be my last one.'

Although Ma detested drink she felt obliged to let Maw

have hers, and Maw would sing her party piece and favourite song – 'No Regrets'. She was always happy when she was drunk, and she'd tell us how much she loved us all and that we were the best weans in the world. She'd grab hold of us and start dancing in an old-fashioned way, staggering and knocking things over. She never seemed to tire and was the life and soul of her own little party. When Maw had a wee drink in her she would ask me if I would remember her and miss her when she was gone, and she'd grip my hand hard. Of course I'd remember and miss her and I told her so. She'd ask me if she had been good to me through the years, and she'd go on about her wee Atty and tell me that she was scared to die because she wouldn't know what would become of Atty and her sons and grandsons. 'Oh, if only yous would settle down then I could die in peace,' she told me.

To hear Maw talk like this really frightened me. At night I would pray for Maw, asking God not to take her away from us. Sometimes life can be so beautiful amidst all the hardship and suffering – and it's this that makes it all worth living for. It was great to watch Maw open up her presents and to see her two useless eyes give a sparkle. Inside I'd cry, but no one looking on would notice. I'm sure my reason for seeming hard-hearted when it came to showing my innermost feelings was a defence. If my folks had really known what my love for them meant to me I reckon it would have hurt them more. Maybe they didn't think I was giving them all the love they deserved and so continued loving me in the hopes that one day I would return it. If only they knew....

At about this time my pal Eddie Dobie and I thought we would rob a farmer who delivered eggs to the estates. We knew he kept his money tucked into his Wellington boots. He looked like a big country yokel so we imagined he would be an easy target. Eddie decided that he would steal some chloroform from his science class and knock Wullie unconscious so that we could get his Wellington boots off. He got the chloroform and hid it. I'd never done anything like this before, and it seemed more of a good laugh than a robbery.

One night Wullie came to Garthamlock to collect his egg

money, and we were ready to pounce. We watched Wullie's big, clumsy shape move up and down the streets, collecting from the messengers who worked for him; we followed him for a while, giving him plenty of time to collect most of his money. Some of the Garthamlock Young Team were out looking for their pals, but we stayed in the shadows so they wouldn't see us. If they had known what we were doing they might have wanted to join us, and we wanted all the money to ourselves.

Once the street was empty we made our move towards Wullie's little van. He looked as clumsy as ever in his huge Welly boots and dungarees. Eddie had a rag and I watched him soak it with the chloroform. We walked up behind Wullie, and before I knew it Eddie was up on the farmer's back and I was trying to wrench his Welly boots off his legs and even though Eddie had the rag over the farmer's mouth he kept shouting, 'This is a robbery.' Wullie was swinging Eddie about like a rag doll. The rag fell to the ground, but Eddie wouldn't let go. He started punching Wullie about the head, but Wullie threw him over his shoulder with the swift movement of a judo expert. I couldn't move for laughing, and even Eddie was in fits of laughter. After that I decided that I would stick to simple stealing. My fear of gaol was long gone, the old desire to steal was strong, and I couldn't help myself.

15 THE BIG HOUSE

In September 1973 Broono and I were walking down the street singing when some plain-clothes policemen stopped and searched us and demanded to know where we were going. They ordered me to get into their car and told Broono to be on his way. I was put into the back seat where the police started harassing me. Broono held on to the handle of the car door and said if they were arresting me then they'd have to arrest him too, so they did. I asked Broono why he didn't go home when he had the chance and he said in his comical way that if he had gone home without me, my ma and family would have half killed him. In court we were both fined ten pounds for a breach of the peace.

One day there was a running battle in the field behind Garthamlock with the gang from a housing estate called Cardowan. I heard that my young brother Joseph was there so I went to get him, fearing that he could be seriously injured as he was only nine. In the middle of the fields was a small burn that ran between Garthamlock and Cardowan. We were on one side and the Cardowan gang on the other, and each was wary of entering enemy territory. By the time I got there the Cardowan team were beating up one of the Garthamlock boys and there was panic amongst our own boys as they were outnumbered. There was only one thing to do, and that was to charge at them as fast as we could. My pal Peter Henderson and I charged at the other team and others followed, brandishing steak knives, hatchets and broken sticks and screaming

150

abuse and threats. They let the guy they were beating up go and we gave chase, right into their own estate. There were too many of them for us to handle, so we headed back across the fields over the burn and on to safe territory – but then we saw the police coming towards us in their jeeps and panda cars. We were caught between the police and the gang beyond the burn. People were dropping knives and scattering in every direction. Peter and I stuck together and dived into the burn, which came up to my knees. I was soaking and filthy, and I could hear the gang from Cardowan shouting to the police that some of us were hiding in the burn.

I scurried through the burn as quietly as I could, but the police heard me. There was no way out except to surrender. As I made my way up the side of the burn I put my hand out for the policeman to help me out, but he kicked me back in and I went under the water. When they finally got me out I was so filthy and wet that none of them wanted me in their car. Eventually they drove us to the police station, where we were charged with mobbing and rioting and breach of the peace and locked up in a cell. There I stripped off all my clothing and wrapped the one woolly blanket around me while I scrubbed my clothes in the water from the toilet pan. We were refused visits from our families and denied tobacco and a change of clothes. Peter was a first offender, and I laughed when I heard him shout to the turnkey that he wanted his 'rights' and a solicitor too. They just told him to fuck off.

Next morning we were taken to the Glasgow Sheriff's Court, and appointed a lawyer through the Legal Aid system. We were both refused bail and remanded in Longriggend for a social inquiry and background report. Peter was shattered – he'd never been in gaol before and he didn't really know what lay ahead. In the gaol bus he complained that the handcuffs were too tight, but the warders paid no attention to him even though his wrists were beginning to swell. I wasn't too happy because I had only meant to do a good deed and get our Joseph away from trouble, and I had ended up in trouble myself.

I told Peter all about Longriggend on the way there, but he

thought I was kidding him. He soon changed his mind. We were marched into reception, and made to line up outside the 'dog boxes'.

'Listen for your names and answer "sir!"' one of the warders growled to us, but when it was Peter's turn to answer his name he failed to say 'sir' and was slapped about the face until he did so. He hesitated, unsure whether or not to attack the bullying warder and on seeing him hesitate other warders ran over and started threatening him and daring him to make a wrong move.

I met a couple of guys in there with whom I became quite friendly. One was called Mulsy and he was in for gang fighting and attempted murder. At a carnival somewhere on the south side of Glasgow he hit another gang member on the head with a hatchet. It went in so deep that it was said that Mulsy had to put his foot on the guy's head to pull it back out again. He was quite a good kid in his own way, but one bad deed had branded him as a sort of mad man. He was sentenced to eight years. My other new pal, 'Fingers', was a good kid. He was very pally with John Grimes and they went out stealing together. 'Fingers' was so affected by Longriggend that he eventually hanged himself. The warders laughed and joked when they described their grisly findings to some of the prisoners. It was sickening. The bastards who governed this place had much to answer for – they made up rules to suit themselves, depriving prisoners of what few rights they had. Who would believe that untried prisoners weren't allowed radios or photographs – or weren't even allowed to talk at their recreation? Some guys said that when they got out they'd come back and give the warders a hard time, or even take their revenge on the warders' families.

Peter told me that he couldn't handle the place and thought of committing suicide. I don't think that he was alone in thinking that way, though most guys tried to pretend that being locked up had no effect on them.

Peter and I appeared at Glasgow Sheriff Court and were found guilty of breach of the peace. The mobbing and rioting charges were dropped. The judge sent me to a young offenders' institution for three months, but Peter was fined and allowed home. I was sick, even though I'd got only three months. As Ma said, it was a waste of life.

The young offenders' hall is one of the five huge buildings in Barlinnie, and it is known as E Hall. It is the same size and shape as the other halls, but the regime is much stricter. It reminded me of the American-type gaols with huge galleries. All the guys on the four galleries looked down at us new admissions on the ground floor and called our names. My own name was called, and I looked up to see John Henry and another guy from Garthamlock known as Forry. Both were in for serious assault. We stood quietly with our towels in our hands, waiting for the warders to allocate us our cells.

In E Hall we all had to wear blue shirts, whereas the other cons in the gaol wore red striped shirts. The attitude of the warders was much the same as that at Longriggend, so I knew what to expect. I was put into a cell on the third gallery with two other guys. John and Forry gave me some tobacco and soap and toothpaste to help me out till I got my wages.

After slop-out next morning we were taken to the dining hall for our breakfast – a bowl of pig-meal, a thin round sausage, two slices of bread and a small piece of margarine. We were given our food in plastic or steel bowls. I then had to see the doctor, and go through the usual humiliating routine; after which I was passed fit for slave labour, and taken to what was known as the 'scrap party'. Our job was to strip old copper piping from its oily wrappings. It was filthy work, yet we were given only one shower and one change of clothes a week, and we were lucky if our weekly wage earned us an ounce of tobacco. Each day after work I would strip off all my clothes and stand in a basin of water and scrub myself with a nailbrush to get the oil off my skin. For our daily exercise we were marched around a small yard – if it was raining or too cold then we took our exercise inside.

Most of the guys in young offenders' went around in little gangs just like they did outside, and if a guy had an argument with someone from another gang the chances were that there'd be a battle and weapons would be produced – and it was just too bad if someone got hurt. Grassing wasn't tolerated – those who did it were shunned and put into protection for their own safety. Rape cases and child molesters were also protected, and they weren't allowed into the workshops with the others. They were given work to do in their cells, and when it came to exercise time they were separated again.

There were tobacco barons among the young offenders, and throughout the prison system: if a guy wanted to borrow half an ounce of tobacco he would have to pay back double the amount borrowed. Some got themselves into debt and couldn't pay up, and they were beaten up or went into protection; there were always fights over non-payment of debts. I didn't smoke much then, so I never went near the tobacco barons.

We were told that we couldn't write anything about our lives in gaol, whether in letters or in book form. I guess the reason for this is that the authorities have much to hide. Every weekend someone seemed to crack up and slash his wrists or smash his cell window and his locker. These incidents seemed to put a bit of life into the gaol: guys would howl out of their windows and under the doors, and their shouts would echo round the huge halls. We'd listen to the warders scurrying into the hall to get to the guy in distress, and we knew what was coming to him when they got to him. As soon as we heard the thuds and screams we'd kick or bang on our doors with our mugs, and shout for them to leave the guy alone.

Some of the guys on the ground floor were on punishment and locked up for twenty-three hours a day, often without cigarettes and sweets. They'd wait till the warders went off, and then they'd shout up to us for a smoke and a match. We would give a bit of tobacco each and send it down by line. I knew how it felt to be locked up in a concrete tomb with no tobacco – and so did the authorities, which was why they did it. Every morning guys were released, and we'd watch them go downstairs with their door cards and towels, but for every one going out another would come in that same night. Sometimes guys who thought they were being released were turned back at reception because they had outstanding fines and

154

charges; sometimes the police were waiting at the gate to re-arrest them.

Craigend was a new housing estate next to Garthamlock. Many of the Barlinnie warders moved there with their families, and soon the Garthamlock Young Team were fighting with them and smashing their windows. The warders came out in their uniforms, pretending to be police, but they were recognised for what they were. They knew the kids who had hassled them and waited till they came into the young offenders', when they took them into the notorious cell 43, where all the beatings-up took place.

The only time we young offenders got close to the other cons was in chapel. The chapel was huge, and was used as a cinema and for concerts. It was also notorious for the stabbings and slashings that took place there. One Sunday I was in the chapel and was whispering to my pal next to me when the priest stopped saying the mass. I didn't care much for this priest, who was more like a warder than anything else. He looked at me and my pal, and brought us to the attention of the warders. As a result, I was taken to cell 43.

My heart was in my mouth, and I dreaded what lay ahead. The cell was empty, with nothing but bare walls with some names scraped into the dull paintwork; and, as in other cells, the window was high up and closed. As I paced up and down the cell, nervously wondering what to do, I panicked and jumped up to the window, looking for a way out: I was so desperate that I tried to squeeze out of a hole I couldn't even get my hand through. I could hear the jingling of keys and warders shouting. It's a frightening experience waiting for a gang to kick the shit out of you when you know that there's nothing you can do about it.

The spy hole in the door went up, someone called through, 'Just you wait, bastard,' and the latch fell down hard. When the door opened I saw them piling in, but somehow I cut off and can only remember the floor coming up to meet me and the room reeling round. I never felt any pain till it was all over. After they had left I lay there till they gave me a basin of water to clean up my blood and let me back into my own cell. My face was swollen and my body ached, and just before they let me out of cell 43, a surgery warder was brought in to look at me and ask if I had any complaints! I knew that if I said that I had been beaten up by the warders this would only mean more trouble, so I said I had no complaints and he left. I was more angry about the surgery warder than I was about those who gave me the beating.

We were allowed two visits every three months, so Ma always made an appearance and was forever begging me to get a job and settle down when I got out this time. I never did tell my ma about me getting a beating as it would only have caused her more worry. Ma had a pal called Mary Carroll and they looked very much alike. Everybody thought that they were sisters, and they were always together. Mary was a good laugh and she wore very stylish clothes which made her very attractive. She was brought up with Ma in the Gorbals and at one time in her teens she courted my Uncle Tam. Whenever Ma went visiting me, my dad or my brothers, Mary always drove her there. I told Mary about the warders and how they treated us and even told her about the beating I got, but I told her not to tell Ma, and she wouldn't. Most of my pals had a fancy for Mary who was married with a family of three sons: Jim, Michael and Martin. I had a fancy for her myself but I never told her in case she attacked me and told my ma. I called her 'Auntie' and she treated me like her own son, always eager to do things for me and running to gaols and police stations for me along with Ma. Mary looked a million dollars and wore plenty of expensive jewellery, but the thing she was liked most for was that she was down to earth with everyone.

My one ambition was to be a country singer, and I often dreamed of going to Nashville, Tennessee, the home of country music. I made a guitar out of a plastic basin: I punctured six holes in it just below the rim, threaded twine through the holes and tied the twine at the bottom of the basin. It sounded very tinny, but it did the trick and I sat there each night with my basin, singing. The guy in my cell made a sort of mouth organ out of a plastic comb and a cigarette paper, so we had a good sing-song and a laugh.

156

The night before my release I couldn't sleep and paced up and down my cell. I couldn't wait to be free. As soon as my door opened I was outside like a greyhound out of its trap. I emptied my pot and basin, grabbed my door card and towel and headed downstairs with the others who were being released. I said goodbye to my pals and left them whatever I possessed. We were made to wait in the hall till the reception warders came for us, and I was never so glad to see the bastards in all my life. I was taken to the reception area and put into one of the 'dog boxes', which had my name written on it; inside was my suit, and I hurried into it and felt better. I was locked in and made to wait for my porridge and tea, which I didn't eat. Then the door opened and I was told to come out and follow a warder. We were given our personal property and bus fares home, and then marched away towards the main gate. Once again we were stopped and asked our names and birth dates and a few other particulars; then we were moved on, getting even closer to the gate. The door opened to reveal the decent world in all its splendour, and I felt great to be alive. I was overjoyed to hear the huge door slam shut behind me and to walk down the drive away from the 'Big House'. The things that I had taken for granted – like colourful clothes and cars and buses – were now a luxury. It was a great feeling as I headed for 999 Gartloch Road. Ma was up and waiting with my breakfast.

16 MORE PORRIDGE

Maw was in bed, so I went in and had a talk with her. She was really pleased that I was home again and gave me a hug and a kiss that brought tears to my eyes. She didn't seem to change or age at all, and I thought she would live for ever. Ma asked me to get a job and settle down, but despite my promises I knew I wouldn't: work scunnered me. That same night I went out stealing.

I went to visit my Uncle Atty at Gartloch Hospital, and if he wasn't in one of the locked wards I would walk round the grounds with him and we'd talk about the good old days. My heart went out to Atty and I wanted him home to stay with us. Everywhere we went patients and nurses stopped to say hello to him – he was one of the most popular and well-liked men in the hospital.

Occasionally Ma's older brother paid us a visit. Uncle Alec was small and wiry and in great physical condition. He played the guitar and accordion and would entertain the family at the fireside. We'd all be happy, especially Maw who joined in the sing-songs, her feet tapping merrily on the floor.

'Don't you be getting involved in any of these gang fights,' Ma said to me as we stood on our veranda watching people at the quarry screaming abuse, brandishing weapons and charging each other. Ma saw some of my pals hitting other gang members with weapons and shook her head in disgust, saying that they would end up murdering someone and that I wasn't to bring them back near the house. I told Ma that it wasn't my pals who were fighting but Ma knew all right and told me not to try and pretend to her I didn't know. Maw got her bit in, saying that she could identity some of my pals' voices and even mentioning their names. Ma knew I was out stealing, and she got angry with me and said I was taking her for a fool.

One Sunday about eight of us went to Airdrie to break into an electrical shop containing things that could quite easily be sold to punters. I walked up to the shop window to see where the best and dearest stuff was situated. It was early afternoon and the town was quite busy. John Grimes and Aldo and the others were around the back of the shop, preparing to remove one of the bars from a window while the others kept an eye open for onlookers and police. Each of us earmarked items to go for. I fancied a few small but very expensive radios which I had seen from the shop window. Eventually we burst a bar in the back window, which left enough room for us to get through. I went in first as I was the skinniest, and passed out whatever my pals ordered so long as it could fit through the hole. I felt like a shop assistant. I discovered a small leather pouch with money in it, and passed it out to John Grimes. Amazingly enough, my pals who hadn't been able to get through the hole suddenly climbed through when they learned there was money inside.

In the back shop we waited a while, listening, but no one heard anything, so we made our way into the front area on our hands and knees. People were standing outside the window, looking in at the household equipment yet never knowing we were there. Whenever the front display window was free of passers-by we darted further up the shop and hid behind something else. We continued in this fashion till we reached the items we were after. Some people on the outside stood looking in for what seemed ages and I wondered if they'd ever go away. Then I saw my chance and, quick as a flash, I leapt up from behind a fridge and grabbed hold of the radio I wanted.

Unfortunately the radio was chained to a good many others, and as a result they all came down on top of me. We had to

159

leave everything and get out fast, scattering into the back shop in full view of all the people looking in. Even though we had panicked and were frightened, we were all laughing. One at a time we wriggled out of the hole.

This bit of bad luck didn't put us off, for we broke into some more shops not too far from the electrical shop that same afternoon; then we headed home to Glasgow and sold most of the stolen goods to our punters, who thought of us as a nice bunch of kids.

When I wasn't stealing I was thinking about it. My dad always said, 'Johnnyboy, as a thief you're hopeless – get a *job*,' but I carried on with a blindness that saw me through. I was jailed yet again on a shop-lifting charge. Broono was with me, but this time he got away and I was sent again to the young offenders' institution in Barlinnie for three months. I never got used to being locked up and it tortured me every day I was there.

Some of the old-timers were allowed to mix with us doing work. They were known as 'jakeys' and 'winoes', and they had spent most of their lives in gaols. They always asked us to give them some cigarettes or to keep our cigarette butts for them and they would tell us stories about themselves when they were young. Some of their tales were fascinating, and I loved to listen to them. Although I wasn't much into reading I often wrote lyrics and verses, sometimes about the old jakeys:

Ode to Crazy Joe

'I may be a down and out, my boys,'
Said the man called Crazy Joe,
'But young luck was mines way back in time,
And this hand was never slow....
A hand that shook the world
And was raised for Kings and Queens.
I had my words with mayors and lords –
and I drank with the should-have-beens.
Yeah, would you believe I had it all

when the gang was much in debt,
I was there, and quick to share,
Say, give us a cigarette!
Give me a cigarette, boys, to fill my lungs with smoke
There's pleasure in it for a bum like me
Who stands with an empty poke.'
So we gave him up some cigarettes
And he snatched them like a thief
And the hand that once had shook the world
Was now shaking like a leaf.

In the winter the police would round up most of these old jakeys to save them from freezing to death.

The cells in Barlinnie Prison had an inadequate heating system: every cell had a hot-air ventilation grill, yet no hot air ever got through them because over the years they had been blocked up and painted over many times. There was much talk about new heating systems being installed and new toilet facilities at the end of each of the five huge halls, but nobody knew when this was supposed to be.

Cell searches were regular, and warders would spend ages looking for things we weren't supposed to have. Some guys were put on report for having a tinder box and for very minor things. Minor or not, they were still locked up in solitary confinement for a few days or weeks. The governor couldn't send a man to the punishment block for more than fourteen days without a visiting committee being involved. The people who make up these committees are civil servants employed by the Secretary of State for Scotland. They have more powers than a prison governor: they could lock up a man for twenty-eight days punishment and forfeit as much remission as they liked, and they could also recommend that a prisoner be kept in solitary confinement till the governor saw fit to take him off – which could be for as long as a year.

As I said before, many judges try to stamp out violence by giving longer sentences, but that fails. The prison authorities try to stamp it out with their steel-capped boots, and that too fails. Often I wanted help in these places, but I had no one to

161

turn to and never even knew how to ask for it. The system wasn't geared to offer the help most guys needed. I'm not saying that prisons shouldn't exist or that society shouldn't be protected: all I'm saying is that the system in prisons is wrong. The regime is counter-productive, and not in the best interests of society. Prison is geared towards destroying a man rather than offering help. It saddens me to think of the many people who were sent to mental hospitals because they couldn't fit into such an unnatural environment.

Some warders actually believed that we were subhuman and treated us as such, but we on the other side saw them as the dregs of humanity. 'Evil is the man who holds the key to another man's freedom' – that's how most prisoners summed up the warders.

17 BACK TO ST JOSEPH'S

Tony Tamburrini, my pal from St Joseph's, had moved to Garthamlock with his family, and when I was released we started going about with each other again. He and I and Gak would go stealing together. One day I suggested that we go back to St Joseph's Approved School in Edinburgh and see how it had changed since we were last there in 1970.

It was really strange to see once again the big mansion building and the fields that I had so often run across when fleeing from authority. We sat near a wee wall which we had often climbed over, and spoke of what now seemed to be the 'good old days'. I took in everything – the football field where Ma sat with me on sunny visiting days, the exercise yard, the circles in which I had been made to stand.

One of the first things that we recalled was the Killiecrankie dormitory and we laughed at the thought of our wandering about in our Willie Winkie nightgowns. We wondered whether any of the same Brothers and teachers were still there, and we decided to go in and challenge the bastards. As we crossed the yard and through the door which led up to the head Brother's office we joked about running into one of the worst Brothers, and how it would be hard not to slap him on the head for all he had said and done. We saw no one, which was strange, but then we found out that none of the boys lived in the building any more. The authorities had built another two cottages, which meant that every kid in the school was housed in one of them. I knocked on the head Brother's door, and we were told to come in. The room was much the same as it had been, but none of us recognised the Brother sitting behind the desk. He was the new head, and I told him we wanted to take a look at the school and to see some of the Brothers and teachers whom we'd known. He told us that there was only one Brother whom we would remember – and remember him we did! We went to his office on the ground floor and knocked on the door. The tall, thin Brother with grey hair looked bewildered as he tried to put names to our faces, his finger resting on his lips. One at a time he studied us – 'McGachan?' and then 'Tamburrini?' and 'Steele?'. He invited us in for tea and a talk about our days there. He asked us what we thought of him when we were under his care, and we told him he was a bastard. He didn't seem surprised or upset by this, and he told us what he thought of us then. We ended up having a debate about physical and mental torture – not forgetting our Willie Winkie nightgowns and the little circles. He admitted that a lot of unpleasant methods were used that shouldn't have been. This was a man who used to tell me that it was time I came to my senses, and now it seemed he had finally come to his.

18 A BAD GAMBLE

Tony, Gak and I went on a stealing spree up and down our part of Scotland, most times getting not a lot and other times nothing at all. But we didn't stop – it was like a sport. Selling the stolen goods was easy: getting the right price was the problem. Sometimes we were ripped off by our punters, who claimed the police had raided their home and taken away the stolen goods. Tony was a mad gambler, so any money he stole was put on the horses or cards. He would walk up and down the betting shop biting his nails as he listened to the results. I hated the depressing atmosphere in the betting shops, and when Tony went in for a bet I stayed outside.

Ma occasionally went to the bingo hall to try her luck, as did Tony's ma. I was talking to my ma there one day; she wasn't too pleased to see me with Tony, whom she disliked and she couldn't hide her feelings. I stood in front of her so that Tony wouldn't see her face. As we left, Tony had a shot at the one-arm bandit that stood in the entrance of the bingo hall. I tried to get him away, but up he went to the cashier's window for change so that he could play it. We started arguing. I said if he wanted the money that bad why not steal the fucking bandit! But he wanted to steal more than the bandit; when he went up for the change at the cashier's window he spotted the money bags which contained the prize money. I went to have a look and there it was, just as Tony said. The woman gave me some change and we stood talking, pretending

165

to be interested in losing our money to the bandit. The cashier's window was quite long, with a door at the end of it. There were two or three women behind the glass, and an usher on the outside, busy showing people in. We decided to snatch the prize money. We had no weapons, nor did we need any – it was simply a case of kicking in the door. From inside the bingo hall we could hear men and women having a good time, and occasionally the door would open to let people in and out. I had just put my first tenpence into the machine and pulled the arm when a wee old woman wearing a headscarf came up and said she would wait her turn for a shot. We had to get her away somehow. Then I won the jackpot. I couldn't believe it – I'd never won a thing in my life. The wee woman was hooting at my good fortune and said she only hoped she had the luck I'd had. I told her to take the money and keep it. She must have thought I was joking, but when I put all the silver into her bag she bolted out the door in case I changed my mind.

Tony crashed in the door and went in, with me behind him. The three women screamed for the police while we grabbed the money. Before I knew it we were on the street, Tony running in one direction and me in another. I could hear women shouting from the bingo hall that some bastards had stolen the pay-out money!

Tony told me to follow him since he knew the area better than I did, so I turned back and followed him up a dead-end street – straight into the police who were parked there. They switched on their headlamps and the flash of lights nearly blinded me. I turned and ran back the way I was heading, still clutching the money. Tony followed and behind him, the police. We darted through back courts and stopped here and there to listen, then we moved on again. We thought we had lost them, so we chanced crossing the busy main road and mingling with the crowds, but they saw us and gave chase and we were off again, running as fast as we could down a long deserted road with a wall down one side. There was a break in the wall so we nipped in, but we were trapped. The police had spotted us. There was nothing to do but hide the money, so we buried it in the thick mud at our feet.

166

The police blocked our entrance, shining their torches in our eyes. Tony made a bolt for it, but was caught halfway down the street and they grabbed me and started kicking my face and legs. The police asked us what we had been up to. Straight away we said that we had been up to nothing. 'You must have been up to something – why else should you run away?' one said. I couldn't believe it – they didn't even know what we had done. Tony said he ran because he owed an unpaid fine, and I told them that I had only run because Tony had done so. It was quite funny standing on top of the money while we were being questioned by the police, and it seemed as if we were going to be let go any minute! Then they asked us where the suits were. 'Suits?' I thought. I didn't know what they were talking about and told them so. They said they knew we were selling suits which had been stolen from Tom Martin's, the tailor's shop, so although they hadn't a clue that we had stolen the bingo money they took us along to Shettleston police station.

We were put into a little detention room and some CID men came in and asked us what we were up to that had made us run away. We stuck to the story about Tony owing a fine, and they told us that we would probably be charged with breaking into the tailor's shop. They left us alone for a while – but when they came back they had the money with them. I denied ever seeing it before and again they left. When they came again they were laughing, and they told us that we would be attending an identification parade for robbing the bingo hall of several hundred pounds. Next morning we were taken to court and remanded in custody at Longriggend.

Probably more than a hundred prisoners passed through Glasgow Sheriff Court each day. It is said to be the busiest in Europe. I was sentenced to six months in a young offenders' institution and Tony was sent to Borstal. The judge couldn't give me more than six months because it was only a summary court. I would have to be in front of a sheriff and jury in a higher court for my sentence to have been made longer. As we were being marched out, I turned and waved good-bye to Ma and Mary Carroll, who had run her down to the court. They shouted over to me, telling me they would come and visit me. Then I said goodbye to Tony. I could be home in four months with time off for good behaviour, but Tony had to do at least a year in Borstal before he got home.

At Barlinnie I was put through the usual routine. When the doors opened I noticed many familiar faces and I was asked what I was in for by those I knew. Everybody was happy, in a sense, to see someone they knew – it was a feeling of security in an insecure world. My brother Jim and Broono were in, each serving an eighteen-month sentence for robbing a bookie's shop, and Jim had an outstanding charge to go up for at the Glasgow High Court, along with my Uncle Billy, for holding up a jeweller's shop and serious assault. He and Uncle Billy both got six years. I told Jim that when I got out I would help break him out, but he said he wouldn't want me to do that. Jim's wife was shattered at his sentence. She never knew of his robberies – he never told her anything. My dad was home when we were in the young offenders', and he came to see us. He looked as if he had just come back from Spain rather than a six-year sentence. He was very tanned and, as always, smartly dressed. He sat there and preached to us both about not getting involved with crime, and how I was to get myself a job when I came home. As usual, he told us that if any of the warders were messing us about we were to get their names and let him know as soon as possible.

I was sent to work in the cobbler's shop with Jim. It had a few bench tables scattered here and there, and it looked empty compared to other sheds in the gaol. The warder who ran the shop was a fair and decent enough guy, who knew my dad. He never bothered with anyone as long as we did our work and looked as though we were busy. He didn't mind us smoking as long as it was out of sight. He was the sort who was only in the job for the money, a happy-go-lucky man, always smiling and talking to us like human beings, and he told us that he disagreed with the brutality of the system.

I wasn't a cobbler, and I was put on to a machine which seals plastic bags. It was crazy. There I was working for a wage that would hardly buy me an ounce of tobacco, yet I wouldn't work for a good wage when I was out!

One of the decent warders pulled me up one Friday just before tea, and told me I was in serious trouble as one of the warders had found a sealed bag of glue which someone had dropped on the dining-hall floor. Because the bag was sealed and I had been working on the sealing machine with another guy, we were being blamed. I didn't think it a serious matter, nor did I remember sealing the bag. As far as I was concerned the machine was there for anyone to use whenever they wanted. Many prisoners made fancy tobacco tins and jewel boxes, and they needed glue to stick the wood.

That night I heard through the grapevine that an older con in another hall was in the gaol infirmary suffering seriously from sniffing glue! I had visions of some poor guy dying in the hospital. You can make a living in gaol by selling glue to other prisoners – whether for making models or for sniffing – but I had never sold a piece of gaol equipment to a prisoner in my life, nor had I ever sniffed glue.

After breakfast we stayed in our cells, because Saturday wasn't a work day. At about ten in the morning I heard, 'Third flat! Send down Steele!' I could see two warders on the ground floor looking up at me, and it seemed that they were whispering between themselves. When I reached the desk on the bottom floor they took me into a cell they used as an office, containing a wooden desk and a filing cabinet. They asked me what my job was in the cobbler's shop, and I told them I was on the machine which sealed plastic bags.

'And what do you know about this here?' one of them said, showing me a sealed bag of glue. They were standing on either side of me in an intimidating manner, but I told them the truth: that I knew nothing of it and that I wasn't the only one who worked the machine. They said that they had spoken to the other guy, and they believed him when he said he knew nothing about the glue: but they wouldn't believe me. I realised then that they were only wanting to blame me, and that my denying it wasn't what they wanted to hear. The cell door was

169

closed over so that no one could see in. This told me that something more was to come and I tensed my belly muscles so that a punch wouldn't take the wind from me. It came full force, but I never felt it. This irritated the warder and he punched me again, and again I didn't feel it.

'It was fucking you who sealed this bag!' they kept shouting, showering me with saliva. I told them it wasn't. 'It fucking was!' they screamed – and, taking off their hats and putting them on the desk, they pounced on me, punching and kicking me to the floor. 'Admit it!' they said as they kicked me on the legs, body and head. I wanted to scream for help but knew that would be pointless. I kept throwing my arms up to protect my face and head, and each time I did they would kick my belly and chest, and when my hands came down to protect those parts, they aimed for my head. They made contact, yet they never hurt me. The thing that hurt was the thought of dying there in that cell. I could feel the crunching of their boots on my head and body.

I don't know how long they kicked me about. I think that my youth, size and build had deceived them, in that they thought that after a few kicks I would gladly confess. Each time I denied it the worse the kicking became. Each time the kicking stopped I felt the pain in my body; when they started kicking again I couldn't feel it but the thudding noises were terrifying. Eventually they stopped and told me to get up. I thanked God that they had stopped and clambered to my feet, using my hands to help me climb up the wall. I was given a paper handkerchief to clean the blood from my nose and mouth. I didn't know where the blood was coming from, nor did the warders who stood before me scrutinising me. They told me not to be foolish and admit it and make it easier for myself – 'You'll be sorry before the weekend is over, boy,' the older of the two said.

They put me into one of the punishment cells, not far from their desk at the bottom of the hall. There was no bed, no table and no chair – nothing except for me and my thoughts. I was not the hard case they now thought me to be. I cursed myself for not admitting it and getting it over with. I promised myself that when they came back I would tell them I had sealed the bag of glue. My body was aching so I had to sit down in a corner. With each move I made it hurt, sending sharp pains through me. Outside my cell door I could hear activity and of course there was the usual yelling from the warders from one end of the hall to the other. I could hear my pals and my brother Jim calling my name from their cell windows, but I couldn't answer in case the warders heard me – and even if I'd wanted to I couldn't because I was so sore that it would have been hard for me to climb up to the window, some six feet above the floor.

'Haw, Johnnyboy! are ye awright down there?'

'Ir they setting aboot ye, wee man?'

'Kin ye hear us shoutin, can ye, pal?'

The door opened and the same two warders came in. 'Are you still going to deny it, Steele?' – and so the beating started again. They were like two mad men as they kicked me, and – what's worse – they had a licence to do so. No one tried to stop them, no one came to investigate the noises that came from the cell. They left saying they would be back, and that sooner or later I would admit it.

I was aching all over with sharp and frightening pains. Why the fuck I wouldn't just say it was me, I'll never know. They came back again after dinner, only this time it was two different warders. I knew one of them had a bad reputation as a 'dog'. He squatted down beside me and told me he wasn't going to take any of my nonsense – he wanted an answer, and it had to be 'yes'.

'Maybe you wouldn't tell the others, but you'll certainly tell me,' he said. I didn't want another beating and decided I would say what they wanted to hear, yet I denied it again, and immediately put my hands up to protect my head – but no blows came, and when the warder stood up I thought that he had given up. That was until I saw him unbutton his jacket and take if off and give it to the other warder to hold. He didn't seem to be in any hurry. He made me stand up and while I stood he started slapping me on the face. I really wanted to hit back – my rage gave me all the strength I needed.

171

When he saw his slaps had no effect, he started punching me on the belly. With each punch he shouted, 'Admit it', and I took great pride in saying, 'Never!' I could see the expression on his face change each time I shouted, 'Never!' It got to the stage that I was daring him to have another punch, and another and another. I was like a mad man standing there under a rain of blows, blinded by the tears that were streaming down my face. I was still shouting, 'Never' when they closed the door on me. I had my mouth to the bottom of the door and kept up the shouting. 'Bastards!' I shouted, hoping they'd come back so I could defy them more. I threatened to harm their families – I even shouted, 'Garthamlock Young Team, ya bass!'

They didn't come in, which surprised me. Instead they gave the door a few kicks. Afterwards, when I had cooled down, I regretted having shouted, regretted even having denied it, and then came the pain and aching. When the door opened again my heart was pounding in my chest, but it was only them throwing in my tea and knocking it all over the floor, which they thought quite funny. 'Never!' I said, my face screwed up with contempt. When they closed the door I heard one say that I was a 'fucking loony'. The food lay where they had thrown it, for I had no intention of eating it. My mind was racing. 'What next?' I wondered.

My cell door opened and a warder put in a pisspot which was filthy and had urine in it. 'See you in the morning, cunt!' he said as he slammed the door. As soon as they had left, my brother and my pals were shouting down to me asking how I was and wanting to know what cell I was in so that they could pass me down tobacco. I was really glad to hear their voices – it was great to have people who cared for me in this hell hole known as the 'Big Hoose'. It was agony climbing up to the window. I thought that my ribs were broken – each time I jumped and grabbed hold of the bars I had to let go again because of the pain. I finally managed to hold on long enough to answer a few of their questions. I told them I was fine and what cell I was in. They passed tobacco along the cell windows by string, each guy passing it on to the next till it reached the

172

cell above me, and from there it was passed down to me. This was a luxury, and I thanked them and jumped off to roll myself a smoke. I never slept a wink the whole night through, and by morning I hadn't a smoke left. My mind had been made up before the door opened: I couldn't take another beating. I was in terrible pain from the last ones, so I was going to admit to the bag of glue. I could hear the warders collecting their cell keys and cell doors opening and closing as they checked the numbers before opening up for slop-out.

It was Sunday, which meant there'd be no breakfast in the dining hall – everyone got breakfast in their cells. After breakfast was the church service and then chapel. I was kept to last. They got a passman to empty my pisspot, and then I was given my breakfast – one boiled egg, two slices of gaol-made bread and a cup of watery unsugared tea.

Then they came in again and tried to get me to admit it. I don't know why I said 'no' when I had already decided that I was going to confess. Several times that day they came in to beat what they considered the truth out of me. After the last slop-out for the day was called I could hear them outside my door. I was fucking terrified of what lay ahead. I would have to admit to it or I was going to end up being kicked to death.

The door opened and I knew they meant business. There were about a dozen of them, all looking at me. The PO told me to get to my feet, and I was shaking all over with fear. 'Still sticking to your same story?' he said. When I said I was he drew back his fist. I turned my head to the side so that his fist wouldn't land square on my face, but 'Get your blankets and get up to your own cell,' he said. It was a reprieve. I was glad to be back in my own cell and to lie on the hard, lumpy coir mattress.

Next morning when I was slopping out and filling my basin with water some of my pals and neighbours came into my cell to find out what happened. When they saw my bruises they shook their heads in disbelief – I was blue all over.

Somehow my dad got to hear about it – word travels fast in prison. We heard that he had made some inquiries about the name of the PO who had been responsible for me getting the beatings. Word was sent out to some of my pals on the estate, and they wrecked a few warders' cars and smashed their front windows in retaliation – and even looked for their kids at the local school.

The day I got out my dad was waiting outside the prison gate in his car. It was a beautiful morning, with the sun shining, and I felt that life was worth living. A few days later I was away stealing again.

19 SCOTTY AND THE GUN

Most of my pals from Garthamlock had married and settled down or were living a quiet life. 'Get yourself a job and settle down,' my dad said. He told me that he was giving up the life of crime, and that we should have a go at it together. I'd never heard him talk like this before. I've never even heard him talk about his crimes. Maybe he was tired of it all. . . .

I never thought about the damage that all his gaol sentences may have done to him. I wonder now if he was in as much pain as I was when I was locked up, or whether for some reason he too found it hard to stop being a crook. He said he was going to settle down and grow old along with Ma, who deserved a better life than the one we had offered her.

The phone seldom stopped ringing for my dad when he was home, and nearly every day people came to see him. He was very popular and well liked. His pals came from everywhere, and were every colour under the sun. They told me that he was a 'diamond': sometimes I wondered if we were talking about the same man.

One afternoon I answered a knock on our door. There were about six men there whom I'd never seen before, but I knew they were from the Underworld. The smallest one asked if my dad was in. I went and got him from his bedroom, and he was delighted to see his pals – particularly Toe Elliot, a well-known Glasgow gangster.

From what I could make out, my dad and Toe had become

175

pals in prison. I went to my bedroom and listened to my records while they sat talking in the living room. After a while the door opened and in walked Toe Elliot, who said he would like to speak to me. I was surprised and wondered what he wanted to talk to me about, but before long it became obvious that my dad had sent him in. He told me that my dad was worried about me and dreaded my getting a big sentence, and about how prison can affect people and their families. This guy has a cheek, I thought, as I'd heard he had done untold damage in the city.

'Listen to me as a friend and don't waste your life in gaols,' Toe said. He couldn't sit still, and as he moved about I could see that he had a gun in the waistband of his suit trousers. He was dressed like a tailor's dummy with his fancy suit. He was very small, yet even so he had all my attention. He was a character, and I had to respect him for trying to make me see sense. He said that the police had been after my dad for years, and if they couldn't get him then they would get me, to hit back at my dad. I had heard this many times but it didn't mean anything to me, since I didn't know what my dad had done in the past that was so bad. Before Toe left he gave me twenty pounds for a night out at the dancing: I bought a tool-kit for break-ins with the money.

I was staying at Lana's house, and I went round to see my ma and the family. My dad had fallen out with Ma, so he was staying with one of his friends. Ma wasn't looking too good so I tried to cheer her up. Scotty, the Cairn terrier Dad had bought for Brenda, jumped all over me when he saw me, and Ma asked me to take him out for a walk in the fields. I had to be careful in case the police came by and spotted me – it was best for me to keep walking or they might pull me for loitering. Scotty disappeared in the long grass, so I had to hunt for him. I could hear him growling, and I thought that perhaps he had caught a mouse. Then I spotted him. He had something in his mouth and was shaking it wildly. It was a bag of some description.

We were a few yards from the social club on the Gartloch

Road when I caught hold of him and took the bag from him. I was for throwing it away but something made me look inside. I thought I was seeing things at first: this was the first gun I had ever held in my life. Something told me it was real, and I put it back in the bag. I was frightened to mess about with it in case it was loaded and went off. I looked around to see if anyone was watching me but the only people I saw were going to the social club. I searched all the other bags that had been dumped there but only found empty cans and bottles.

Sometime before this a man had been gunned down and killed in the Gartloch Road. The man who was shot was a pal of Toe Elliot's, and his killer also tried to shoot Toe but missed. Not long before the shootings the social club had been held up and robbed at gunpoint. My dad was questioned about this, but he could prove he was elsewhere at the time.

I decided to take the gun home with me to show my pals, and find out what they thought of it. My dad had always warned me and Jim never to bring anything stolen into our home and I seldom did, but this was different. I wanted to know if the gun worked, and I didn't want to hide it anywhere else in case someone found it.

I carried it under my jacket, and once I was home I went out to the veranda and hid the gun under some old lino. Ma never went near this part of the veranda which contained much of our junk. I told a few of my pals that I had found the gun, but they didn't believe me.

I went around to Ma's a few days later. No one was in and I made myself something to eat after checking to see if the gun was still where I'd left it. I was eating when there was a knock on the door. It sounded like a policeman's knock. I panicked and thought of climbing out of the window. Scotty was barking for all he was worth. I sat still till I heard whoever it was walk downstairs, and when I peeped out of the side of the curtain in the living room I saw a stranger walking away. Whoever he was he put the wind up me, and left an eerie atmosphere in the house.

The phone started to ring and I answered it to my dad. He asked me if Ma was in, and when I told him she was out shopping he said he was coming round to collect some clothes. Not long afterwards he appeared with his pal John. My dad said that he had seen police in plain clothes sitting in a car in the Gartloch Road, and it looked as though they were watching our house. 'Are you sure you haven't been up to anything?' he asked, looking me in the eye. Then he asked me if I had anything in the house that I shouldn't have. I thought about the gun in the veranda but didn't say anything about it, even though I was worried. My dad was getting his clothes from his bedroom when there was a knock at the door – just like the knock I had heard before. He opened the door, and pandemonium ensued, with him cursing, threatening and demanding to see a warrant. He wouldn't let the police in, and I could hear them saying, 'If you've nothing to hide, Andy, then you've nothing to worry about!' I hoped that he wouldn't let them in till they'd got a warrant, so that I could throw the gun into the canal or somewhere safe. The police said they simply wanted to have a look at what was in the box he had brought into the house with him.

My dad finally let them in, thinking he had nothing to worry about. There were only two of them at first but soon there were six, with some more standing below our window, and they searched every nook and cranny in the house. While this was going on my dad was cursing and threatening the police, and warning them not to plant anything in the house. I recognised some of the crime squad from previous raids on our house and from the police station.

Just when they seemed to be satisfied that the house was clean one of them asked my dad if they could look on the veranda, and he opened the door with the key that hung from a nail in the wall. I thought of telling them what was there, but the longer it went on the more frightened I became.

My dad and one of the policemen disappeared on to the veranda. 'What's all this, Andy?' the policeman asked, and my dad told him it was old wax cloth and some junk belonging to his sons. He was searching through the junk himself, and passing it on to the policeman. I expected to hear a shout from my dad at any moment – he would automatically have assumed that they had planted the gun there. But the shout never came, and I was still in the living room when another member of the serious crime squad came to our door, holding the gun with a pencil so as to keep his fingerprints off it.

Only later did I find out exactly what happened on the veranda. When he saw the gun, my dad knew straight away that I had brought the fucking thing into the house. He panicked and threw it over the veranda and into the garden below, where the other police were standing and saw it come down. He hadn't realised that the police were there as well.

When he and the cop came in from the veranda he gave me a dirty look. I was so ashamed that I had to look away. I thought of owning up there and then, but I feared the consequences and kept my mouth closed. Just then one of Ma's insurance men came to the door with a little box in his hand. He got a terrible fright when the police pounced on him, searched the box and demanded to know who he was and what his business was.

My dad and his pal were arrested. John was released soon after, but my dad was remanded in custody at Barlinnie on a firearms charge. When Ma came home I told her that he had been arrested: she was shattered and turned very pale.

My conscience was bothering me at the thought of his being locked up because of my stupidity, and with that on my mind I made a statement to the police, who came to Ma's house. Maw sat with me so that she could be a witness to the facts. They asked her to leave, but she refused, saying that she might be blind but she wasn't stupid. Maw was scared, as I was, that the police would make a false statement to incriminate my dad.

My dad pleaded guilty to throwing the gun over the veranda in the High Court in Glasgow. I didn't know whether to laugh or cry when I picked up the newspaper the following day to read of his eighteen-month sentence and saw the headlines 'SCOTTY THE WEE WIRY CAIRN TERRIER FINDS HIS MASTER A PACKAGE OF TROUBLE!' It told the

179

story, ending with how Scotty was run over shortly after finding the package. And so it was. I was walking to the bus stop with my girlfriend Carol one night, and had taken Scotty with me. He was hit by a car when crossing the road. My dad later said that he would have thrown him under a car after all the trouble he had caused.

20 DEAR JOHN

I had fallen in love with a lassie called Carol. She was only sixteen but she looked older and was very mature for her age. She was beautiful. When I was with her I wasn't really interested in thieving – probably because I was scared to lose her if I got put in prison. We were with each other most nights. People were beginning to think that I had settled down at long last, and they asked me when the big day was. But the 'big' day never came....

One night in December 1976 I met Tony, whom I hadn't seen for a few weeks, and we got talking. He was amazed at my change of attitude now that I was with Carol – he couldn't believe that I was settling down, and we both had a good laugh about it. Tony was on his way to steal some money when I bumped into him: he said he was going to take the 'takings' off the driver of an ice-cream van, and he even had a key that fitted the door of the van. He had another two guys with him, and he asked me to go with them. I went, but it was decided that I should watch for the police as I was too well known in Garthamlock and might be seen. So I stayed in the shadows – for all the good it did me!

Tony and the others got the money, which wasn't much, and I was arrested soon after. In the police station I was messed about by the police because I wouldn't tell them who was with me. I was shattered when I thought about Carol – it was torture to be in love and so far apart. I realised what it must be like for those in gaol with families of their own. I was so shattered that I felt like grassing Tony's name to the police, hoping I would be let off or only given a short sentence. But I knew I couldn't and wouldn't, no matter what. I tried to imagine giving evidence against him at court, and the thought of the puzzled and unbelieving look on his face made me burst out laughing!

I was charged with assault and robbery and was to appear before a sheriff and jury at the High Court in Glasgow. The maximum I could get was two years, but if the sheriff thought I deserved more than two years he could then remit me to a higher court.

Carol visited me four or five times a week while I was in Longriggend. I thought about her all the time. I even thought about hanging myself if she left me while I was in there, and I told her so. We weren't allowed photographs, but I got her to smuggle in a couple of herself. I wrote to her every day, and I received a letter from her every day; and every day I was falling deeper in love. 'If only I hadn't met Tony that night,' I kept thinking.

There was a really bad blizzard when I was at Longriggend. The snow was so deep that a tractor had to bring the food to the gaol because no truck or van could get through. It was on such a night that my name was called for a visit while we were sitting in the dining hall watching television. As I made my way out between the rows of prisoners seated at long tables, one of the warders shouted from the other end of the hall, 'Who the fuck would want to visit you on a night like this?'

When I reached the visiting room I was chuffed to see Ma and Carol sitting there. They were soaking wet, having walked through the knee-deep snow. Carol was wringing her trouser legs out on the floor, but they both had a good laugh at their wild journey. I was so proud of them. I was the only guy in the gaol to get a visit that night. I promised that I would get a job when I came out and that I would never go stealing in my life again – and once again I really meant it this time.

Carol was having a hard time of it with her dad, who wanted her to stop seeing me. He told her to go out and find herself a decent guy. I could understand his not wanting his daughter to get hitched to someone who was in and out of gaol; most Glasgow villains had similar views even though they themselves had been in and out of gaol too. It wasn't a case of their wanting their daughters to have the best – they just didn't want their daughters to have the worst.

We weren't allowed any physical contact but we found a way without being seen. I would take a shoe off and Carol would do the same, and we'd put our feet together and whisper to one another.

Ma and Carol were convinced that I had nothing to do with the robbery, and I never let them know otherwise. I was going to deny that I had robbed the van, but I was warned by my lawyer that if I pleaded not guilty and was found guilty I could get remitted to the higher court and face a sentence of anything up to seven years. On the other hand if I pleaded guilty, I could get off with one year for not wasting the court's time. This was my first indictment and that would help.

I was transferred from Longriggend on my twenty-first birthday and moved to the Barlinnie untried hall to await my court appearance. Carol still came to see me; although I was grateful to her, the visits were terrible since we could only see each other through a sheet of glass and talk to each other through a wire mesh. I was glad when it was my turn for court – and I hoped to get out. In the cells below the courtroom, I made up my mind that I would plead guilty. I couldn't stand the thought of being remitted to a higher court for sentence. One good thing was that the van driver hadn't been physically assaulted or injured in any way although he'd been threatened.

I was called for trial in February or March 1977: I pleaded guilty to assault and robbery, and was sentenced to eighteen months in gaol. Immediately I regretted pleading guilty and wanted to tell the judge I was innocent. I kept thinking about Carol, who was in court, crying, and I didn't know how I was going to get through my sentence without her. I re-read all her letters every night, and every day when I came back from work I would go to the warders' desk on my gallery to see if there was any mail from her.

I managed to get through my sentence without getting into much bother with the warders: all my trouble was with Carol. A few months into my sentence she stopped writing to me or visiting me. Anything could have happened to her – I thought that maybe she was in hospital, and that was why I hadn't heard from her. I hadn't a clue, but I kept writing to a friend of hers who lived down the stairs from her, and asked her to pass my letters on. Eventually Carol answered my letters and put my mind at ease in a strange sort of way. She said that she couldn't take much more of her dad's nagging her about me and that she was sorry for the way it had to end. As I read the letter, the tears were streaming down my face. 'I'll never forget you, Johnny,' and 'I hope you'll always remember me for as long as you live,' she wrote. The trouble was I couldn't forget her, couldn't get her out of my mind. I couldn't eat my food, couldn't swallow. I'd heard about guys slashing their wrists or killing themselves because their girlfriends had left them, but I could only make sense of it when I was going through that bad patch myself. Some of my pals were worried about my not being able to swallow my food and they advised me to go and see the doctor. My pal Teddy from Greenock said that it could be cancer of the throat, and that I had better go and get it checked out. I tried eating little pieces of food, thinking it might help: it got to the stage that when I ate my soup – which was watery at the best of times – I had to wash it down with a mouthful of water, and even then it sometimes wouldn't go down and I'd spit it back into the bowl. But I never did go and see the doctor about it.

Just before I was due to be released I was informed by a warder that I had an outstanding fine and would have to serve extra time if it wasn't paid. I wrote to my ma and asked her to get my dad to pay it for me. He refused, saying he wanted nothing to do with me. I cursed at my old man like one possessed. But one evening about a week later I was sitting singing in my cell when I heard a warder shout, 'Send down Steele, that's his fine paid!' Ma had got the money together and bought me out. I was never so glad to get away from it all. Lana and Ma were there to meet me at the gate. I wanted to give them a big kiss and a hug but something stopped me from doing so – probably I was too shy. . . .

My dad was out of gaol, and Ma and Lana told me that he said I was an embarrassment to him. I felt like going home and kicking his fucking face in. I had had enough of him and all his nonsense.

'It's all his fucking fault anyway,' I told Ma. But much as I would have liked to have given my old man a beating, I didn't. Maybe that was part of my trouble with him, my not hitting back. Ma begged me to stay away from Tony and to settle down.

21 A BIG MISTAKE

When I got home my dad was there. He wouldn't talk to me because of the gun incident, and it was quite clear he didn't want me in his house, so I went to live with Lana.

I didn't know what to do with my life. I was too shy to get a job. I found it hard to work with strangers, and couldn't even ask for a job without feeling awkward. Henry Healy's store job had been enough for me. I lacked confidence. I would have loved to be a singer but I didn't have the confidence even to hum in front of a stranger.

The last time I stayed with Lana she got a phone bill for £2,765. Her phone was meant to be cut off, it could not take incoming calls, so I didn't think the calls would register when I started phoning America. I phoned the wife of my favourite singer, Jim Reeves, and spoke to her for hours. It was great, and I went on phoning America for about five weeks. During this time I had no interest in going out stealing. If my pals turned up I told Lana to tell them I wasn't in.

All the people I phoned in the USA seemed overjoyed to talk to me. I started phoning any old number and speaking to whoever answered the phone. I never told them the truth about my life – I made out I was working hard and had never been in trouble with the law. Some of them asked me to stay, and others said I was the first Scotsman they'd ever spoken to. Sometimes I was on the phone to one person for as long as eight hours. They always asked me if I wore a kilt and seemed disappointed when I said no. One night I phoned a number in Kentucky and a girl answered the phone. 'Have you heard of Jesus Christ?' she asked, and she told me that the Lord had meant me to phone her. She was a Mormon. I spoke with a woman in Texas who told me she grew up with Jim Reeves and played me records over the phone.

I had written a couple of songs at the time, one of which was 'The Ballad of Jim Reeves'. Jim Reeves' wife wanted me to send it to her on tape, and I arranged to meet her when she came to Britain for the Wembley Country Music Festival. I was all excited at this, but I never did sing my song and send it to her, nor did I meet her at Wembley. Everybody tried to persuade me to go, but I was too shy to go alone. You should have seen my sister's face when the phone bill arrived – and mine!

I met Tony a few days after my release. All he could say about my misfortune was 'sorry'. I had to accept it as bad luck and held nothing against him – and we went on stealing together. His ma had moved to another housing estate called Ruchazie. He told me that she had a debt collector who came to their house and that he always carried large amounts of money with him. It sounded easy enough and I agreed that we should rob him. Tony said that since the guy knew him and could identify him, he should stay out of it and leave it up to me and two friends of his, Joe and James – one of whom had a fish knife which he intended to use as a frightener, and nothing more.

When the debt collector came out of Tony's ma's house we were waiting on him in the stairway. The plan was that Joe and James would hold his arms while I took the wallet from his pocket, but that wasn't how it turned out. As soon as the guy saw the three of us standing there in masks he panicked and started to lash out. The other two ran off and left me to fight with the guy, who refused to hand over the money. Every time I tried to put my hand into his pocket he kicked and punched me. One of the two who had run away had dropped the knife on the landing, so I picked it up and pointed it at the guy and demanded the money. I had no intention of using it on him, but he grabbed the blade of the knife while trying to pull it out of my hand and cut himself. When he saw the blood he told me to take the money and leave him, and I did.

On the way downstairs I ran into the other two, and raged at them for running away. We met up with Tony and split up the money, which came to about a hundred pounds.

Tony and I met a guy in Garthamlock whom I knew quite well. He had heard that we had robbed the debt man in Ruchazie, and he gave us some advice on doing robberies. He told us we should go for people with plenty of money, and that some people living in a house nearby who owned taxis and a café kept their takings in a wardrobe. If we struck on the night he suggested we might make several thousand pounds. Of course he would expect something for himself. . . .

Once again, Joe and James were involved. On the night of the robbery we put masks on, and each of us had a knife. As we stood in the dark in the back court we were more nervous than excited. I was selected to go up to the top landing and knock on the door. We could hear sounds coming from the street below, people talking and laughing, and televisions from the nearby house. My heart was pounding as I waited for the knock to be answered, and when I heard someone coming I was ready to run. This was the first time I had ever been in a situation like this, and I just didn't feel right. I don't know why I didn't turn around and get away from there. It turned out to be the biggest mistake in my life.

The door opened and a woman stood there; she was in her twenties, and wearing a house coat that came to her knees. For a split second it didn't dawn on her what was happening – then I saw her eyes shift quickly from one point to another and terror set into her face. Someone from behind me dashed into the house, pushing the woman into the middle of the hall; I followed, and then the others, and we closed the door behind us, still not knowing who was in the house. But there was no time to worry now. I ran into a room and searched the wardrobe. Tony ran into another. I heard him say there were two guys in the bed. 'Don't fucking move!' he told them threateningly, and they didn't. Joe asked the woman where the money was, but she told him there was none in the house. I searched the wardrobes again and chests of drawers but I found nothing. The woman repeated that there was no money in the house, but I said we had information that it was there. She said that whoever told me was lying. She began to argue with Joe, and he told her that if she didn't stop being cheeky he'd beat her up. But she wouldn't let him bully her, and gave him a mouthful of abuse.

I decided it was time to leave and get as far away as possible. I was really sick at the thought of having gone to all this trouble without getting the money we were after. The others wanted to search again, and started taking jewellery and the little money there was lying about. One of them even stole the television meter.

I felt better going down the stairs than I had coming up, and I felt even better when I was in the dark back court with the cool breeze on my face. Pulling off my mask felt good. It was horrible to be under the fucking thing. I was sorry for what I had done back there ... so fucking sorry.

Tony knew some people who would buy the jewellery we had taken, and then he took me to another house in the Parkhead area belonging to a friend who knew people who would buy stolen goods. I was introduced to the family, who seemed okay. The son was a thief and had done time. Tony said he was 'solid', meaning he wouldn't tell the police a thing, but before long the police had caught up with us and we were all arrested and taken to a police station.

The CID told me to give them a statement. I refused to do so, and was kicked and punched. 'Come on, Johnnyboy, the others are giving statements,' one of them said. 'Come on son, co-operate with us and we'll put a good word in with the judge for you.'

Although they didn't know it, I felt like giving them a statement: it's just that when I got caught in a situation like this I cut myself off mentally and couldn't talk to anyone. They moved me to another room and removed my trousers for forensic tests. I was handcuffed to a radiator while a policeman in plain clothes spoke to me nicely and tried to persuade me to give him a statement.

Once the CID man realised that he wasn't getting anywhere he left the room and another took his place. He eyed me while he took off his jacket and glasses, and told me to start confessing or else I would be a sorry boy. I didn't answer, so he started doing karate on me and screaming. I had had beatings before from the police, but I had never witnessed anything like this.

I was eventually uncuffed from the radiator and, still half-naked, I was taken into the room where Tony was. He too was handcuffed by one hand to the pipe at the bottom of the radiator. He was kneeling on the floor watching the blood pour on to the lino from a deep gash in his face, just below his eye.

Then we were taken down to the cells. After a while the cell door opened and a turnkey told me I was to be fingerprinted. I knew this was untrue, because fingerprinting wasn't done in this station. I was taken upstairs to a room in which there were six or seven CID men. I knew at once that I was in trouble, still more so when I heard the door click shut behind me. One of them was sitting at a desk with pen and paper, which he pushed towards me. When I refused to sign a statement one of the CID men got up and pulled down the blinds on the window – and then they all started kicking and punching and screaming at me to sign and save myself a lot of trouble. I could hear their grunts as they kicked and punched me. I was terrified by the thudding of their boots and by the black flashes in front of my eyes. The old fear was there, but no physical pain. I never attempted to hit back, and this only encouraged them. I heard one of them ask for a truncheon. He held it in his hand, beating his open palm. Two others pulled me to my feet. There was a silence as the one with the truncheon asked me to give them a statement.

I felt the blood drain from my head and the coldness in my skin that told me I was going to pass out. I felt like retching. I could feel my face being slapped as I stood there with my eyes closed, the tears running down my face. Maybe they

190

thought I was crying because I had had enough, but I was crying with rage more than anything. Then the one with the truncheon told the others to put my penis on the table top, at which I panicked and lashed out. I began screaming abuse and challenging them to fight. My only concern was that they didn't get my penis on the table top. I wriggled and squirmed and tried to crawl away under the tables and chairs. They told me to calm down, and that I would rot in gaol; after which they began to talk to me as if I was their friend. One of those who had beaten me gave me a packet of cigarettes just before he closed the door of my cell.

We were transferred to another police station. I wasn't given my trousers – any trousers – until I went on an identification parade. I was fingerprinted and photographed and a blood sample was taken.

At the ID parade I was picked out by the debt collector as the one who had assaulted him. The woman from the house came to identify us, but she failed to recognise me. The police charged us with thirteen robberies and one conspiracy to rob a post office. When we saw the charges we couldn't believe them: I had committed two of them, the debt collector and the robbery in the house. Joe and James gave statements to the police saying I had been involved in both: the police told me I should get my own back by giving them a statement incriminating Joe and James, but I refused to do so.

I was taken to Barlinne to await trial at Glasgow High Court – my first High Court appearance. I met some pals of my dad's there, and they tipped me for anything up to four or five years in gaol. My only hope was to deny the charges and be acquitted.

My lawyer tried repeatedly to get me bail, but it was refused. I gave him a statement about the beatings in the police station and the business of the police trying to get my penis on to the table. None of this seemed to have any effect on my lawyer – maybe he was used to hearing such stories and was hardened to them.

My trial was set for June 1978. I was charged with robbing the debt collector and the house, robbing an ice-cream van, attempting to escape from police custody, assaulting police and conspiring to rob a post office.

The debt collector had identified me as the man who had robbed him, and there was some forensic evidence to corroborate this; the woman from the house described the threats of violence made by one of us; and the evidence of Joe and James was another nail in my coffin. When I gave my evidence about the police and the beatings I told the truth, yet when my counsel questioned them about it they pretended to be deeply offended by such allegations and denied them under oath. I lied when others told the truth, and I told the truth when they lied.

We were all taken away downstairs to await the ringing of the bell that would tell us that the jury had reached their verdict. In the cells I spoke to Joe and James, who said that the police had beaten them to extract the statements. I blamed myself for getting involved with them in the first place. What angered me was that when they gave their statements incriminating me, they never admitted to threatening the woman, nor said that I had put a stop to Joe's threats.

While I was talking to them the bell of the south court rang and the four of us were taken up the narrow stairs to the dock in the courtroom. I was found guilty on two charges of robbery, Tony on one charge, and James and Joe on three charges. Passing sentence, the judge said he had no doubt I was the ringleader. Something inside me died when I heard him say I would go to gaol for twelve years.

I remember hearing a cry from the balcony at the back of the courtroom. I was shattered. How could I get through such a sentence? I held on to the railing in front of me, hoping not to collapse. I didn't want to give them that pleasure. I thought that maybe he meant twelve months and that he'd probably correct himself – but no, this was for real.

I then heard the judge sentence Tony to six years in prison, and Joe and James to five years each in a young offenders' institution, but while they were being sentenced I stood there in a kind of daze, looking at a world that had collapsed around me. I didn't even have time to hate the judge or the police

192

officers laughing at the back of the courtroom – there'd be plenty of time for that. My thoughts were with my family, and those close to me. My dad's words kept coming back to me – 'They'll fucking crucify you, son.'

22 THE APPEAL

I was entitled to appear before an appeal court, and the thought of my sentence being halved stopped me from going round the bend. Even the CID man in charge of my case said I'd get my sentence reduced on appeal.

Back at Barlinnie I was placed under strict observation. This was routine for all long-term prisoners for a night or two; a lot of them try to commit suicide. Suicide was the furthest thing from my mind that night, and yet I felt I was dead. It pained me terribly to think of the hurt I must be causing my family, and to think that I had lost all their love and affection. I'd ruined my whole life, and ruined Ma's too. I'd been a failure all my life: nothing had ever gone right for me, and nothing could surely go right for me now. I was alone with the truth, and the truth was even more painful than twelve years in prison.

I was taken to the prison doctor for a check-up. He hardly looked at me, but asked if I felt fine. Felt fine! I was shattered, but who cared? I said I'd like to come off strict observation. The doctor agreed, and I was taken away to join a party that made and repaired mail bags. It included all the new admissions and all the old-timers who'd been coming in and out of gaol for years. The clothing I had on would have fitted a man twice my size and weight – even my shoes were odd and a size too big. I was equipped with grey trousers, a grey jacket and plastic shoes: humiliating and degrading clothing, but I was too frightened to complain. To argue would only end up with my being beaten and put on report.

I was glad to be taken off strict suicide observation. No one had bothered to check up on me – not once did a warder come to my spyhole to see if I was still alive in my cell, from which my wooden locker and bed and chair had all been removed as well as my clothes. But I knew that I was trapped in prison, and what's worse, that I couldn't do my time. There's an old saying amongst prisoners: 'If you do the crime you must do the time.' It was the manly thing to do. Not being able to do the time was seen by others as a weakness. I was to spend some six and a half years in solitary confinement because I couldn't do my time, and during those years I kept trying to get away from it by digging through walls and sawing bars. In some ways my weakness saved my life.

My appeal was heard at the Edinburgh High Court by three appeal judges. Two of them had bad reputations amongst the criminal fraternity, but my lawyer and Queen's Counsel were optimistic that I'd get my sentence reduced. There were a few prisoners up on appeal that day. Everyone – warders included – thought that I would be the only one to get a result. As soon as I entered the appeal court I was aware of an eerie silence, and the staring eyes of the three judges upon me as if I were some sort of subhuman. My QC said my sentence was far too long and asked the judges to reduce it . . . but naw, they didn't seem to think me too hard done by. I left the courtroom with my hopes shattered. My QC said he was sorry for me and that somehow I'd just have to get on with it; then he shook my hand and left.

It was like being sentenced all over again. I wept, and almost cracked up – then I thought about escaping, and it made me feel better and helped me over my depression.

Walking around the exercise yard I heard a voice calling, 'There's one thing I can't stand, and that's a sneak sentencing my pal to twelve years.' It was Gak. He was always in doing time; he was a great comfort to me because he was such an unconscious comedian, and we used to talk about St Joseph's.

I was told to attend an induction board to see which gaol I would be allocated to. We were taken to an empty recreation hall, where we were informed that we would be sitting an examination, and that anyone who refused to sit it would automatically go to Peterhead Prison – the equivalent to America's Alcatraz or the Siberian camps, up in the cold north of Scotland next to the North Sea and reserved for Scotland's most dangerous and hardened criminals. I sat the test. I was asked if I'd ever had any illnesses, ever been in a mental institution, ever been to a special school, had fits or black-outs or wet the bed. I was asked if I knew what the words on a sheet of paper meant, and told to write a sentence which was dictated to me by a warder; then they took notes on my family background. I was called over by a man from the prison department, who said he would recommend that I go to Edinburgh gaol or Perth gaol. At least I wouldn't be going to Peterhead. I may have had a bad deal in the courtroom, but it seemed the prison authorities were prepared to give me a better chance.

I was given a week's notice that I'd be going to Peterhead. I went to the principal warder and told him there must be some mistake, but he smiled and said they never made mistakes. When I asked to see the governor, he told me to fuck off and do my time.

Jim came up to visit me. He was shattered when he learned of my sentence and of the transfer to Peterhead, and said he had no intention of letting me do the time. He told me he was going to stop the gaol van with his pals; they'd be using shotguns to get me away. I was glad my brother wanted to break me out, this is what I'd have done for him, but I was against shotguns being used. I knew – as everyone did – of Jim's capabilities. He gave me an even bigger shock when he told me that my dad had made the arrangements for the breakout.

I wondered if it would work, and too, what would happen if it were to fail. That night at about 12:00 I was told that there had been a shooting in a pub in Garthamlock – my

neighbour told me he had heard it on the radio. I wondered.
... In the morning someone came and told me that my brother
Jim was on the run for the shooting.

I left Barlinnie in handcuffs for Peterhead. We had to stop
at Perth Prison for our dinner and a change of buses. Perth
Prison is the oldest in Scotland, and it looks it. I saw my Uncle
Hugh there and he told me he was very sorry to hear I'd got
such a long sentence. He looked much older, and his hair
was greying. My heart went out to him even though he had
murdered my favourite auntie, Ruby. I didn't eat my dinner;
I just drank some tea and stood looking out a window, watching the Perth prisoners exercising.

Before we reached Peterhead we stopped for tea and sandwiches at Aberdeen Prison, where I met my Uncle Billy who
was still serving the remainder of a six-year sentence. We
hugged and shook hands before I was handcuffed again and
put on the bus for Peterhead. As we drove I watched the
countryside fly past. I hadn't known Scotland had so many
beautiful scenes – even the slums had an attraction.

PART
TWO

23 THE DRAFT TO HELL

There stands a gaol by the sea
You say reeking bad with sin,
And although there are men who don't get out –
There are men who should be in!

Some say it was the devil's den
That erupted out of hell,
And there's some who say, in their philosophical way,
'It serves its purpose well . . .'

But I'd like to tell a story,
And *facts* I promise too
That these gaols are *full* of decent men –
But I leave that up to you.

And if you find my judgement sound
Then I guess it says a lot,
For the worst of men who lay in here
For the good in them to rot.

So there was I, handcuffed to a strange face. A killer? A rapist?
A robber? A thief? What did it matter – he was to be my
neighbour for God knows how long. At the back of the prison
transport bus there was a familiar face or two, there were
smiles here and there, and the sound of chattering filled the

air. I had nothing much to smile about. Men on the same bus were serving less than half of what I had got for blasting men with shotguns and for serious assaults and robberies, and here I was – a petty thief by any standards, an innocent in comparison with these guys. Of course I felt sorry for myself.

Peterhead Prison stood alone and dreary-looking with its twisted granite walls and high security fence – and I wished my dad and Jim were there to get me out. Before I knew it the massive electronic gate had closed behind us, cutting us off from the outside world. The turnkeys began removing the shackles from the prisoners as we drove through a series of prison gates to one of the halls. Country music was playing somewhere – I could hear guys singing and playing their guitars at their tiny cell windows. As we stepped out of the bus there was an exchange of banter before the turnkeys could silence it with their threats. They shouted to the guys to get back from their windows. A turnkey ran over to where the shouting came from, his face screwed up like he was giving the world a dirty look and defying someone to shout at him at close range. His eyes swept the rows of windows, but no one answered him. He seemed satisfied, and walked back to where we were standing. Another steel door was opened, and we were taken through to the punishment block and put into a small cell.

The cell into which six of us were locked was about eight feet long and six feet wide, with one piece of wood on hinges attached to the wall to form a bed. The six of us all crammed on to the wooden bed and sat as comfortably as we could. We had one pisspot and it smelled like a sewer whenever it was opened. Some of the guys had been in Peterhead before, and they told me that we wouldn't stay in the punishment block as it was reserved for the mugs who couldn't do their bird the easy way. That was a relief, because I didn't think I'd survive being locked up here. Someone nearby was screaming a torrent of abuse at the world, and there was no music playing or singing of songs.

The cell door opened, and I was taken to a small reception area and made to strip in front of six warders. They told me to bend over and spread my cheeks, which I did to mocking

202

laughter. I felt degraded and hopeless and I wanted to kill. A warder asked me questions in a strange Highland dialect. 'Fit like is your name, loon, eh?' – What's your name, boy? – I didn't have a clue what he was saying, and after about five minutes another warder intervened. I was given an ill-fitting grey-coloured dirty-looking jacket and trousers, and an old pair of shoes: my own suit was taken from me and hung away till I needed it again. I was then taken back to the cell where the others were smoking and figuring out which hall we'd be going to. A Hall had a reputation for trouble-makers – if you can call a man a trouble-maker for fighting a system that humiliates and degrades him. D Hall was adjacent to A Hall, separated from it by a brick wall so as to break up the numbers and make it easier for the warders to manage.

B Hall was different in atmosphere from the others. The guys made the best of it: during recreation periods they'd play guitars and have sing-songs, and occasionally some guy would get taken away for being drunk and disorderly and offending the good order of the most brutal gaol in Scotland. Except in C Hall the prisoners had all their meals in their cells. C Hall was called the 'training hall' by the authorities. As such it had two television rooms, two snooker tables and flowers and plants scattered here and there. There is – or should be – a set of rules provided for each prisoner on entry, but in C Hall the rules were different. By being in C Hall, you were supposedly a better class of prisoner. Some guys actually believed this, but most knew the warders were giving them a load of shit and that this so-called training hall was merely a stepping stone to another gaol. The governor and the warders tried to convince prisoners that their best move was to the training hall, and whenever visitors from the Prison Department came round they'd be given a tour of C Hall. But there was *no* training whatsoever.

After we had been changed and fed we were taken through to B Hall by some warders. It was decaying and haunted-looking. There wasn't much activity as all the prisoners were locked up, but I still could hear country music playing. A warder was at my side, the noise of his boots echoing throughout the hall. Suddenly the music stopped and we could hear guys shouting from under their cell doors that the draft was in and asking our names. I kept on walking up a flight of stairs, where I was met by a short fat warder who allocated me to a cell with two others.

I heard a voice calling my name. It was one of my dad's friends, Big George. He got one of the warders to open my door so that he could talk to me as I was his pal's son. Big George was powerfully built and as strong as an ox. He hadn't changed much since I first met him when I was fourteen years old, back in 1970. As I was talking to him some other guys looked in and asked me how long I was doing and where I came from. Many of the cons knew my dad and had known me when I was a wee boy. 'How is your dad?', 'Is your wee maw still alive?', 'How are your uncles doing?', 'How is your ma keeping?' 'Twelve years you said?', 'Who did you kill? ...'

They advised me to try for a job in the cookhouse. George, who was the bookie at Peterhead, got me a huge bag of sweets and some tobacco and soap and toothpaste. I was warned that the place had informers, and to be careful what I said to others. My dad had no enemies amongst the prisoners, he was well liked and respected, but he wasn't too popular amongst the warders, as I came to know. Coming from Peterhead and Aberdeen, the warders mocked prisoners from Glasgow for thinking of themselves as 'hard' men.

B Hall had been condemned many years ago and used as a store, but now it held its human stock to full capacity. My cell was badly lit, and badly in need of a wash and a coat of paint. The concrete floor was cracked with age. On my first night I never slept a wink, but spent my time looking out of my window. I'd been in many cells in my time, but now I felt more trapped and helpless than ever, thinking of the long years ahead of me. Here was I, classed as one of Scotland's danger men – I could have been a pickpocket, and they'd have put that tag on me. I was twenty-two years old and looked about eighteen, but I felt old in heart, old and weary and finished with life. Some said I was still young and had my whole life ahead of me, and that twelve years would fly by.

But I didn't believe it. I couldn't bear to think that I'd be in for that long, even with four years off for good behaviour.

Between C Hall and B Hall was the exercise yard with its two goal-posts, where the prisoners played football at exercise time each day for an hour, if the weather wasn't too bad. But the weather was always bad up there in the north of Scotland. The gaol was always full of seagulls screaming for food all day and night. It was a small gaol, and so were many of the cells. Some of them were known as 'iron lungs' – they were only seven foot long, and if you stood in the middle of the floor you could touch the walls on either side, and the ceiling. Other cells were called 'Peters' – the code name for a safe or vault.

During the exercise period I saw my dad's pal, Derek, coming towards me with his arms out to embrace me. I was embarrassed when he gave me a hug. Everyone in the yard was staring over at us. We walked together and I had a lump in my throat as I listened to him talk about the affection he had for my ma and Maw and Brenda. 'How will your ma cope with it this time?' he asked.

After a few days, I was moved out of B Hall into D Hall. D Hall was much the same as B. In the middle of the floor was an old table-tennis table and a television set, and there was a hot-plate from which food was served. There were cells on either side of the ground floor all the way down the hall, and on each of the four floors there were two slop-out sinks, two toilets and two sinks for filling our plastic basins with hot water. All the halls were of the same design. The galleries were very narrow, with hardly enough space for two men to walk side by side, and floored with thick black-grey slate. At the end of each gallery was a hot-plate which sat in front of a sink and a steriliser for the steel food trays and bowls, and behind the sink was a huge arch-shaped window, heavily barred. All the cell doors were painted green, and made of thick wood. High above was the loft and roof with its skylight windows; there were beams running from one end to the other, coated with dust.

From where I stood on the fourth gallery I could see the entire hall, including the PO's desk which was at the main door of the hall; it had a huge sheet of wood over it to protect warders from falling objects. Every so often someone would throw something at one of the warders from a gallery and then dive into a cell and hide.

My new cell-mate introduced himself as Bill, and we began to talk and make the most of one another's company. After a while I heard the wall next to my bed being knocked on. I went down to the pipe which ran through all the cells and called through the little gap. 'Is that Andy Steele's son?' a voice asked. Its owner's name was Rab, and he was a good friend of my dad's. He was in an 'iron lung', and had been since he arrived there. He had refused to move out when the warders offered him a bigger cell – he told the warders that it didn't bother him any, but he told me it did. He had a huge beard which made him look as though he'd been in for a hundred years. I became friendly with him, and would sit and listen to him play the guitar like a master, or sing for him while he played.

I was taken in front of an induction board to be allocated to a work party. The board consisted of the governor, a welfare officer, a psychiatrist and a few others. When I was asked where I would like to work I said the cookhouse, but was refused. They told me I would be going to Number 5 work party, the tailor's shop – the security party where the potential 'trouble-makers' were housed for their work duty.

When the time came to go to work we were taken out to the exercise yard and lined up in our work parties. The warders shouted at us to get our hands out of our pockets – no one was allowed to have their hands in their pockets, whether in hail, rain or snow. As each party was marched across the yard we were counted and re-counted. To get to work we had to walk in twos through a huge gate manned by warders, and past the football field. Next to the field was a hilly piece of land like a dump, and behind it was a brick shelter housing the toilets. There were little sentry boxes at strategic points around the field. The dirt road we walked down was known to all as the 'Burma Road'. Straight ahead of us was a row of old granite sheds, and to the left was a lone building which looked like a fortress. This was the tailor's shop. All around this area was a huge granite wall.

I was told by the warder in charge of the party that I was to work upstairs with the security prisoners; when I told him that I wasn't on security he threatened me with the punishment block. I could tell I'd have problems with him in future. All the prisoners in the security party had told me I shouldn't be upstairs. I was put on a sewing-machine, but I pretended I couldn't work it or even see the needle and was told to sweep the floor instead. Our wages were just under two pounds a week for five days work, from eight to four each day.

On the top floor of the tailor's shop there were four rows of sewing-machines – two on either side, with a passage-way down the middle. Just by the stairs were two other machines and an ironing-board table. Next to them was the toilet with its three-quarter-length door that showed the legs and head of anyone using it. If you stayed too long in it the warder would be over to investigate the delay. Behind the ironing-board was the back shop, where prisoners worked cutting material. I soon got to know the guys in the shop and stopped to talk to them as I made my way around their machines sweeping the floor.

We wore grey uniforms – those prisoners who were con-sidered a security risk were kept in 'greys'. Prisoners on the security party are deprived of a lot of things, including football in the football field, education classes, PT in the gym and hobby classes. A red light is kept on in their cells at night so that they can be watched. Escapees had to put all their clothing outside their cell door each night before lock-up.

Some prisoners couldn't do their time and were put on the sort of medication which is given to psychiatric patients. They walked about like zombies, hardly knowing where they were or who they were. They were laughed at by others, but it was their way of surviving.

The guys there had various hobbies. They made caravans and boats and dolls' houses out of matchsticks; since we weren't allowed knives or cutting tools, the only tools they had were old razor blades or some sort of home-made implements, but this didn't stop them from making some classy stuff. I wandered about the hall on my own during recreation till one night a couple of guys asked me to sing for them while they played guitar. The three of us sat in a cell singing while some others sat nearby to listen. They enjoyed my singing and soon everyone was aware that I was a good Country singer, or at least that's what they told me. If we were watching a movie and some guy was singing in a gaol, or maybe even a cowboy singing, the guys would shout: 'There's Johnnyboy!'

On Sunday mornings there were religious services, and exercise in the yard for half an hour. Catholics and Protestants were separated during Sunday morning exercise. I don't know why this was. There was never any trouble over religion as long as I was there, nor did I ever hear of any. On Sunday afternoon there was recreation from two till four.

Saturday and Sunday were visiting days. The visiting room had tables and chairs, but along each table was a plank of wood to stop anything being slid across. Even though some of our visitors had to travel well over a hundred miles to get there, they weren't able to buy tea or biscuits at the prison. Visits lasted an hour and had to be booked in advance: prisoners were allowed two one-hour visits every three months. Sometimes Ma would arrive dressed like an Eskimo because it was so cold. I had never experienced such cold before – during periods of heavy snow the seagulls would tap our cell windows with their beaks for food. Ma still talked to me like I was a wee boy, so it was no surprise when she refused to buy me some pornographic magazines which I'd asked for.

One day while I was brushing the floor in the tailor's shop a warder asked me if my dad had been in Aberdeen gaol. He then told the other warder who was with him that my dad was a fucking animal, and that he had put his finger up a warder's arse and run him around the gallery to humiliate him. I walked away without answering, but I could feel their eyes on my back. During my tea break I asked the older cons if they knew anything about what I'd just heard. It was true, and there was more. I was told that he had made a spirits bomb and left it inside the hot-plate where the warders dished out the food

208

because they were giving such small rations to the prisoners. The bomb was meant to go off when the warders were standing round the hot-plate, but there was no one near when it exploded. They knew it was my dad, but they couldn't prove it. I learned that he hated the warders and was forever threatening them with gelignite bombs. They seldom went out of their way to hassle him because they knew he meant what he said, and they feared him as a result. I was told that my dad had blown up a few places when on the outside, including a house on the south side of Glasgow belonging to an informer who was giving evidence against one of his pals. A gelignite bomb was planted on the window ledge, and although it did terrible damage no one was in the house at the time. They said that if anyone needed explosives or guns and ammunition, my dad was the man to get them.

Bill, my cellmate, was okay, and we got along fine even though we were crammed in. He taught me a few chords on his guitar, and we would sit and sing each night. His father-in-law, Watty, was known as 'the Godfather', and had been sentenced in Glasgow's High Court for a trail of robberies. Bill himself was serving four years for intimidating witnesses at the Godfather's trial. Watty worked in the tailor's shop with me and I found him sincere and friendly, contrary to what the papers said about him. He used to sit at his machine and tell me about his past. He had been in Borstal along with my Uncle Tam, and he used to sit and listen to Tam singing Al Jolson songs.

The tailor's shop was full of dangerous men, of that there is no doubt, but they were not of the kind to stab or slash someone just for the fun of it. If there was a stabbing or slashing there was always good reason. It was a jungle and it had its own rules. Visitors to the gaol were always brought into the tailor's shop so that they could see Scotland's most dangerous men. I would hear the governor tell visitors what crime so-and-so was in for, and describe him as a monster. They gave visitors the impression that the prisoners were terrible people who should be feared. It was the same story every time visitors came around, but a thief's only a thief and a murderer's only a murderer when he's someone else's son, or is unknown to us. I can't count the times I've read in newspapers about people who want prisoners to be more hard done by than they already are. Of course, the authorities in charge of the prison system – governors, warders, ministers, psychologists and psychiatrists – all think along the same lines, but it's a different story when one of their own kind is imprisoned. Then they fall over each other to make excuses for their fallen friend, and off he goes to the gaol with the easiest regime, with all the help he needs and a cushy job.

The tailor's shop was always full of chatter: the guys would talk about their families and loved ones and pals and show each other photographs. You'd think they hadn't a care in the world. Yet underneath the talk and laughter was a silence that could almost be heard.

> There's a beggar in the heart of me
> And he pleads for not a lot,
> But he'll be the bleeding death of me
> For the things he hasn't got –
> And what the hell he's got in mind
> Can never be as such
> Because to ask for a little freedom
> Is to ask for far far too much –
> But he'll be the bleeding death of me,
> Of that there is no doubt,
> For its hard being on the inside
> With the beggar wanting *out*.

> There's a beggar in the heart of me
> And he's got a lot to say,
> And its 'Aww, hey!' this and 'Aww, hey!' that
> And 'Aww hey, come away!'
> But he'll be the bleedin' death of me
> Because of that and this
> And it's this and that and other things
> The beggar seems to miss.

210

There's a beggar shares my eyes each day
And he looks beyond the pale
But he drops more than he ever drinks in
And its seldom he sets sail.
He'll be the bleedin' death of me –
(Or maybe my rise and fall)
Still, I'll spare a smile, for one so vile
As the beggar in us all.

Some of the guys used to sit and whisper to each other in the hall, exercise yard and sheds, plotting to escape or riot. The fewer who knew about such things, the better – there were grasses to worry about. I had been there a few months when word went round that there was going to be a work strike. Some of us also refused to eat that day. For my part I was fined half a day's wages, as were the others. This was my first report at Peterhead. Our complaints about the conditions went unheeded. Some prisoners said the food at Peterhead was better than at Barlinnie, but that didn't mean it was any good. It was bad, and by the time it came from the cookhouse it was often cold. This used to cause trouble for the warders, and sometimes resulted in fights or a hunger strike. There were many work strikes as well: the prisoners would walk out, sometimes because there was no heating on the coldest of days, sometimes because a prisoner had been put on report by one of the warders. Strikes were common, and every day off work meant the loss of one day's remission or the cellblock for a spell. Other work parties would come out in sympathy, and the warders and governors would brace themselves for serious trouble.

The warders often threatened us with 'Yi'll be ganging 'ben the hoose, loon!' – what they meant was 'You'll be going to the punishment block, lad.' The cellblock was their pride and joy, and if anyone stepped out of line they were sent there. Some guys were terrified because of its reputation. It stood on its own, a two-storey granite building with cells on one side only, eight cells on each floor. Prisoners weren't allowed to mix with anyone – solitary confinement was the main part of the punishment. It was a prison within a prison. It was rumoured that blood was coated into the walls from the beatings handed out there.

If we wished to make complaints about a warder or conditions we had to request to see the governor, who would then investigate – and, if need be, give us a petition so that we could write to the Secretary of State for Scotland. Making such complaints could mean being locked up for making false allegations – even though they weren't false. There were often fights between prisoners and warders. If one was prepared to fight with – or rather 'assault' – a warder, one had to accept the consequences: being charged with assault, and beaten up by a gang of warders.

Many of the prisoners smoked hash, which helped them stay calm. I was introduced to hash while I was there, but it didn't do for me what it seemed to do for the others. Instead of feeling calm, I panicked and thought I was going to crack up. I left it out after that for quite some time.

Archie, the guy who was doing life for shooting and killing in the Gartloch Road, and trying to shoot my dad's pal Toe Elliot, was in D Hall. I was quite pally with him. Archie was about thirty-five years old and had fair hair which he kept short. There was a wee bald patch at the back of his head about the size of a penny – he said it was a scar left by a hammer during a gang fight, but I knew it was a bald patch.

Seven prisoners in A Hall rioted one afternoon and tried to smash their way through and burn the roof off. One of the guys involved was my wee pal Tam from St Joseph's, who was serving life for killing his best pal. They couldn't get through, so they started throwing petrol bombs at the warders and locked themselves in a cell when the warders came after them. In D Hall we didn't know what was happening. We heard the riot bell ringing and we were all locked up for a while. The seven guys stayed in the cell for some days before coming out, when they were taken to the punishment cells and locked up till they went in front of the visiting committee to be disciplined.

Tony Tamburrini was transferred to Peterhead and put into

my hall. It was great to see him again. I was moved in beside him and we had some good laughs together – as well as sad times when we reflected on our past and regretted having done what we did. Ma sent me curtains, a table-cloth and a record-player to play my country music. From my cell window on the fourth gallery, I got a great view of Peterhead harbour and the sea. I'd stand there for hours watching the ships in the distance and wish I was on them. But Tony and I soon started arguing over trivial things, and I decided it was best we parted friends rather than enemies.

Derek got me into A Hall with him. He'd had a letter from my dad asking him to look after me and make sure I didn't get any hassle from anyone. He did his best to put some happiness into my life. He'd come into my cell with mugs of tea and ask me to sing the country songs he liked. We'd look at each other's photographs: like me, Derek was sentimental, and whenever he spoke about his friends and family I could see the beggar within him come to the surface. His eyes would fill with tears, and mine would well up too. Derek made fun of it later by saying, 'We were sitting there crying like it was the end of the world.' Derek was due to go down to Barlinnie on accumulated visits to see his missus and twin sons – in Peterhead a prisoner could save up enough visits to go to a gaol nearer his home and stay for a few weeks, and once the visits were finished he came back to Peterhead. The night before Derek left we swapped photographs: I gave him pictures of Ma, Maw, Brenda and my dad in exchange for pictures of his sons. Next morning he came into my cell with my mug of tea and some biscuits and we had a good talk and a few songs together, then he left for Barlinnie in his usual happy-go-lucky mood.

I never saw Derek again. He committed suicide in his cell soon after arriving at Barlinnie. It was hard to imagine that someone like Derek could hang himself. Most guys in Peterhead were shocked and saddened. I cried when I learned of Derek's death. The prisoners gathered a collection, donating money from their weekly earnings to help pay for the funeral as a sign of respect to Derek, but the governor refused to let

213

the money out. A year later Derek's wife hanged herself in her home in Carntyne.

I'd watch the warders from my window as they went out the gate and headed for home, laughing and talking amongst themselves. From my cell I could see the small visiting room on the other side of the seventeen-foot wire fence topped with rolls of razor wire, and at weekends I'd watch the visitors arrive. It was great to see them in their many-coloured clothes, as in prison everything was dull, grey and black. Next to the gatehouse was the main office: there was a little garden round it with a few flowers in bloom, as if they were trying to impress the visitors.

I was sorry I left my cell in D Hall with Tony for company. I had a nice view of the North Sea from that cell and I spent time looking out at the boats in the distance. The waves were really high at times; one moment a ship was in sight, the next it was gone. I thought they had sunk, then they reappeared.

I couldn't do the time and I didn't want to live, but I didn't want to die either. I wanted to start life all over again and enjoy it, but it was too late for that. I thought about the others who had been through what I was going through and wondered how they managed it. Some thought I would have trouble getting through my sentence because I was too young to handle it. I didn't read much, I never could concentrate on a book. I never even found the time to learn the guitar, for my thoughts were all about the gaol. I hardly slept, which left blue circles under my eyes.

I was locked up in solitary confinement in December 1978 for attempting to escape. That weekend I had been out to the football field to see a guy I knew who was in another hall. He was playing football, and I wanted an opportunity to talk to him before Monday morning. The football only lasted about half an hour because it was too cold. I came out of the granite toilets to find that the park was empty except for a few warders. They were relieved when they saw me.

214

'Where the fuck hiv ye been, loon?' said one.

I was asked my name and when I said Steele I wasn't surprised to hear a warder say, 'Andy Steele's son?' They searched me and made me strip to my underwear. When they didn't find anything they took me to the punishment block.

My heart was pounding as I walked across the exercise yard, a warder holding on to me on either side, up to the double doors of the punishment block. One of the warders kicked the doors hard. A latch was pulled back and half a face peered out at us. The latch closed and the door opened to reveal five or six warders. They were staring at me like they meant to do me harm. I was pushed inside and the door was locked behind me.

They didn't know which cell to put me into – someone said I was to be taken upstairs, another asked who I was and why I was there. The place was deadly silent, but I knew there were prisoners around because I could see their bedding outside their cell doors. I was taken into a cell with two doors. The warders again stripped off all my clothes and searched them outside the cell, locking me in and leaving me naked. One of them shouted through the spyhole that I would get my clothes back when I told them what I had been up to when I disappeared in the field. I heard the others laughing. Then the door opened again and the same warder said that some prisoners were shouting that the 'mole' had been caught. I said I didn't know what he was talking about. 'I'm only telling you,' he answered.

The window in the cell was some six feet from the ground; the walls were damp with condensation and the paint peeling and bubbly; the roof was shaped like the roof of a caravan, resting on massive granite walls; the wooden bed was worn with age.

Every so often my cell door opened and the warders looked in and said that if I'd dug through the walls of the tunnel. I'd have been eaten alive by rats or that I'd have been suffocated by the gases from the sewer. Eventually I was told that I was on the governor's report for attempting to escape by digging a tunnel in the football field behind the toilets. Then the door

215

opened, and in came the governor and his warders.

'I've no doubt your father and the Paddens have put you up to trying to escape,' he said to me through clenched teeth, one hand gripped tightly round my arm. I denied their having anything to do with it, but he said he didn't believe me and that he knew what kind of family I came from. I thought they were going to beat me up, but I was only shoved around a little, after which they left me alone. The governor said that I wasn't to have any books in my cell during the day. My bedding was taken from me during the day and given back at seven in the evening. I wasn't allowed my photos, nor any soap or shampoo. I was kept locked up for twenty-three hours a day, and it began to get to me.

'On yer feet, loon, for the governor's visit!' I stood to attention, which seemed to please the governor, who looked on with a grin. Every day they tried to make me confess to digging a tunnel. I pretended I hadn't been with the other prisoners because I'd been fighting with another con in the toilets, but then they wanted to know whom I'd been fighting with. I kept telling them I hadn't been down any hole in the field, but 'fucking liar!' was all they said to that. I felt I was going mad.

When the governor came in one day and asked me to confess, all my worries and fears and the usual pounding of my heart suddenly vanished. I said in a squeaky voice, 'If I tell you who it was, sir, will you promise not to hit me?' It was great to see the looks they gave each other, as if to say the wee boy was ready for breaking. The governor seemed in his glory, and promised that the warders would not hit me. This was all I was waiting for, and I took great pride in telling him to fuck off, and all the others too. I called him a glorified turnkey and a lump of shit. I felt my legs come away from me as they punched and kicked me. The madness lured me on, and I kept screaming obscenities at them and telling them that they'd have to hit harder if they wanted to get any information out of me.

When they left me I sat in the empty cell gloating on thoughts of revenge. I wasn't taking any more of this kind of life. That

216

same day a warder asked me if I wanted to see the prison psychiatrist. I said no.

I was taken before the prison visiting committee and the governor. Two men in their fifties and an older-looking woman were seated behind the governor's desk. I was made to stand before them and give my name, number and sentence. A warder stood on either side of me to restrain me should I make a wrong move. The woman had a hat on, which gave her a snobbish look – a typical little granny. Her wee beady eyes were all over me as I stood there in my slippers and grey uniform. I thought that she was eyeing me up for the kill. ...

The warders gave evidence that I had been attempting to escape, yet not one of them said he had seen me come out of or go into a tunnel, nor was a single witness produced to say that I had. After the evidence had been given I was told to wait outside while the committee came to its verdict! I hadn't been allowed to cross-examine any of the witnesses, and I was refused a lawyer to act on my behalf when I asked for one. It was all cut-and-dried, and I knew I would be found guilty. I was sentenced to twenty-eight days solitary confinement with no privileges, and forfeited sixty days of my remission. I asked for a petition to the Secretary of State, but was refused.

They had me on strict security; my clothes were put outside my door every night, and a light was left on. There were two ventilator systems in the cell, one of which was supposed to bring in hot air, the other fresh air: the vents had steel grilles over them and there were dead birds behind them which had fallen down from the loft above. I was allowed one blanket during the day to keep me warm. My shoes and jacket weren't allowed in my cell at any time. There were three exercise yards outside my window: each 'pen' had fifteen-foot walls with rolls of razor wire along the top.

In the halls prisoners are exercised indoors during inclement weather, but in the punishment block it's outside or nothing. We weren't allowed to talk out of our windows or to each other during exercise. The warders made a point of being strict so as to put us off going back again. During slop-out a group of warders watched me at all times and followed me wherever

I went. 'Hurry up, loon!' they'd say as I filled my basin and slopped out my pisspot, but I always took my time because the longer I was out of the cell, the better I felt.

One morning the warder who had told me about my dad putting his finger up his pal's arse in Aberdeen gaol told me to put my bedding and blankets outside the door. I folded up the blankets neatly and hung them over the railings. The warders pulled them off and threw them on to the floor, saying they weren't folded well enough; then they stood in front of me, chewing gum in an exaggerated way. I picked up the blankets, threw them over the gallery and told them that they could fold them up themselves if they weren't satisfied. Other warders came running up to see what was going on, and they all attacked me. After this I refused to take in my mattress and blankets. They were furious about this because they wouldn't be able to come in at six in the morning to take my bedding off me. I was freezing that night.

I was kept in the punishment block for fourteen days, after which the governor let me back into the hall to complete the rest of my punishment in my own cell. I spent Christmas in my cell while the others were at recreation. The warder wished me a Merry Christmas and slammed my cell door hard, rattling the bolts to annoy me.

When Ma wrote and asked me how I was keeping I told her I was fine and that she wasn't to worry. Sometimes I got a letter from Maw which was written for her by Brenda, and I always became emotional and had a good cry fearing that I would never see her outside again. My mind was made up. I couldn't possibly get through this sentence in one piece, it was fucking killing me. At nights I would get up and pace the floor in my bare feet and smoke one hand-rolled smoke after the other, plotting or reminiscing about my past.

A few days after I came off punishment, Archie, who'd been suspected of trying to escape, was thrown into the security party. We sat together in the tailor's shop and discussed our experiences. Like me, he had been brutalised in the cells, so we decided we would do something about it. Archie, Davy, Wee Smiddy and I decided to wreck the punishment block,

218

which was the warders' pride and joy, and so ruin their cushy job of locking up and beating up the prisoners. All the others in the security party were aware of what was going to happen and helped in whatever ways they could, giving us tobacco and sweets and biscuits and other odds and ends that would come in handy in case we were up on the roof for a few days. Some of them encouraged us to burn it to the ground, others thought we were crazy for doing something that would only get us into serious trouble.

It was six below zero when we stormed the cellblock through the roof. The snow made it difficult to walk on the slates with our haversacks on our backs. Once on the roof we started smashing the skylight windows with iron bars and ripping up the slates and throwing them down into the yard below. It felt great. Through the broken skylights I watched the warders panicking and shouting, unsure what was happening. It must have sounded as though there were a hundred men on the roof. The four of us took pride in terrorising the warders as they ran about trying to dodge the glass and slates.

We smashed through the wood under the slates and climbed down into the loft to shelter from the warders in the yard who were throwing bricks at us, and we lit a small fire there. We could hear the others shouting from their cell windows, roaring at us to burn down the torture chamber that so many of them had suffered in. The chief warder tried to persuade us to come down, promising that no one would get hurt. I told him to fuck himself and threw a brick at him, and he scurried away. We knew they would beat us up when they got us down, but it didn't worry us – we were too busy smashing the building up and working out our frustration. Any bricks we got from the wall we kept for ammunition to throw at the warders if they tried to get near us.

By evening I was black all over from smashing down walls. I couldn't stop smashing the place up – when the others were resting or taking their tea break I went on making huge holes in different parts of the wall. We climbed through these holes into the cells area and barricaded the doors so that the warders couldn't storm the building. We smashed toilets and sinks and

219

ripped out pipes. Water was squirting everywhere and we were soaked to the skin.

The warders had got the prisoners out of their cells and taken them to B Hall before we had a chance to break them out. All the cell doors had been locked, but we tried to bust them down, and smashed light-switches and spyholes and door-handles. The steel gate that led through to reception was locked; this was a setback, since we'd hoped to get the warders' tea-bags and coffee and biscuits as our own supplies had been eaten or lost. We demanded to be given our dinner, but were refused. We were cold and hungry, but we laughed as we watched the warders stamping their feet and rubbing their hands to keep out the cold.

Every now and then we went on to the roof to throw bricks at them and chase them back if they came too close. One of us kept watch while the others slept in case the warders stormed the building. We agreed that we would tear into them with anything we could lay our hands on if they stormed us – we knew we had no chance of winning, but felt we had nothing to lose.

Some of the other governors tried to talk us down, and they were very polite about it! They spoke to us like human beings for a change, but in return they were showered with verbal abuse and flying objects. One of them waved his fist at us and shouted, 'Just wait!' We knew what he meant, but we laughed at him. All the other prisoners were kept locked up and off work: the warders were scared to let them out, but went around the halls beating up guys for shouting encouragement out of their windows.

We stayed up there for three days and nights, tearing the place apart like madmen and doing as much damage as we could. At night we gathered round the fire and talked about our families and our pasts. We agreed that we would do it again once we were back in circulation – which suited me because it was easier to wreck the place than to accept it. Before long we were weak with exhaustion and hunger. The warders stood eating on parts of the corridor roof or in the yard, and they'd throw crusts of bread on to the roof as if they were feeding dogs. They never threw up any more when I started jumping up to snatch the crusts of bread, to eat them.

From the top of the cellblock I could see warders everywhere, some of them sitting in dark corners with grey blankets wrapped around them to keep out the cold. They had all been equipped with riot helmets, shields and sticks like baseball bats. We came out at night under cover of darkness and threw slates and bricks at them, and laughed as they ran for shelter.

I decided that I was going to break through the roof of reception and get the warders' kettle and tea-bags, and whatever else there was to eat. Smiddy and I tore up the slates and then smashed through the roof into the loft of reception. There were no windows, so we had to depend on a cigarette lighter for some light. The steel mesh in the ceiling was difficult to get through, but through the broken plaster and the mesh I spotted the warders' tea-bags, coffee and biscuits on a table. We jumped up and down on the steel mesh, and the next minute the two of us were lying on the ground with half the roof about us. For a second I was stunned and then we gathered the foodstuffs, and a guitar which was there. Before we left I sang a song among the rubble, while Smiddy did a tango with the warders' kettle.

As soon as we appeared on the roof with the kettle and the eatables the warders tried to knock us with a shower of stones. Once back inside the cellblock loft we all cheered and laughed at our good fortune; we even went on to the roof to have our tea break so as to wind up the warders. Some of them laughed at our audacity, others were livid.

The governor was away when we first went on to the roof, and only came back a few hours before we came down. In fact it was he who talked us down. We had taken down the barricades, and were throwing boulders at anyone who tried to come in, when he came walking in shouting, 'Hold your fire!' We did, and he marched up the staircase and on to the gallery, looking up at us looking down at him through a huge hole in the wall. He told us to come down and give him a list of our complaints, but we refused, thinking it was a trap. He then told us to come down one at a time and talk to him.

There were no lights working in the cells, but a warder who was with the governor had a torch which he shone on our faces as we went down to say our piece, climbing down a makeshift rope on to the mountains of rubble and bricks on the gallery. We had to be careful how we went as there was broken glass from the skylights everywhere.

As I made my way slowly along the gallery, heading towards the governor, the doors downstairs opened and I ran back the way I'd come. I heard the governor shout to whoever was downstairs that they were to get to fuck, and I saw him shining a torch at whoever had come in, who quickly left again. When I realised that the governor was being true to his word, and that he wouldn't let another warder in, I went back again. We went to the archway near the top of the stairs, where the burst pipes were still running. I could see from the light of the torch that I was black all over and I almost burst out laughing – as did the governor, who said he liked my hat, which I'd stolen from reception. Above us were Archie, Smiddy and Davy, sitting round a huge hole with bricks in their hands. The governor kept reassuring us nothing would happen, and he never even raised his voice to me. I got the feeling that he had some sympathy for us – he told me that if he was in my shoes he'd wreck the gaol too. He laughed when he heard about my putting the toilet pan through the skylight of his orderly room. I'd wrenched the pan off the wall and dragged it on to the roof by rope. Just as I was about to throw it through the skylight I heard a roar of laughter from the guys in their cells, so to give them some entertainment I shouted, 'Here comes the governor,' as I threw the shit pan through the skylight, breaking his big wooden desk.

We sat together on the rubble, and I told him that I was rioting because I'd been framed by the warders over the escape charge, that I couldn't cope with the length of my sentence or the prison regime, and that it was easier and less painful for me to rebel than accept. Then I listened to him, and it was Johnnyboy this and Johnnyboy that. He said I should send a petition to the Secretary of State and appeal against my sentence for the attempted escape charge, that he was doing his best to change things in the gaol, and that he didn't agree with the regime either. But when the warder asked me if I'd like to come downstairs with him and the governor so as not to get into any more trouble, I took offence and told him to fuck off: the four of us were in this together and there was no way I would leave them now.

The governor tried to persuade me that I had proved my point, and that there wasn't much left to smash – if only he knew what I was thinking. He told me that if and when we came down, there would be no brutality. We would be kept in cells on the top landing of the surgery until the visiting committee charged us, and once the cellblock had been repaired we'd be brought back over.

When we'd all seen the governor we sat round our little fire and decided what we should do; and then, late at night, we came down. They took us over to the surgery, where we all shook hands as we parted, never knowing if we'd see each other again. It was the parting that hurt, more than surrendering. For the three days and nights that we were up in the loft we had all four become really friendly and close.

The governor had told the warders that if anyone put a hand on us they'd be charged with assault. He meant it, and they knew it and were furious, but they were too scared to say anything to him – which was why many prisoners liked and admired him. I heard the warders complaining to each other about the governor's attitude: they wanted to break our bones for what we had done, yet this man prevented them. He told the warders to make sure that we were all bathed and fed; he put a special guard on our doors, and warned the warders that if anyone got into our cells to beat us up the warder in charge of the cells would be held responsible. The warders had to make us ham, eggs and tea at three o'clock in the morning: one of them said to another as he handed me my food, 'Fucking great, isn't it, they smash up our gaol and he's got us pampering the bastards!'

We were guaranteed that there'd be no beatings, but as was only to be expected, they kicked me about the cell over in the surgery. Before I was beaten up I was given a medical examination by the surgery warder, who was looking for cuts and bruises that I may have got when I was on the roof. Then I was taken upstairs to join the others. The cells in the surgery had steel grilles as well as thick wooden doors, and as I was dragged to a cell I passed Smiddy and Davy, naked and filthy black, standing behind their steel grilles, looking out at me. Smiddy had his leg through the steel grille, trying to kick the warders.

Every day in my cell I sat by the window and looked out to sea, reminiscing as usual. I imagined I was at home and sitting at the fireside with Maw and Ma, and I'd sing to them too – it helped me through the hard days. Archie sent me some books, but I never read them. When I wasn't singing I was plotting and scheming as I paced up and down the little cell floor, my hands behind my back. I must have walked miles this way: I'd take six paces forward and stop inches from the wall, turn around and take another six paces back. I became so used to it that I could do it with my eyes shut so I could rest as I walked. I ate even less, and I only picked at my food. Nor did I feel like sleeping: I often stayed awake all night, hating the world because I wasn't part of it.

Every now and then an urge to commit suicide would come over me while I was eating, or reading a newspaper, or thinking about home. It was like something clinging to my back: I'd try to shake it off in a blind panic, and a voice in my head would be shouting, 'Naw! Naw! Naw! Don't do it!' I'd run back from my cell window so that I wouldn't hang myself with my sheets. I couldn't get away: I was trapped in my little cell, which seemed to get even smaller. A voice in my head was shouting for me to press my bell and alert the warders, but I knew that if they saw me in this state of mind they would send me to a mental hospital. I panicked even more at the thought of going there to vegetate and die inside. I only managed to come to my senses when I thought of escaping – it was like a safety-valve.

I tried talking to God at times and asked for strength to help see me through the hardship. I would say things like, 'Awww, if only you would give me one little chance then I'd take it and make the best of it.' If he ever answered, it certainly never reached my ears.

The visiting committee came to see us in the surgery in January 1979. I was given a jacket and made to wear my over-large slippers before I was marched in by a dozen warders. The chairman was a youngish-looking woman and they all eyed me as I came into the room. Again I was refused a lawyer. I listened to the warders giving their evidence, indifferent to what they said about me. The whole exercise was pointless, as I knew I would be found guilty. I even thought it was funny to hear the warders take the oath on the Bible and swear by almighty God to tell the truth.

I was found guilty. The chairman thought it terrible that I had recently been in front of a committee for attempting to escape. I would have to suffer the consequences of taking part in a riot which had caused some £30,000-worth of damage to prison property. I was to forfeit 365 days remission, and sentenced to a further twenty-eight days solitary with no smoking or wages, and a fine of twenty-five pounds. On my way out one of them said, 'Let this be a lesson to you.'

We all got the same sentence, and they took us back to the cellblock to serve out our punishment. It didn't take long for them to repair the cells, as they felt insecure when they were not in use. The noise of hammering and drilling was deafening.

One morning the warders came in and held me spread-eagled on the concrete floor. One of them then stood on my belly with all his weight and told me I was just a silly little boy. The madness came over me and I laughed in their rotten faces, and told them I would get the last laugh. I heard Archie, Davy and Wee Smiddy shouting and banging on their doors and the warders left me to attend to them.

Whenever they brought me my food one of them would hold the plates while the others stood by, ready to attack if I made a move. 'Thanks, arsehole,' I'd say, so they stopped handing me my food and left the plates on the ground. I knew they sometimes spat in my food as I could see the spittle. They probably hadn't been too pleased when they recovered their kettle from the loft to discover someone had shat in it.

225

A few days later the governor came on his rounds, and I heard him screaming from one of the cells above me. Apparently he was attacked by and had got into a fight with one of the prisoners, and had been slashed on the neck. I could hear all the warders shouting and kicking the guy. There was pandemonium in the cellblock, and warders were running in and out in a panic. We all began banging and kicking on our cell doors, yelling at them to leave the guy alone. The governor was shouting at us at the top of his voice to shut up. The prisoner had to have stitches in a wound on his face where he had been slashed during the fight, and the governor had two butterfly stitches in the back of his neck. The governor then came to my door with a mob of warders who looked as if they were dying to give out more beatings. He had his battered hat in his hand and his tie was open as if he needed air; he was shaken and white-looking as he screamed at me, 'Don't you imagine that your dad or the Paddens frighten me, Steele!' He started shouting that he would fight anyone – he was getting more furious by the minute. Then he went away and threatened a few others in the cells nearby.

For weeks all the talk in the gaol was of the incident, but the whole thing was hushed up by the authorities.

Just before I got out of solitary confinement the governor told me I would be back. He never said a truer word – I intended coming back....

24 BACK WITH A VENGEANCE

Back in circulation with the other prisoners I didn't feel any better; this seemed just as bad as solitary confinement. I couldn't go anywhere without guys commenting on how pale and thin I was. One of my dad's pals gave me some vitamin pills, saying they would help.

About this time, Jim had been tried for shooting the guy with a sawn-off shotgun in the pub in Garthamlock. He was found guilty and sentenced to twelve years; I was in the exercise yard when I saw him come out of the hall towards me. I was all choked up, but I tried my best to hide it.

Jim's wife had left him, saying she couldn't take any more, but I never said anything about it. I told him what had happened to me since my arrival, and he said he wasn't going to stand for their bullshit and their wanting to torment us because of what our dad had done in the past. Although he was only eighteen months older than I was, Jim tended to treat me as though it was eighteen years: he was the typical big brother.

Ma and Dad and the family came to visit us regular and Mary always seemed to be there. The visiting room was split in two with one half for those on protection and in the punishment block. Ma wondered why I was put into this visiting room at times, and to stop her from worrying about me I told her it was because I was sometimes given the job of the trustee. She seemed to be satisfied that her wee Johnnyboy was a trustee.

227

Archie was moved into my hall and we became even closer. We would talk about rioting and escaping each day; I couldn't stop talking about it now.

One evening the warders were in my cell going through everything twice while I stood in the gallery being searched. All the other prisoners were locked in their cells. One of the warders told me to take my clothes off and bend over so that he could look up my arse. I refused and the other two came out of my cell and threatened me with violence if I didn't do what I was told. I wanted to attack the bastards but I started laughing at them and they went back in again. When they came out of my cell smiling deviously I knew I was going to the cellblock for something – and that 'something' was a prison rules and regulation book.

The next morning the governor asked me what I was doing with another prisoner's rule book, and I said I was reading it. 'You can't even cope with the rules in society,' he bawled. 'What chance do you think you have of coping in here?' I never answered. He told me he would give me a 'warning'. That was a cracker – him giving me a warning, it should have been me who gave him a warning. When someone is placed on a governor's report, there's no such thing as 'not known' charges or 'not guilty' charges – it's a warning.

The governor was transferred to Barlinnie Prison as the number-one governor of Scottish gaols. Before he left he told me that he was a specialist in breaking the spirits of would-be-hard-men like me.

In October 1979 I was again in front of the visiting committee for rioting and assaulting warders. There had been a lot of tension in the gaol – many of the prisoners were getting unnecessary hassle, and there was much talk about rioting and killing the warders. At first Jim, Archie, Smiddy and I thought of escaping, but then we decided to riot and try to stop the brutality and witless persecution.

I went to Big George, the bookie, and asked him for twenty ounces of tobacco for the 'hold-out' in the cellblock after we had stormed it. Most of the prisoners knew what was going to happen, and, as before, many of them wished us luck and offered to help in any little way. We were given iron bars, sweets, tobacco and tinned meat. The gaol was alive with excitement and I felt good – this was better than bare existence any day. The night before the riot I couldn't sleep, and didn't want to, either; I paced the floor thinking of the following day. At slop-out I talked to Archie and Frank and Jim in my cell. We had all we needed, and were satisfied with the way things were going. The Godfather came in and tried to talk me out of the riot, fearing I would end up being killed by the warders, or getting years added on to my sentence. He had tears in his eyes when he realised that he couldn't get through to me. 'Think of your poor wee ma,' he kept saying.

When we met in the exercise yard we all had iron bars under our coats. Guys were watching from their cell windows, waiting to see what was going to happen. The prisoners were even more excited now that we were ready to tear down the punishment block – and the warders hadn't a clue what was going on. Even the gaol informers wanted us to destroy the cells, and some of them even wished us all the best!

As soon as most of those involved in the riot were in the yard, about ten of us pulled out our iron bars and chased the warders away while we walked round to the back of B Hall to get on to the roof of some sheds there. The warders ran away in terror, screaming and it felt great to watch them go. There were rolls of razor wire behind B Hall to prevent anyone from getting on to the roof, but I got through them without much difficulty and the others threw their coats and jackets over them and walked across. By now riot bells were ringing in every part of the gaol and all the warders had come rushing to the yard, but when they saw our weapons they kept their distance. We climbed on to the long workshed roof alongside B Hall, which led to the corridor roof and the punishment block. Everyone was at their windows, cheering us and dropping food, sweets and woollen jumpers from their windows. Some prisoners became so excited that they broke their windows and furniture. We started smashing the shed roofs and the old picture house which contained the church, the chapel and the gymnasium. The noise of smashing windows and wood was deafening. There was a madness in everyone: we couldn't give a fuck about the consequences, or at least I couldn't. Some of the prisoners sang to themselves as they smashed and tore at the gaol. Jim and Archie were on the punishment-block roof, and I could hear them shouting down to the warders in the exercise yard and throwing slates at them. I climbed up a drainpipe on to the roof of B Hall – somehow I got through the rolls of razor wire that were wrapped round it without a scratch. Once on the roof I could see the warders in the yard, who were furious when they saw me up there with my iron bar, smashing the skylight windows and slates. I could hear guys shouting, 'Johnnyboy is on the roof!' and a cheer went up from the guys who were locked in their cells in B Hall. The warders tried to knock me off by throwing stones and turning on their power hoses. Breeny managed to get on to the roof with me. Before I knew it, it was getting dark. The warders, in their protective riot gear, were everywhere, even on the corridor roof below, and they had trapped the others in the loft of the punishment block, pelting them with bricks and stones and concentrating their power hoses on them if they tried to come out of the hole they had made on the roof.

Breeny and I had no food or tobacco with us, and we couldn't get off the roof to join the others. We couldn't even get into the loft in B Hall because it was full of warders. They came to the loft door and tried to sweet-talk us down. Breeny wanted to give himself up, but I tried to discourage him by telling him they would smash his head in. The warders heard me say this, and they told him not to pay any attention to what I was saying. I could tell Breeny was in two minds. He asked me how we could possibly get back down on to the punishment-block roof to join the others, who had a small fire lit in the loft and had all the food. We couldn't get off the roof because of the warders on the corridor roof, and if we climbed back down the drainpipe they would be able to reach up and hit us with their riot sticks.

I told Breeny we could jump off at the front end of the hall and land on the corridor roof, twenty feet below. We would then be only four feet away from the hole in the cellblock roof, and the warders were some fifteen feet away from that. Breeny said I couldn't be serious – dropping from such a height on to solid concrete would cause my spine to come out the top of my head. He didn't want to know, and decided to surrender.

I was frozen and had no jacket or jumper on, and I could smell cooking from the hole in the roof of the punishment block. Every now and then one of the guys there popped his head out and told me that they would try to work out some way to get me down. Breeny gave himself up to the warders in B Hall at the loft door; we shook hands before he left, and he gave me his jacket. I was sorry to see him go, and I lay there wondering if they would beat him up. I could see over the wall to the quarters where the warders lived: I could see their families at their windows, and some even sitting on the roof to get a better view of what was going on. Some of their kids shouted at me, calling me an animal and a madman, and to upset the warders below I shouted back at them, 'The governor is fucking yir ma!' They turned the power hose on me for this, and I clung to the roof fearing the bastards would knock me into the yard below. They also had flash lamps which they shone on the roofs so as to keep an eye on me. I thought about getting off unseen and making a break for it, but wherever I moved a flash beam followed me. I lay on one end of the roof, keeping my head down while stones landed all round me. I lay looking at the stars, feeling peaceful, wondering about them. I could see daylight coming in across the North Sea, and I knew I had to get off this roof soon.

'Okay! I'm surrendering!' I said, jumping up and raising my hands above my head to let them know I had no weapons. I shouted to the warders below not to throw any more stones, as I had had enough and was coming down. Jim and Archie and all of the guys in the cellblock loft came out and stood in the open looking at me and wondering what I was going to do. I told the warders at the left door that I wasn't going down with them – I was going down the way I came. They said it was far too dangerous and that I could slip and fall to my death. As I climbed on to the top of the drainpipe, which was well greased to prevent anyone climbing it, I saw warders coming out the loft door to try to stop me, so I slid down till I reached the rolls of razor wire. I got tangled up in the wire while the warders below were laughing and rubbing their hands with glee, but I managed to get back on to the drainpipe and tore my clothes from the wire.

The warders on the ground thought I was surrendering, but once I had got under the wire on the pipe I leapt on to the long workshed roof just above their heads. One of them shouted up to me, 'Hey, loon, I thought you were giving yourself up!' I told them I was – not to them, but to the warders on the corridor. It was still dark, but many of the guys in their cells were awake and had been watching all night. I heard some saying things like, 'Fuck sake, did you see that?' and I knew they meant my climbing through the razor wire – wire that everyone said could not be breached without bleeding to death.

I walked along the ridge of the workshed roof, trying to look defeated and dejected. To my left were the prisoners and to my right the warders. I told them that I was giving myself up to them as I didn't trust the others. This seemed to please them, and they coaxed me on. I kept on walking till I reached the end of the long roof, and then stepped on to the corridor roof. I could hardly contain my laughter as the warders made way. I turned to the left and walked to the hole in the roof, where the boys were cheering and patting me on the back. The warders were furious and began shouting at each other for letting me get away so easily – and then they started throwing stones and turning the hoses on us.

I was livid when I heard there were still guys locked in their cells below us, and that the warders had no intention of letting them out. There were about sixty warders in riot gear on the bottom floor, wating for us to come down. I climbed down to the gallery and barricaded the stairs so they couldn't get up, then I looked in at the cell doors to see who was there. The guy who had slashed the governor was still there, and another guy was up to his knees in water – the warders had aimed one of the power hoses through his cell window after he'd smashed the glass with an iron bar which Smiddy had passed him through the ventilator system from the loft. Further along I found a prisoner fast asleep, so I banged on the door to wake him up. He was known as 'the Bear', and he had been getting treatment from the gaol doctor – something called Largactyl, which leaves people like zombies. It took me about ten minutes to wake up this poor guy. He had a massive beard, his hair was unruly and matted, and he didn't even know there was a riot going on. I told him I would break him out of his cell but he didn't want out, all he wanted was some tobacco, and when I gave him some through the spyhole he thanked me and went back to bed. I felt sorry for him – he was dead inside. I then went to help the other guy out of his flooded cell. I smashed away at the door from my side, while he did the same from his.

Jim shouted at me to come back on to the roof as the new governor was in the yard and wanted to talk to me. He was standing in the yard below there with his umbrella, looking like he was posing for a photo. Joe McGrath shouted down, 'Where's wir dinner, ya fucking wee bam!' He wasn't amused, and told us if we wanted to be fed we would have to come down. We threw slates at him and at the warders, who galloped away across the yard; then we started singing 'I belong to Glasgow'. The warders turned on the power hoses, so it was back to work inside for me. I managed to get the guy out of his flooded cell, and we took his cell door off and threw it over the gallery. Up in the loft, we fed him and gave him some dry clothes. Then we went out on to the roof to let them see that we had broken the guy out of his cell, displaying him like a trophy. My hands were a mass of cuts and bruises, but that didn't stop me tearing up the building – I wrapped some torn sheets round them which made them less painful. All around us guys were smashing up this and that, while others kept the fire going and made tea and sandwiches.

Again I looked over the gallery and saw the warders beneath us in their riot gear. They had commandeered an empty cell on the ground floor where they made coffee and tea. I edged down the stairs so as to count them, and they stared at me in disbelief for having the audacity to venture so close to them. Jim and Archie told me to be careful in case they got hold of me, but I knew that if they tried to rush me I'd have been back on the roof before they were halfway up the stairs, and the warders knew it too. To get back into the loft I climbed a sheet rope that hung from one of the rafters through a hole in the wall. We decided that the only way we'd get the warders out of the cells was by hurling down at them the thousand and so bricks we had at our disposal. We knew the warders had been told to stay there so that we couldn't come down and cause further damage.

Most of our food had been ruined by the hoses or was underneath the rubble. I suggested to the warders that they could have the remaining prisoners in the cells in exchange for food and bandages and some antiseptic lotion for my cuts and bruises. They said they would have to phone the prison department to ask permission, and would let us know later.

From the roof we could see a dozen or so newspaper reporters and cameramen outside the gaol, shouting up to us to ask what it was all about. We shouted back that we were rioting because of harsh conditions and brutality – but we couldn't talk to them for long because the warders kept throwing stones at us. A light airplane was circling overhead, and we could see a TV camera in the window. We listened to radio reports, according to which the authorities had estimated the damage at a million pounds.

The warders told us they could agree to the exchange we'd suggested. We demanded the food and medicine first, and it was delivered to us. A surgery warder brought over the bandages and lotion and had a good look at my bruises and cuts. He told me I needed an injection in case I had poisoned my bloodstream, but I refused, so he cleaned my wounds and bandaged some of the deeper ones. All the time he was cleaning my wounds he kept telling me what a nice guy I was and how silly I was to be rioting. As I listened to him I was on the alert in case any of the warders came upstairs to grab me, and they'd been warned that if they did the surgery warder could get hurt. He was a bit nervous as he stood there bandaging while I was smashing the wall with an iron bar in my other hand.

We let two warders come upstairs to take the guys out of their cells. They were obviously terrified, but we assured them they would come to no harm as long as the others below didn't try anything. The Bear came out of his cell and laughed when he saw the mess the cellblock was in. The warders couldn't wait to get away from us – this was the first riot of its kind in a Scottish prison.

After this we got ready to attack the warders on the ground floor with bricks, iron bars and anything else that was handy. It felt as though we were in some housing estate doing battle with another gang – the only difference being that we knew we couldn't win.

Jim, Archie, Frank, Joe, Wee Smiddy and I climbed down the sheet rope quietly, our iron bars strapped to our bodies. I was the first down, and I crept along the gallery, straining my ears for the warders below me. They were boasting about the overtime they were getting from our misery and bragging about what they were going to do to us once they got us down. As soon as we were all down from the loft, we leaned over the railings of the gallery and started hurling bricks at the panic-stricken warders, who ran back and forth with their shields above their heads to protect them. The noise was deafening. Some of the warders tried to fight back, but many of them ran out of the double doors and stayed there. When we saw this we headed for the staircase and made our way down, swiping at the warders as we went. We didn't know it then, but it seemed that the whole gaol could hear the battle, including the reporters on the other side of the wall.

Eventually we drove all the warders out. In their hurry to get away, some of them dropped their riot shields and sticks and we took them on to the roof with us to show them off. About half an hour later a newsflash on the radio reported that we had been seen on the roof with warders' riot gear. The authorities told the reporters that we must have found the riot gear in a cupboard, and we had a good laugh at this.

To our surprise, about sixty guys in B Hall began rioting

when they were opened up for their exercise. They threw furniture over the galleries and barricaded the one set of stairs in the hall, and they planned to get on the half-wrecked roof and destroy it completely. The windows I had smashed when I was on B Hall had been covered over with sheets of tarpaulin, which were now hanging down into the hall after being disturbed by the wind. Guys were climbing up them, but only a few made it. They forgot to barricade the doors on the galleries that led through to the adjacent hall and the riot squad stormed in and beat up anyone in sight.

The first we knew of all this was when Joe, who was watching the warders through a hole in the loft with a pair of binoculars he had found, told us that Ronnie and others were on the roof of B Hall. We were all really glad to get some support – particularly as the warders had told us earlier that the other prisoners weren't interested in us and were all perfectly happy. Although some of the guys in my loft hadn't got on too well with some of those in B Hall, the guys on the B Hall roof were suddenly our best pals in the world.

I told Jim that I'd try to get some food to the guys on B roof if they'd keep the warders at bay. I filled a bag with sweets, chocolates and tobacco and strapped it on to me, but I couldn't get out of the loft because of the power hoses. The warders had filled the cellblock with so much water that the fire brigade had to pump more water into the gaol to prevent them running out. We were drenched with water coming through the roof: we made a sort of tent out of some tarpaulin, but even that let in water.

One of the double doors below us was open and the warders were hiding behind a steel mesh, shining powerful lamps through it into the darkness. They had a power hose on, which made it almost impossible to get down the stairs. I managed to climb down with some others, and we crept along the gallery until we reached the far wall, directly above the double doors. I was carrying an iron bar shaped like a golf club, and I leaned over the gallery railings and smashed at the lamps through the steel mesh. Frank held on to my legs to stop me from falling as I swung wildly with my club.

236

At the far end of the ground floor, near the reception door, was a huge wooden cupboard in which the warders kept property belonging to the prisoners who were on punishment. We needed it to barricade the double doors with and prevent the power hose from hitting us, so that we could get into reception and collect our personal clothing which was stored there. Jim, Frank and Archie agreed to try to move the cupboard provided I somehow kept the hose away. So, with Joe holding on to my legs I hung almost upside-down over the railings, I swung my iron club at the observation panel through which the warders aimed the hose. I don't know whether I hit the warder behind the panel, but he drooped the hose, which fell inside, soaking them. Then I jammed a plank of wood into the observation panel and held it there till the others had managed to move the cupboard. I laughed when I heard the warders cursing and trying to smash the plank of wood so as to get the hose through the panel. When I looked to see what the others were doing at the far end, all I could see was a huge cupboard moving towards me. I heard the warders grumbling when they saw what we were up to: they withdrew the hose, and we put the cupboard in front of the double doors.

Negotiations began, and we were promised a public inquiry into brutality if we came down. Some of the guys wanted to agree, but others including me, told the warders to fuck off and said that they should get our MPs and lawyers in to see us first.

We put on our own clothes and felt like human beings again, but before I changed I had a bath in the huge water tank in the loft, washing myself with a bar of gaol soap and a floor scrubber and singing for all the warders to hear. I was joined by Wee Smiddy, who came for a swim. After my bath I went on to the roof with the others. The warders weren't too pleased to see us dressed up and looking human again. Despite my change of clothes I went on wrecking as much of the cellblock as I could while the others sat about: I just couldn't stop myself.

The new governor asked to speak to us on the roof, so we went out and listened to him. He told us that he might be able to get a lawyer in from Peterhead to see us, and that he would be there when we came down to make sure there was no brutality. I told the governor I wanted my own lawyer from Glasgow, and Jim shouted that he wanted Perry Mason.

Some time later the lawyer from Peterhead came into the exercise yard to speak to us and listen to our complaints. He said he could guarantee that there'd be no brutality if we came down now, and that he'd talk to us in our cells. We went back into the loft and argued amongst ourselves. For four or five days we'd been in control of the cellblock – the guys in B Hall had given themselves up earlier because they were cold, wet and hungry. Brian, who was serving life, wanted to give himself up, reckoning enough damage had been done, and Joe thought the same – and then Jim, then Frank. . . . I wanted to stay: I knew I'd get a beating from the warders, and it was better up here than down below. Smiddy also wanted to stay, as did the guy I'd helped to break out, and Archie and Mac, whom I'd known in Larchgrove, and Tam, my wee pal from St Joseph's. There was no vote taken on it – we each just made up our own mind – but the atmosphere on the roof had changed now that some of us were going down.

We went back on to the roof, and Jim told the lawyer they were coming down with the assurance of no brutality. The lawyer sounded pleased at this, and must have assumed that Jim was speaking on behalf of all of us. A ladder was put up against the front of the building to enable us to come down into the exercise yard. We all shook hands and wished each other the best. I had tears in my eyes as I watched Jim going down the ladder. When those who wanted to go had disappeared from sight we went back into the loft and sat about smoking, straining our ears to hear any screams – but they never came.

'What about the rest of you?' the governor called up to us. I went out on to the roof, and there he was standing in a military posture and holding his umbrella. I told him to fuck off, and he told the warders to take up their positions again.

Back inside, I began smashing everything in sight. The next thing we knew thick smoke was making its way into the loft,

238

suffocating us. I could hear the warders shouting, 'Die, you bastards!' I wrapped a wet rag around my mouth to prevent me from inhaling dangerous fumes. The smoke was so thick I could hardly see in front of me as I staggered about, groping for the hole in the roof. Archie and the guy I broke out of the flooded cell managed to get out, and surrendered to the warders. I eventually found the hole, but when I tried to climb out the bastards started throwing stones at me and turned on the hose. I was choking in the smoke; I could hear Smiddy choking too as he groped for a way out, and I pulled him to the floor where the smoke wasn't as dense. By this time the warders were on the roof above, shouting that we weren't so fucking tough now. We crawled under the huge water tank, hoping the smoke wouldn't be so thick there, but it was; I could feel pains in my chest when I breathed in, and I was afraid I was going to die.

I don't know how long we were trapped up there in the smoke, but eventually I felt myself being dragged through water and on to the rafters. I felt I was dreaming when I opened my eyes and saw the warders holding me, and I felt so tired that I only wanted to rest. It hurt to breathe, and although I could feel the breeze on my face, that high-pitched sound in my ears warned me that I was going to pass out. I was overcome by fear. Someone told me I was all right, and I was lifted to my feet by two warders in riot gear. I felt dizzy and tried to sit down again, but they walked me to the end of the roof where a ladder had been propped against the side of the building. Smiddy was behind me with two other warders, and when I looked over my shoulder I saw him staggering about and groaning like he was drunk. They made me stand there for a few moments before taking me down the ladder with one in front of me and the other behind, holding on like they were scared to lose me. When I reached the bottom rung other warders in riot gear put my arms up my back and frog-marched me towards B Hall. Suddenly I was sorry for having got involved in the riot, and I wanted to scream that I was sorry. As I saw them all standing there in the gauntlet fashion, I panicked at the thought of what lay ahead for me. I saw them raise their riot sticks and move towards me. I cursed them and challenged them.

I came to in an empty cell. I still had my own suit and shoes on, and I lay soaking wet on the floor. I could hear shouting and doors banging. I tried to get up but I couldn't, so I crawled to the door. As I lay there kicking at the door, my body wracked with pain from the beating, they came crashing in on me with their sticks and shields. I thought I was in for another beating and I panicked – I was too scared to fight with them now. Two of them were hanging over me with knives while the others held my legs and hands. I thought they were going to kill me. I tried to move but I couldn't. They started slashing my suit with their knives, ripping at it as though they were plucking a chicken. I stopped struggling so that I wouldn't get injured, and let them slash and rip my clothes off till I was naked. I was trembling with fear and shock: they must have interpreted this as weakness, for they told me I wasn't so fucking tough now and kicked me, trying to provoke me into fighting with them. The governor appeared and asked me if I had any complaints. I told him no. It was the madness within me again, the stubbornness and hatred. Surgery warders then came with needles and asked me to roll over on my side so that they could inject me with penicillin. When I refused they said they couldn't give a fuck and left.

There were about sixty prisoners locked up in B Hall, but many were moved to other gaols. Warders from other prisons had been drafted into Peterhead to help keep things under control, and were sleeping on mattresses in the gymnasium. B Hall had been like a condemned building at the best of times, but now it was really bad. I was neither fed nor given a pisspot that day, and I asked for neither. I peed up against the wall near the door. Nor did they give me any bedding or a blanket, but one of the guys above me lowered down a jumper which I was thankful for. Mac was in the next door cell, so I crawled over to the heating pipe and we spoke quietly to each other. He had had his two front teeth knocked out when he was made to run the gauntlet, and every few minutes he had to spit out blood. I learned through the pipes that some of those

240

who had surrendered to the lawyer were beaten up once he had left the gaol.

That night there was much talking and shouting under cell doors to each other. I heard Jim, Archie, Joe, Frank and the others calling my name, and it echoed throughout the hall. One of the warders was also shouting 'Johnnyboy' in a squeaky voice, as if trying to make a fool of me. Everyone was asking who had set reception on fire: no one seemed to know, so it was put down to the warders.

I got myself to my feet and limped up and down the small cell holding on to the wall for support. My legs were black and blue and covered with cuts. Painful as it was, I kept on moving. I had hardly slept all the time I was on the roof, and had seldom stopped smashing walls. My body was wrecked, but my mind wouldn't let me rest.

Next morning the warders threw me in some prison clothes – they were far too big, but I put them on – and I was given a pisspot as well. Then I was opened up for my breakfast and I limped all the way to the hot-plate and back again. My legs were swollen, and I was sorry I'd refused the penicillin injections. The hall was being repaired, and the noise of drills and hammering was deafening. Mac and I could hardly hear ourselves talk at the pipe, so I just sat there singing to myself and felt the better for it.

A few days later Mac called me to the pipe and told me that Ma was on the front page of the newspaper, claiming her sons had been brutalised. I got the newspaper from him, and there was a photograph of Ma below huge headlines. I loved her for this and felt sorry for her at the same time; I cried as I read her words. 'I know my boys are no angels,' she said, and then went on to say that we weren't animals either. The warders were furious at Ma's allegations. The bastards gave me cold food, and sometimes I found slivers of glass in it so that I had to check it very carefully. Some of the guys said they could taste piss in their soup.

We were taken out to see the prison doctor for an 'examination'. He sat at a table in the middle of the hall, surrounded by rubble and broken glass. 'Any complaints?' he asked as I

241

limped towards him, but before I could answer the warders took me back to my cell. He did the same with nearly everyone that day, yet there he was in the newspaper next day denying any evidence of brutality! Some of us complained to the governor, who told me to write down everything, including the names of the warders who had assaulted me, and put what I had written into a sealed envelope so that he could look into my allegations! I took the paper and pen from him and wrote, 'Get the police in.' I wasn't prepared to give this bastard a statement in case he abused it in some way. He demanded to know more, and asked who had beaten me up. One of the warders with him was a face I remembered, and I pointed to him and said, 'There's one of them.' But he only shook his head and told me to write it all down in detail for him. I said I wasn't prepared to do that.

A few weeks later the visiting committee came to the gaol and gave us a mock trial. Just before the visiting committee arrived, one of the governors had put notices up to the effect that the rioters on the roof were responsible for destroying the prisoners' property. This didn't bode well for our getting a fair hearing from the visiting committee. The notice was later taken down and smuggled out to my dad, who took it to his lawyer along with other complaints.

When it was my turn to go into the orderly room to face the charges I asked for a lawyer to represent me, and again I was refused. The charges were read, but I shut my ears to them and to the evidence. I knew what the outcome would be. I lost a further two years remission from my sentence, which meant that I would have to do eleven years out of my twelve. I was also locked up in solitary for twenty-eight days, and told that Rule 36 was to apply after that. Rule 36 means that a prisoner is kept locked up in his cell for twenty-three hours a day: it's really just another name for solitary confinement, except that the prisoner is allowed a radio and a small wage to buy stuff from the canteen. He may have to work for the wage by sewing buttons on to shirts. I was told I had to pay another twenty-five pound fine for damages, though I hadn't yet paid my first one.

The Procurator Fiscal set up an internal inquiry into the allegations of brutality, and some warders were charged with assault. My dad visited me, but there wasn't much I could say because warders were standing behind me listening to everything we said. Jim was there too, and we both sat in the same box talking to my dad, who couldn't conceal his rage and hatred for the warders. He threatened them with murder and mayhem, but they only smiled. This so antagonised my dad that he turned to his pal and said, 'If you see any of their subhuman kids in the street, just run the bastards over!'

They weren't laughing now – one of them ran to get the governor. They asked my dad to step outside for a moment, and we could hear him telling them they had made a mistake in fucking his sons about. A senior warder stormed into the visiting room shouting, 'Terminate this visit!' and calling Jim and me 'bastards'. Jim spat at the warders, picked up a chair and tried to smash the unbreakable glass to get through to the governor. I started trying to kick in the glass, too, but I soon stopped to help Jim, who was being attacked. One of the warders pressed the riot bell and the visiting room was filled with their pals, who dragged us away and kicked us down the corridor.

I woke up in my cell and could hear Mac calling through the pipes, 'Are you in there, Johnnyboy?'

I was covered in blood from my nose. At first I thought I was bleeding elsewhere, so I stripped off my clothes and looked my body over, but there were only bruises. Mac told me I had been screaming in pain and had been lying there for several hours. A warder gave me a basin of water and soap to clean myself up. Something inside me wanted to drag him into the cell and bite his throat out, but it wasn't in me to do that sort of thing. What I did have in me was the need to escape from this hellhole, and I swore on Ma's life that I wouldn't stop trying as long as I was inside. I couldn't fit in. I didn't even look like a convict. I looked like a schoolboy, which annoyed me: if I could have, I would have grown a beard and moustache. My soft voice didn't help either.

I was taken in front of the governor, who took more remission from me and told me I would not be allowed visits at the same time as Jim.

One night I felt an uncontrollable urge to kill myself. I thought it was all over for me, then I snapped and pressed the bell, desperate to get out of that cell. In a blind panic I wrecked the windows and what little furniture there was, and I tried to smash down the door, like a man with superhuman strength. Once I had calmed down, the warders took me to the cellblock, where they threw me into a cell and slammed two thick doors behind me. This was the first time I had been in the notorious silent cell, and I stood there in the dark, straining my eyes. It was different from any other cell in that the window was so high that it hardly let any light in. I could hear my own breathing, but nothing else. I felt my way around the damp-smelling cell until I reached a block of wood, rotten with age. That was my bed.

Next morning my door opened, and some warders handed me porridge and tea, some tobacco and matches, which they said were from Jim. I felt dizzy smoking, as it had been weeks since I last had a cigarette, but I put the tobacco down the front of my underpants so that the other warders wouldn't confiscate it – I was still on punishment and not allowed tobacco.

After a spell in the silent cell I was moved back to B Hall and into an 'iron lung'. My next-door neighbour was a wee guy called Keyhole. He told me how the riot squad had charged into B Hall and attacked anyone in their path – one guy who suffered from epileptic fits had been badly beaten up. Keyhole had managed to have one of the most vicious warders charged with assault. Every night guys smashed up their cells and screamed curses at the world outside and every day the governor came around with his usual, 'Morning!' and then was off again. I asked him not to bother coming near my cell, but he said he was paid to look after me.

I was moved back to the punishment block where we made the best of the worst and rioted in our cells and threw our piss and shit out the doors for the warders to clean up. Joe had his radio on full playing 'Jailhouse Rock', and it sounded as if the prison was 'rocking' to judge by the noise of windows and furniture being smashed. After a while the riot squad was sent in, and I heard them going from cell to cell; I listened to the screams and thuds and threats. When my cell door opened, I saw only a mattress – behind which the warders rushed, pushing me up against the wall while others cleaned out my cell, throwing broken tables and chairs and glass over the gallery. I tried to get out from behind the mattress but they held me all the harder, almost embedding me in the wall. They kicked me on the legs till I fell to the floor, and then handcuffed my arms up my back. My only weapon was my tongue, and I used it. They made me pay for that, too. Before I passed out I heard one of the warders shouting that they should leave me alone or they'd kill me.

Next morning I felt like a terrified child. I wanted to cry out, I wanted Ma, I wanted to die. My mind wouldn't stop racing and I had that high-pitched sound in my ears again. I wasn't hungry, but I was cold and thirsty. I crawled over to my bowl and licked up a little milk from the top of my porridge. My fingers were numb from the tightness of the handcuffs. Whenever I moved my arms or hands I cried out in pain. When the governor came to my cell I was sitting in my underpants in a corner. He looked at me and said, 'When I first saw you, you told me that you were going to get through your sentence as fast as you could!' I told him that I had tried my best and had obviously failed since he and the other bastards had made my life so hard. He laughed and went away, the door slamming hard behind him. My handcuffs were removed at dinner time; my hands were swollen, and I rubbed them gently under my armpits till the feeling came back into them.

The smell in my cell was really bad. I had been peeing and shitting on the floor and leaving it for the warders to clear up. They had to hold their breath when they opened the door. One of them tried to convince me that I would catch a disease if I continued my dirty protest – he went on about my nice clean-cut look and how surprised he was to see me living like this. I was surprised to hear him talking to me as though I was

245

his pal, but I wouldn't clean up the mess for him no matter how much he soft-talked me, and I told him so.

When the governor came on his rounds he walked among the piss and shit with a big false smile on his face, as though it didn't bother him at all and then I noticed that he was wearing a pair of Wellington boots. I told him that it wouldn't bother me either if I could wear Wellingtons: he obviously didn't think much of my sense of humour, for he aimed his boot at me and told me to shut up.

I made a hammock from my blanket and tied it to my cell bars, and I ate and slept there – it was better than lying on the cold floor among the filth. It was freezing, but I was getting used to it. We spoke every night about escaping. That was what life was all about as far as I was concerned: somehow I had to get away from this hell.

Some strange and painful spots appeared on my body. I didn't know what they were, and I thought that I might have caught a disease amongst the filth in my cell. The pain was unbearable and had me squirming about, trying to clutch at it with my hands. I was very weak and could hardly muster up the strength to get into my hammock. I shook uncontrollably, and the pain wouldn't go away. It was like having toothache. The doctor refused to see me in my cell, so I was taken down, filthy and in my underwear, to the governor's orderly room. When I told him about the pain and the strange spots, he made me lie on the governor's table and examined me. He then said that I was on the edge of a nervous breakdown, and that I had shingles, a painful, nervous, skin disease.

I was taken back to my cell, where some warders brought me a new mattress and blankets. I wondered what was going on till one of them told me that the prison doctor had taken me off punishment, so that I could take my nervous breakdown in style. They then closed my cell door, leaving me to worry about my health. I was frightened at the thought of a nervous breakdown, and fearful that I would end up in a mental hospital. When the screws opened my door for slop-out I walked out in my underpants, carrying the mattress on my back, and tossed it over the railings and on to the ground floor. My sheets, pillow and blankets (save one) then followed after. I heard all the others shouting under their cell doors to find out what was going on. I was locked in my cell while they went to fetch the governor and a surgery warder. The governor said I was to have my mattress at all times, under doctor's orders.

'Your nervous system is going haywire,' he told me. I told him his prison system was going haywire. He told the warders to put my mattress back in my cell whenever I threw it out. They stood looking down at me as I lay on the floor; as the governor left he said, 'That's what's known as a "broken spirit"!' and they laughed amongst themselves.

Jim was worried about me, as usual, and he wanted to know if I was tucked up in bed. I wasn't, but I told him I was. At night I slept on the wooden bed board while the mattess lay in a corner with the bedding. My arms and legs twitched, and sometimes my whole body jerked violently. The warders refused me my exercise, telling me I was to stay in bed on doctor's orders. I was cracking up in that cell: I had to get out of it, if only for a few minutes.

The doctor painted some medication on the spots on my skin, but gave me nothing to kill the pain – he did offer to put me on a course of Largactyl, but I refused. Before long I seemed to get over my would-be nervous breakdown, and was back to thinking about escaping. Every time I did so I felt stronger and better. It was something worth living for: being subversive was like a tonic and cure to me – I had become addicted to it.

One day I asked the governor if he could help me get off the security party, so that I could settle down, and told him that I had been put on it for nothing in the first place.

'Well,' he said, nodding his head and chewing his lips, 'you'll settle down and stop smashing up my gaol?' I promised him I would.

I knew that my asking to get off security would work, as they wanted to soften me up for going back into circulation.

Even the warders became more pleasant and tried to talk to me. They said there were going to be big changes in the gaol with new toilet facilities and showers, and longer visits, etc. The chief warder said he would try to get me off security. It wouldn't be easy as he would have to convince other people that I was a changed man – 'And don't you let me down!' he said as he left my cell.

'Fuck you!' I thought, and I had a good wee laugh at his expense.

I had been kept locked up for six months, like most of the others. The governor told me I would be going back into circulation, and that I would have to go into an 'iron lung' until a larger cell was available. A Hall was closed for renovation, so I was put back into D Hall. I was glad to see some guys I knew and to talk to them again, and I was given sweets, tobacco and the like by my pals. I was shown to my 'iron lung' by a warder who laughed and joked as if I was his best pal. I took the chair out of the 'iron lung', left it in the gallery outside my door on the second floor, and refused to take it back: the cell was small enough without a chair in it.

I'd been in circulation a few weeks when I learned that I was to come off the security party. The only difference this made was that I wouldn't have to put my clothes outside my door or sleep with my light on at night. The chief warder told me he had managed to talk the governor into taking me off security, and he asked me to promise that I wouldn't try to escape and make him look a fool. I did so, but I had no intention of keeping my promise.

I became pally with a new guy called Thomas, and before I came off security we were sawing through his cell bars with a hacksaw. Thomas had no intention of escaping, but he wanted to help us escape and was prepared to cut his bars. The warders told me they needed my cell for someone else, so they moved me into Thomas's cell, where the two of us worked slowly and carefully on the bars at the weekends and sometimes during recreation, when the hall was noisy and busy. The hot-plate was outside our cell door, and the warders would often sleep on top of it to keep warm. We tried rubbing oil on the blades

248

to keep down the noise, and that helped some. The guys in the cells nearby knew what we were up to, so they'd play their music loud to cover the noise of cutting. On one occasion, I asked Thomas if he was prepared to come out into the hall with me and bring our guitars to sing for one and all, and all the while we could have one of the guys sawing the bars for us and the warders would be none the wiser. He thought it was a great idea and so we dressed up like western singers and went out and mingled with the other prisoners while Frank sawed away at the cell bars. It was working fine, for all the prisoners and warders gathered around and laughed and cheered. But the warder in charge of the hall became suspicious, his eyes everywhere. I noticed, as I sat there singing, he told the other warders to keep their eyes open and then they too moved about the hall suspiciously. So that was the end of our concert.

A fight broke out early one morning in which Frank and Thomas were involved. When they were taken away to the cells I was left to cut the bars by myself. The day after the fight the warder in charge of the hall came into my cell and told me he was glad I was settling down. I played along with him, though it was hard to keep myself from laughing: little did he know that he was sitting in a cell with half the bars cut through. He was even sitting on the hacksaw blade, which was glued to the bottom of the bed. I had to lower my head when I felt a smile spreading over my face. The governor and the warders thought that my not getting involved in the fight was proof that my spell in the punishment block had paid off, and that I was settling down.

25 HOMEWARD BOUND

Jim and Archie were going to Barlinnie on accumulated visits. I decided I would go with them, if I could, and come back with some new hacksaw blades. Before I left I painted the cell bars and filled in the cuts with woodfiller. I did a good job, and I felt sure it would pass inspection.

It was great to see Ma again with my sisters, Lana and Brenda, and of course, my dad. We had a family reunion in two small cubicles, smaller than telephone boxes with a sheet of armour-plated glass and wire mesh to separate us. Soon after we arrived at Barlinnie and I got some new hacksaw blades from my dad, a guy from Peterhead was brought down. At Peterhead Big Tony did repairing jobs – mending and painting and rewiring – and even though he was a trustee we trusted him and knew he would never grass on any of us. When we met he looked kind of worried, and then he told me that the warders at Peterhead had found my half-cut cell bars – he had been there when they welded them back together. My heart was in my mouth, and I expected a hand to fall on my shoulder any moment. I felt much better when Big Tony told me that he had learned from some of the warders that they weren't going to have me arrested at Barlinnie: they'd get me when I stepped off the bus back at Peterhead. I was going to have to escape from Barlinnie.

With a few others we could trust we tried to figure out the best way to escape. I knew there was a hatch leading on to the

roof in a cupboard-like room in the top gallery showers. The
door had only a Yale lock, and sometimes it was left open so
that prisoners could regulate the water. In the ceiling was a
steel-barred gate with a security padlock on it. Above that was
a wooden door leading to the roof. To one side of the room
was a shaft with pipes going down to the ground floor.

We had found a way out – now we had to figure a way off
the roof and over the wall. There were many ideas bounced
about and rejected.

We told my dad what we had in mind, and he said he would
help us, though he wasn't too happy about me and Jim wanting
to escape. Broono came to see us with his wife, and he too
wanted to help us get out. We saw and spoke to Alex Howatt
each day. It was great to hear that Alex, a pal from way back,
had started cutting through the padlock on the steel gate.
During recreation he and his pals would say they wanted a
shower, and while the shower was running one sawed the
padlock, another watched out for warders while pretending to
wait his turn at the shower, and another pretended to be
mopping the floor. But the teeth of the hacksaw blade wouldn't
grip, and it kept slipping, so Alex decided to burst the padlock
off with an iron bar. He took most of its insides out, but still
it wouldn't budge.

Although they sometimes only got five minutes' work done
in one night because other prisoners were in the vicinity, Alex
wouldn't give up. He was aware that the warders at Peterhead
would be waiting for us on our return. In the end he told us
the padlock wouldn't come off – his hands were almost raw
from handling it – and that he would have to saw through one
of the bars on the steel gate.

The day before we were due to escape we came back from
recreation and went into the dining hall for tea. My heart
was pounding and my belly turned at the thought that Alex
and his pals might have been caught. Then I saw Alex come
in, and as he passed our table he gave us the thumbs-up
sign.

'God bless ye, Alex,' I thought as he passed by. We were all
happy now and winking at each other. I couldn't eat a bite of

food – Jim and Archie said I was so thin that I could have slipped through the bars without cutting them.

Back in the hall we had a chance to talk to Alex. He told us that they had managed to cut through one end of the bar and that they had bent it down to save us time in the morning. It was pointing downwards, so if anyone walked in and looked up, everything would be over. The warders were really on their toes now, and everywhere I went I felt their eyes following me. After slop-out it was, 'Right, staff, downstairs with your numbers!'

Back in my cell, I paced the floor as the hours ticked by. Eight steps forward, then eight steps back, throughout the long night.

Next morning – Sunday 22 June 1980 – I was up and waiting when the warders opened my cell door. The sun was shining brightly, and the world wasn't such a bad-looking place after all. I brought my clothes in and got ready fast. I had a letter from the prison welfare officer in my pocket. He had written something like 'Dear Mr Steele, as regarding the "open" visit with your grandmother, you will have to go on request to see the hall governor.' I had already seen the hall governor, and it was he who had told me to go and see the welfare officer. On the bottom of the letter I wrote in bold letters 'FUCK YOU, BASTARDS, I'll just go home and visit my maw' and pinned it to the wall above my bed, knowing they would find it when they searched the cell. Jim came in to ask me if everything was okay, and I said it was. He had decided to walk upstairs to the top floor: I couldn't risk following him in case the warders stopped us, so I had to rely on him or Archie coming down the shaft from the top floor and opening the Yale lock from the inside.

Jim went upstairs and I joined some other prisoners who were carrying their pisspots and towels and shaving gear. I stood by the cupboard door, and after a while I heard a slight rapping. A warder was standing nearby with his legs apart and his arms folded, chewing gum. He kept looking at me, and I was worried that he would stay there till slop-out was over. I hadn't much time left; in a few moments breakfast would be brought into the hall. Prisoners were coming and going with their pots, and still the warder stood there. I saw my pal Aldo at a sink, pretending to shave, and I asked him to distract the warder. Aldo stood up and stared at the warder, who began to shift nervously from one foot to another. I threw a tantrum and told him to go and get me the fucking governor as I wasn't taking any more from him and his staring. It worked, and the warder walked away. I shook hands with Aldo and entered the cupboard, locking the door behind me.

It was pitch-black in there. I could hear sinks being filled and prisoners talking, Jim's and Archie's voices coming down the shaft. I climbed into the shaft and went up fast, groping for holds. The dust almost choked me. I could smell the dry wood as I climbed up. When I reached the fourth gallery, Jim and Archie pulled me out and into the cupboard. I squeezed through the cut bar; then I crouched on the steel gate and put my back to the wooden door a foot or so above me. I managed to open it, and the sun lit up the little cupboard.

I climbed out on to the flat roof at the end of the hall, and could see for miles and miles. I sat there marvelling at the view, waiting for Jim and Archie. Jim came out, but Archie was in a panic. He looked up at me and told me that he couldn't get through: he would have to go back inside so as to give us a chance to get away. He had both his arms and his head through the hole in the bars: I pulled one arm and Jim the other, but for a long time we couldn't budge him. Eventually we pushed and pulled him through on to the roof.

We kept as low as possible so as not to be seen from the warders' houses in the street below. I crawled to the edge of the roof and looked over. Below me was the huge, thick prison wall that kept us in. We were at a great height, above the security camera which was looking down along the bottom of the wall, watching for anyone trying to scale it.

Jim and Archie were getting worried. A brand-new mountain-climbing rope had been given to us by a guy who had just got out of Barlinnie: he had delivered it to a 'certain party', who was supposed to bring it with him that morning. We smoked as we waited, and I kept my eyes on the street below.

We could hear the warders and passmen going round the cells with breakfast, banging the cell doors. Jim and Archie wanted to get back to their cells before they were discovered missing: they assumed we had been let down, or that something had happened to the guys on the outside. I told them they could go down if they wanted to, but I wouldn't. Jim made his way over to the trap door, but I stopped him. I told him that for all we knew the guys could be parked somewhere in the street, not be able to see us because we were so high up. I stood up to my full height, walked to the end of the building and looked up and down the street, like a pirate looking for ships. Suddenly I spotted a black car creeping round a corner. It was them! There were four of them, and the driver waved up at us. The car stopped and the guys got out.

We had stolen a reel of tape from the textiles shed, which we would throw over the edge so that they could tie the mountain-rope to the end of it. One of the guys had a white rope with him, and we threw him down the tape and pulled the rope towards us. Jim and Archie were shocked to see how thin the rope was, and doubted if it would hold their weight. I took hold of it and told them to hold as tight as they could.

'I'll gladly be the guinea pig,' I said, and climbed over the edge of the building and on to the rope, which went straight over the top of the wall and into the warders' garden. It was almost a straight slide down, clearing the wall as I went. I landed in the arms of the guys below, who congratulated me and told me to get into the car and change my clothes. I looked up at B Hall roof and saw Jim and Archie tying the end of the rope to a concrete frame. Archie then slid down into the garden, and Jim followed. As soon as they reached the car, the other three walked off in different directions and disappeared.

The driver took us to a house in the Haghill district. He wished us luck; we couldn't thank him enough for what he had done and the risks he had taken. We danced and sang with happiness once we were inside the house, and roared with laughter when we thought of the warders waiting for me at Peterhead. It was great to be free.

It was then we noticed that the owners of the house were

there, and that they were both in bed and steaming drunk. They were expecting us, and they got up and made us welcome. They couldn't believe I was in prison: they said I was only a 'wee boy', and the woman cuddled me like I was her lost kid and told me I could stay with her for ever. Jim and Archie laughed at my being pampered by this little woman, who was just like my ma in many ways. It didn't take long for us to feel at home, and the woman made us a nice breakfast.

On television we watched newsmen and police describing 'Scotland's most daring escape'. The police warned the public to watch out for us, and our photographs were shown. All police leave had been cancelled, and a massive operation had been set up to catch us. The public was advised not to 'tackle' us should we be seen.

The driver and the other three came back to the house with food and fresh meat, and some money for us to buy cigarettes and drinks. They told us to lie low for the time being as the police were searching half the houses in Glasgow, dragging people in and demanding to know where we were. I couldn't even send word to Ma to say that I was fine – I knew she'd be worrying herself sick. So we stayed put and hoped things would settle down soon.

It was great to look out of the window and see people walking about in colourful clothes and women hanging out their washing; I reflected that I too could have been out there, enjoying life. I always seemed to see the best in life through a window. Jim, Archie and I scrubbed the house till it was sparkling, not just to pass the time, but because we wanted to. We joked about making good passmen back in gaol. We burned our grey prison uniforms, and our shirts, underwear and shoes. We cooked meals and made sure the couple's kids were fed and washed. I'm not saying they were neglected – they looked healthy enough – but their folks being alcoholics didn't help matters. One of the boys told us that he was going down to Barrow's Market to steal a bike, and that he went there every Sunday with his pals to steal. He was a handsome kid of eight or nine with short fair hair, and he was all excited about venturing into the world of crime. We tried to give him good advice, telling him he would only end up being taken away from his family if he was caught stealing, and we managed to talk him out of going stealing that Sunday. They were great kids. When they were tucked up in bed we had to tell them stories before they'd go to sleep.

News came fast, and we learned that many of our pals had been pulled in by the police demanding to be told of our wherabouts. The police had offered to drop serious charges against some people if they told them where we were. From those of our pals who managed to slip in to see us, we learned that Alex Howatt had been locked up in solitary for helping us. They couldn't prove it, though, so he couldn't be charged. Jim and Archie sat by the fire drinking vodka and saying, 'This one is for Alex.' The wee woman got drunk, and she kept filling her glass and saying, 'Here's tae Alex, and the boys who helped ye's!' before swallowing the glass in one gulp. Then they had a sing-song, seated around the fireside. I didn't touch the vodka, but I had a can of lager and sat there enjoying the company and singing country songs.

That night another couple came to the house. The couple who owned the house assured us that we had nothing to worry about, and we chatted away like old friends. They told us that we could stay with them for the time being, in their house in Carntyne and we accepted their offer. We were frightened to stay where we were too long, and feared it was only a matter of time before the owners of the house got drunk and told somebody that we were there.

Early next morning me and Archie, dressed like workers in hats and overalls and carrying some small wooden steps, set out with the couple. I felt exposed and frightened, and wanted to go back to the comforts of the house we'd just left, but we kept on walking. They took us up and down streets, through back courts on to spare ground and along a railway track. Cars kept passing us everywhere we went, and the occasional police van sped by. We passed some teenagers who eye-balled us and, recognising us as strangers in their territory, threatened us and told us to move on. We ate humble pie and did so, though Archie took umbrage at their insults and said he had a good mind to go back and punch their cheeky faces in for calling him 'bald head'.

When we reached Penicuik Street, we were asked to be very quiet, and I found myself walking on tip-toes. The couple lived on the ground floor in a sparsely furnished two-room flat. We were taken to the bathroom to wash our faces, which we had dirtied to make us look like workers, and we were told that we could make ourselves at home while they went to collect Jim. We checked the doors and windows in case we had to make a quick exit. It was a strange feeling to be in Penicuik Street, for I'd played round there as a child. Archie and I sat on the bed in a room facing the street and waited for Jim, hoping that everything was okay with him. Once he'd arrived we made some tea.

Next morning the woman came back from the shops all excited, saying my ma was in the papers. There on the front page was a huge coloured photo of Ma looking worried, below headlines that read, 'Give yourself up, for your own good.' Ma's appeal touched me and I had a good cry. Jim and I were now more concerned about Ma than about anything else, and Archie and the others left the room so that we could have a personal talk together.

Jim asked me to give myself up for Ma's sake, and he spoke sense that I didn't want to hear. I read Ma's words over and over again, wondering what to do. Jim must have been reading my mind, for he said that if I gave myself up to my lawyer I wouldn't be beaten up by the warders. I told him that he should give himself up and I'd stay, but he said it was me that Ma worried more about than anything. I was her 'wee pet', the one who never had much of a chance in life, and all she longed for was for me to get out and settle down to a decent life. As he spoke I could see the worry and sincerity on his handsome face. I told Jim I couldn't give myself up because I couldn't do the time, and the length of my sentence was killing me. I couldn't give myself up, nor could Jim.

We had to wait for further instructions from the others who were trying to make arrangements for us to get down to London, but the police were watching their every move. We

257

were moved back and forth between the two couples' houses. The change did us good and made us feel less paranoid.

My dad got word to us that he had a place for us to go to in London, but that we couldn't bring Archie – he was in for murder, so many people didn't want to know. We didn't want to leave Archie behind after all we'd been through together, so we sent word back to my dad and told him we were fine and in a safe house, and not to worry about us. Archie had dyed his hair jet black, and I had dyed my dark hair blond: it hardly made any difference to my appearance, but Archie was almost unrecognisable. Jim had his hair permed – I saw him sitting in the bathroom with rollers in his hair. He said I looked like a member of the Hitler Youth army, with my blond hair and blue eyes.

At the older couple's house there was a younger man of whom we became suspicious. He said he was more than willing to help us in any way, but he stole from us, and whenever he came back from seeing certain people on our behalf he behaved very nervously. We had asked him to go and see a friend of my dad's and I asked the older guy if he would go and make sure the young guy wasn't pulling any strokes on us, and he agreed to do so. It was dark when they left the house; we made ourselves some tea and got ready to leave when they got back.

When they returned, I noticed that the younger man had a black eye, as if he had been in a fight. The elder guy said he had thumped him for being cheeky. We knew something wasn't right, but the elder guy wouldn't tell us as he didn't want to worry us unduly. He told us that he was to go and see my dad's pal in the morning, and then we all sat round the fire together.

We had just decided that we should leave in the morning when we had an unexpected visitor, steaming drunk and staggering about like he'd been shot. It was an old friend of ours, Shadow, and I've never seen a man sober up so quickly in my life. He stood there in his black coat, swaying from side to side, as he looked from me to Jim to Archie like we were ghosts. He had come to see the elder guy, who was his drinking partner. It was great to see him, and Jim and I rushed up to him and hugged him. Shadow was just like one of our family. He told us that he and T.C. had been questioned about our escape, and that his house had been searched by many armed police.

Jim, Archie and Shadow and the others then had a wee drink, and then we had a sing-song to cheer us up. By now Shadow was quite drunk again: we were worried that he might unintentionally tell someone about us, so we coaxed him into staying and filled him with more drink till he fell asleep on the couch.

After breakfast next morning the elder guy went to see about the message from my dad's pal. He went alone, and the younger one remained with us. He was acting very suspiciously and nervously, so we watched him closely. The last we saw of him he was going to the toilet – and then the elder guy's wife came running in and said that he had climbed out of the bathroom window and was off to get the police. She told us to move fast before they came. She didn't need to say more – Jim and Shadow went one way, and Archie and I the other.

I found it hard to believe that the young guy had really gone to the police – but he had. The police now knew that we were still in Glasgow, whereas some of the newspapers and news reports had said that we had been sighted as far away as Jersey and London. Archie and I ran towards the railway, where we picked up some picks and shovels, hoping to give the impression that we were a couple of workers. I ripped the sleeves off my jumper to make woollen hats. We watched the police cars speeding by in the direction of the house we had left.

We learned later that Jim and Shadow had run out of the house and through the back courts. They had heard someone rapping on a window – it was a pal of theirs beckoning them in. They went into his house and listened to police messages about us.

It was a nice day as Archie and I walked off along the railway; the smell of grass and flowers reminded me of when I was young and used to play here in the summer-time. I took Archie to where I had once lived, hoping to find Dannyboy

259

in, but the building was empty and the closes had been bricked up.

I stood in the back court and looked up at the house I was born in and had so often run away from. If only, I thought, I could turn back the clock ... I had often longed to be there when I was in solitary confinement at Peterhead, yet there I was with not only Ma ... but every policeman in the country looking for me. It was the best I could get out of life, and I snatched it like a thief.

We hailed a taxi and I told the driver to take us to Shettleston. We agreed that should we get split up, we would meet at the Shettleston bingo hall at ten the following morning. It's a pity we hadn't made such arrangements before we lost Jim – now we had no idea where he was. Once out of the taxi I had to keep my head down while passing people I knew. I told Archie that we were going to the house of a lassie I was friendly with.

Marie looked surprised to see us on her doorstep, but she didn't hesitate for a moment as she ushered us in and closed the door behind us. I gave her a big hug and a kiss after which she pushed us into a room and told us to stay there and keep quiet – her grandmother was in the living room, but would be leaving soon. She looked lovely as she went to the window and closed the curtains. Then she left us and went back to her granny.

Every time we heard a car stop we looked out of the side of the curtains to see who it could be – only when we were satisfied that it wasn't the police could we relax in the semi-darkness. Once her granny had left, Marie made us something to eat. There she was, sheltering me once again, as loyal and as friendly as ever: I felt quite emotional as I watched her moving about the kitchen. She said she was worried about Archie being on the run for murder – not because she was in any danger from him, but because harbouring a killer was worse than harbouring a robber. Archie was aware of this, so he told her that we wouldn't stay long. She said we could stay as long as we had to, and that she wouldn't dream of turning us away, but we could tell she was worried. We stayed the night in the living room while Marie went to stay with her sister Christine.

Next morning Archie went to a call-box. I was waiting for him and pretending to be window-shopping when I noticed a couple of Shettleston CID looking at me suspiciously. I tried to keep calm, but when I saw them crossing the road towards me, I bolted through a close without knowing if they were following. It was an area I knew very well, and I ran down a back court which was littered with rubbish and mud before leaping the stairs of a close four at a time till I reached the top flat of the building, where I knocked on a door.

I could hear nothing from below, but was grateful to hear footsteps from within. My pal Lev's dad, Mick, opened the door. He was wearing nothing but his trousers: I didn't know what kind of reception to expect from him, but he threw his arms around me and almost dragged me in. He told me that the police had already searched his house for me, and that I wasn't to worry about their coming back as he wouldn't let them in. I wondered how he would stop them! He took me into the living room where his other sons and some pals of theirs were playing snooker. Lev wasn't there – he was living with his wife at the other end of the city. They gave me some tea while I explained to them what had happened, and told me I could stay as long as I wanted to, and showed me a newspaper with an artist's impression of us sliding down the rope commando-style. Everybody, it seemed, was impressed with our escape.

When Mick went in and woke his wife to let her know I was in the house, she didn't believe him, so they took me in to see her, and there she was in bed, still half sleeping and rubbing her eyes to look at me. She smiled. 'That's not Johnnyboy,' she said.

I told them I couldn't stay any longer, and thanked them all the same. Before I left, Lev's sister Angie helped me improve my disguise, and gave me her sister's one-year-old child to carry as she walked me down to the Shettleston Road to get a taxi. We all shook hands and they wished me luck. I could have stayed there for ever in the comforts of that house. Angie

261

didn't seem too worried as she walked with me down the stairs and around the corner into the Shettleston Road. I spoke to the baby as if I was its father – Angie assured me that I was holding it correctly and told me not to worry.

As we were looking for a taxi a wee woman stopped and told me what a lovely baby it was, and I wondered what I would have done if the police had come while I was holding the baby. When the taxi arrived I put some silver in the baby's hand and wished it good luck in life. Angie took the baby back and gave me a big hug and a kiss, and I told the taxi-driver to take me to the Gartloch Road, about six closes from Ma's house.

As I looked towards Ma's house I wondered what they were doing and who would be in – and, even more so, what they would say when I knocked on the door. I kept my head down as some of my old neighbours passed by. I saw a car with four men inside – I assumed they were police watching my family, hoping they'd lead them to me or Jim. So I turned and walked away to the other end of the estate.

When I reached the flat on the top floor of Tillicairn Road, the door was opened to me by my friend Josie, who lived there with her husband and family. The first thing she told me was that Tony's girlfriend was there. I went to leave at once, since I didn't trust or really like her, but Josie pulled me back in and told me I couldn't risk walking round Garthamlock in daylight. She kept crying and cuddling me and telling the others, 'I told yous he would come to me.' I tried to keep them quiet so as not to waken Tony's girlfriend who was still asleep – and I intended leaving before she woke up. Josie and her husband John made me really welcome.

I asked Josie whether her daughter could ask Lana to come and see me as soon as possible – and to make sure she wasn't being followed. The daughter said they would go to the Easterhouse shopping centre, where they could lose anyone who was following them in the crowd – after which they'd slip into a taxi and come round to Josie's.

Tony's girlfriend got up and came into the living room, someone having told her I was there. She had always said it was me who got her Tony into trouble, and often asked him to stay away from me, but that morning she was crying and hugging me. She told me she had been shattered when I got sentenced to twelve years. She wasn't the person I once thought her to be. She went out to buy me some wigs: as soon as she had left the house I worried that she was only pretending to like me and that she had gone for the police, but John and Josie assured me she would never do that – and she didn't, for she came back with the wigs. Then the door went again, and my heart nearly leapt out my mouth – but it was my wee sister Lana, crying and rushing into my arms.

Lana could hardly speak for sobbing, and I sat on the bed with her on my knee, rocking her back and forth and patting her back to comfort her. I wanted to scream when I thought of how I had ruined my life and the lives of those I loved most. I had never realised how much they missed and cared for me, nor how much I missed them.

Lana told me that the police had searched Ma's house for us, and that they had told Ma that they weren't too bothered about Jim – it was me and Archie they wanted. She was worried that the police would shoot me when they saw me – and so was I after she'd told me that they were more concerned about me than about Jim. After all, when he was still in his mid-teens, Jim had been charged with two attempted murders, and he had also tried to hack off Nero's head. Not long after that he had been charged with the Stepps Hotel robbery and firing a sawn-off shotgun above the manager's head; after which he had been charged with robbing a jeweller's shop, serious assault, attempted murder and shooting a guy in a pub with a shotgun at point-blank range.... And it was me the police were worried about? I was puzzled at this. I could only assume that the prison authorities had given the police a bad report of me.

Lana went off to see if she could get me a safe house out of Garthamlock for the time being. Josie, John and Tony's girlfriend suggested that they dressed me up as a girl so as to get me out of Garthamlock without my being recognised. I wasn't for the idea at first, but when I thought about it it made sense – provided I wasn't caught! When Lana got back they set about dressing me up and putting on mascara and lipstick and a skirt – and, worst of all, a set of boobs that would have put Mama Cass to shame. They tried the wigs on, and decided that a blond curly one suited me best. They were all chatting away to each other as they made me up, chopping and changing me like I was a tailor's dummy on display, and when I complained they told me to shut up. Lana told me to stretch my lips while she was putting on the lipstick so that she could make a good job of it, and when someone tried to pluck my eyebrows I let out such a howl of pain that they painted them instead. . . .

Once I'd been dressed and made up, the girls told me to walk around, then stopped me and told me to walk like them: they started prancing up and down the room! They brought in a mirror so that I could look at myself. I couldn't believe it when I saw what they'd done, and I said to Lana, 'I'm not only younger-looking than you. I'm even better-looking!' This had them all laughing and joking – I was told to watch myself in case I got myself a date with the taxi-driver.

In the meantime, I had managed to contact Archie at the Bingo hall, and it was really good to see him again. Lana's pal took us to a house in Cranhill in the east end of Glasgow, not far from Barlinnie Prison. Whenever we left the house wearing our men's wigs and our new suits we passed some of the warders; none of them recognised us, and we had a quiet laugh to ourselves. Lana and her pals came from time to time to bring us our food supplies and cook for us. A guy we knew gave us some money and advice on passports – and a sawn-off shotgun, thinking it might come in handy should we decide to do a robbery. At first the woman who owned the house thought Archie and I were on leave from the oil rigs, but she soon put two and two together. She told us we could stay, and that she and her son would go and stay with a friend. We couldn't thank her enough, and we apologised for not telling her the truth in the first place.

I went out one night with Lana and phoned Mick and Mary Carol at a neighbour's house to inquire about passports. Poor

264

Mary was crying when she heard my voice on the phone and kept telling me to look after myself. She and Mick were out on bail charged with smuggling illegal immigrants into the country so the police were watching their home and had been listening to their phone calls. All we could do was lay low till things had settled down, only then could we get what was required.

After a while we were moved to another flat on the other side of Glasgow: it was near the top of a skyscraper, which gave us a great view of the city. The guy who took us in was called Wullie, and he was a friend of my dad and of Archie. We had the house to ourselves, since Wullie had not yet moved in with his family. He was still painting and decorating, which suited us since it gave us something to do while we waited for out passports. But next morning we were moved on to another house a few miles away – Wullie said his flat was too dangerous, and he was afraid the police would discover us there. I was quite surprised to find our new house in a residential area with lots of beautiful gardens, and very quiet too, sometimes it was too quiet. We stayed here for a couple of days then had to move yet again, this time to a house in Great Western Road. The guy who owned it was called Watty, and he and his wife made us more than welcome. Archie, Wullie, Watty and another guy who knew my dad sat there and discussed where we should go when we managed to get our passports. Archie and the others then went to see someone in another part of the city while I stayed behind with Watty and his wife. Watty rolled a joint: he told me it was good hash, and passed me it, saying it would help me to stay calm. I took a few puffs while Watty asked me about my experiences at Peterhead, and then something strange happened: I panicked, and thought I was back in the 'silent' cell at Peterhead! The walls of Watty's home were whitewashed, like those in the 'silent' cell, and suddenly the room seemed small and very quiet. I jumped off the couch and ran to the window to see if the street was there. It was, but it was like looking at a silent movie: although I could see the traffic and the people just below me, I couldn't hear anything. Watty just sat there, looking very calm. I accused him of putting LSD in my tea. I tried to get away, but Watty pleaded with me to stay, telling me I was only having a bad trip because of the hash. He told me he would play some music and that would help. God knows what he played on his stereo, but it nearly sent me round the bend. I had to get him to take it off. When Archie and the others came back they were shocked to see how pale I was. I had to get away from Watty's house, so I put my wig on and went out for a walk with Archie.

This was the first time I had ever experienced paranoia like this. Out in the street, I put on my sunglasses and walked with the crowds, still convinced someone had put LSD in my tea. I was terrified that this strange feeling would never go away, and I told Archie I was going to hospital to get the LSD out of my system. He was really worried at the state I was in and kept trying to convince me that I was okay and not to worry. After we'd walked for perhaps half an hour, I told Archie I was going into a pub for a drink – I hoped it might take away the paranoia and the horrible effects of the LSD.

The pub was crammed and stuffy, and no one gave us a second glance. Archie ordered me some lager, and as we sat there he told me he had something to say and not to get paranoid: 'Look over my shoulder at the four guys seated at the table and tell me what you think of them.' I knew he was panicking, and when I looked over his shoulder I saw four men all dressed in shirts and slacks; but what I noticed most about them was their short-back-and-sides haircuts. I was sure it was the police. Archie said to act cool and finish our drinks, and then calmly get up and leave, but I wanted to throw the table at them and run as fast as I could. As we sat there, the escape story came up on the pub TV. Silence fell as the people there heard about our daring escape. Our photos were flashed on the screen, and the public were told not to approach us as we were dangerous and desperate men. That was a good one – we were the ones who were terrified! A wee drunk man staggered over to our table and started to talk about the escape, telling us he knew the three guys who had done it – he even said he had helped to get them out of the country. 'This

266

is just between the three of us,' he whispered. I felt sure he was a copper in disguise, and I peered over the rim of my sunglasses to get a better look at him. We got up and left, with the wee man still rambling on about how he was in the know.

We walked out of the door and into the sunny street. The four men didn't follow us, which made Archie feel better, but I was still convinced that someone had put LSD in my tea. I was in mental agony. I had never viewed life like this before: I was going mad, and was ready to crack up in the street. I tore the sunglasses from my face and threw them away – I was sick of hiding and running, and couldn't take it any more. Only then, when the dark shades were off my eyes, did I feel any better. The paranoia left me, and I felt ashamed when I remembered all I had said to Watty. Archie was relieved that I had come to my senses and said, 'Johnnyboy, don't touch that hash again, for God's sake'. If I had known hash could have such an effect I'd never have taken it in the first place. It was a terrible experience I'll never forget.

At night Archie and I would go for a walk in our wigs and suits, strolling about the city centre as if we were entitled to be there. It was better than sitting in a house waiting for the police to come. We went on trying to make contact with Jim, without success. I asked Wullie to get in touch with my dad so that we could get away to London instead of running from house to house each night, but he said it was far too risky – he was being watched closely by the police. We heard through the underworld that both the young couple from Penicuik Street and the elderly couple had given statements to the police, incriminating T.C. and Shadow, and they were getting police protection in case they were intimidated.

We decided to head back to the house in Cranhill, get rid of the shotgun and make our way to London. The gun was in a locked cupboard on the outside of the house. It was about midnight when we got there, and since there was no one in we had to hang around hoping that Lana's pal, who owned the house, would come back. Two guys approached and asked us what we were doing there. We couldn't argue with them or we could well end up in gaol for breach of the peace. So we had

267

to run away pretending to be scared. As we ran we were in fits of laughter. Archie reckoned the whole world was going mad; this was the second time drunken bums had threatened to beat him and me up, and he was getting sick of it.

Lana came round, and we decided to stay the night and leave next morning. We learned that the police had arrested Jim. He had agreed to meet some guy in a pub, and when he got there the serious crime squad were waiting. We felt sick at the news. I went to a phone box and rang Barlinnie Prison. When the warder on the gatehouse answered, I told him who I was, and threatened murder should anything happen to my brother.

Next morning Archie went out to make a phone call and to buy something for our breakfast. He took Lana with him so that he could pretend he was her husband, and I was left alone in the house. I was in the kitchen pressing my suit when the phone rang. It was Archie. He said that one of the guys who had helped us had been dragged in by the police – and that Archie had given him our phone number on a scrap of paper.

'Johnnyboy, get out of there now!' he said. I told him he was getting paranoid – I couldn't see the guy keeping the phone number on him for the police to find. I told Archie to come back and bring Lana with him. Then I went on pressing my suit. Beside me lay an Adidas bag containing the gun, the wigs and a few other odds and ends.

Through the window I could see two young-looking guys standing at the foot of the path. A red car drew up, and the driver told them to get away.

I grabbed the bag and ran into the bedroom, panicking I hid it under the bed, then ran back into the kitchen. I cursed myself for not taking Archie's advice about getting out of the house, but it was too late now. Suddenly police were all over the street, and cars were screeching to a halt. I could see that the police were armed. They came up the footpath, and one of them was carrying a sledgehammer. The neighbours were shouting out of their windows. The street was full of men, women and children – I saw the two guys who had threatened to beat us up the night before. I heard the police tiptoeing down the hall, so I called out to them not to shoot as I was unarmed and in the kitchen with my arms raised. One by one they appeared, pointing their guns at me. I stood stock-still in case I made them nervous and one of them shot at me. Then one of them said 'It's Johnnyboy,' and they came rushing in and pinned me to the wall. One of the younger ones asked me where Archie was while the others searched me for weapons. I told him he was in London. He wasn't amused and smashed me across the side of my face with his gun. The madness came out in me, and I asked him if he wanted to have another go at beating me into telling him. But the copper in charge told him I was a tough nut and wouldn't tell him anything, he never bothered me again except to help spreadeagle me on the floor and handcuff my arms behind my back.

They then searched the house. They found the shotgun, and laid it alongside me on the floor. Some of the coppers told me that I had pulled off a great escape, and one even patted me on the shoulder as I lay there.

After about five minutes half of them went rushing out into the street to pick up Lana and Archie, who had just got out of a taxi. A neighbour who had seen us in the house had shouted from her window, alerting the police that Archie was there.

Everyone in the street tried to get a look at us as we were taken to the CID cars, and some shouted 'Cheerio!' and 'Hard luck!' In the police station Archie and I were taken to two different rooms. Almost all the police who came in to look at me congratulated me on making such a daring escape: they were really quite pleasant, much to my surprise. They seemed more interested in the escape than anything else. One of the head CID men said that my dad was the cause of all my troubles. I told him it wasn't so, but he was adamant. When they asked me if I had anything to say, I told them that the lassies knew nothing about the shotgun, but I learned later that Lana and the two other lassies had been charged with harbouring prisoners. Sometime later my cell door opened and about half a dozen CID men came in. They said they wanted to know the name of the Barlinnie Prison warder who had taken a bribe from my dad. I told them they had charged T.C. and Shadow when they had nothing to do with it – and they were wanting me to do them favours? They were quick to tell me there was no real evidence against T.C. and Shadow. I said that I thought they would fit them up for the escape by manufacturing evidence, but they swore they wouldn't. I said I needed to talk to Jim and Archie before I said anything – and when they came back they brought them with them!

We cuddled and shook hands, glad to know we were all fine, apart from my swollen face. The CID told us that we should give the door a kick when we had come to a decision. After discussing what would happen to us when we got back to Barlinnie, we told them we couldn't give the warder's name because that would make life worse for us in gaol. They assured us that we would be granted immunity and sent to any secure prison we wanted. All they wanted was the name of the warder who had taken the bribe. We told them we would give them all the information they needed if they stuck to their word about the immunity and not manufacturing evidence against T.C. and Shadow, they agreed.

We were taken to Glasgow Sheriff Court, where we were remanded and returned to Barlinnie. I hadn't seen Lana since our arrest, but I heard she had been remanded in custody at Cornton Vale women's prison.

It was horrible to see Barlinnie's walls and its huge halls looming up again. We stopped for a moment outside the massive electronic gate; then it opened and in we went. A senior warder came over to me; he was shaking with rage and couldn't open the cuffs, nor could he look me in the eye. I knew him for what he was, and how he condoned violence and beatings. When the cuffs were eventually off, the CID took us through the back door of reception and into a waiting transit van. We were driven to a building near B Hall which was used as an office by the warders. The CID men stayed with us all the time, and there wasn't a warder in sight.

Then we were taken to a room on the ground floor and introduced to an elderly-looking man seated behind a wooden desk and told to sit down. He introduced himself as the Procurator of Glasgow and congratulated us on our daring escape. I asked him what he wanted, and he said he believed we had something to tell him! He tried again and again to get us to give him a statement, but we refused. He said we had nothing to worry about as he had made arrangements to have us protected against the warders, and that we could be transferred to any other security gaol we wanted to go to. We were thankful for this. We were then handed over to the prison authorities who took us to E Hall – the Barlinnie training hall!

Warders had been posted outside our doors on the ground floor of E Hall. It was just like being put on protection – only this time we were being protected from the warders. The coppers had stuck to their word. We weren't allowed out of our cells except to slop out and exercise. The hall was run along the same lines as the training hall at Peterhead: no training of any kind was given, yet when the authorities spoke of it they gave the impression that it was all in your best interests! Every time my door opened I expected warders to rush in and do their dirty work, but it never came.

The governor came to see me. He told me he had received a letter from my dad, asking him to stop anyone beating me up. He said my dad wasn't the same man that he had once known – the long-term gaol sentences had affected his head – and that I should think carefully about this. I couldn't guess what the governor was talking about, but I learned later that my dad had threatened terrible revenge if anything happened to me or Jim.

When the governor asked me which prison I wanted to go to, I asked for Dungavel, which is an 'open' prison. He said no way was I going to an open prison – it had to be a high-security one. So I said Peterhead, because I knew that I would go back there anyway.

We were taken back to Peterhead under a heavy escort of armed police.

After we had changed into prison 'greys' we were taken to the punishment block and locked up. I was to be kept in solitary until I was tried in Glasgow for escaping – which could be anything from a few weeks to a year. The Peterhead warders weren't too pleased with me. I had cut the bars in my cell and made them a laughing-stock; one of their fellow-warders was in trouble because of the bribery allegations; and they'd been worried about us taking revenge on them for the harm they'd done us.

There was a huge puddle on the floor of my cell, and the walls were running wet. I asked to see the prison doctor, and was moved to a cell next to Joe – but it was just as bad as the other. At about 8.30 each night I was told to take my clothes off and put them outside my door. One of the warders threw in two blankets, but no mattress. I waited till the warders went away, and then told the night-shift warder, who was new on the job, that they'd forgotten to give me my mattress. He told me I was on 'guard bed' – a form of punishment in which a prisoner is deprived of his mattress – for seven days for smashing up my last cell.

I managed to break off part of a cast-iron shelf from my cell wall. It was shaped like a machete blade, and after dark I began to hack away at the wall separating me and Joe. Joe started digging from his side. The cell walls were about twenty inches thick and made of huge granite blocks which I placed as quietly as I could on the floor. Eventually I saw Joe's finger appear, and then his head. We laughed and shook hands like long-lost brothers.

By the time the warders realised what was going on, Joe and I had taken half the wall away. I was in Joe's cell and we had barricaded ourselves in with the debris and the huge granite blocks. The warders tried to negotiate with us through Joe's spyhole, but we just continued tearing the wall down. Joe was like me; he couldn't do his time, and we swore we would try to escape as soon as an opportunity arose.

We were so exhausted that we fell asleep, and when we woke up the warders were about to force their way in. They took the cell door down, and came rushing in with riot shields and sticks. They dragged me away to another cell, and Joe was taken away to the silent cell. I was kicked and punched to the floor and handcuffed.

There was nothing in my new cell except a concrete block

for a seat and a bed, a thick wooden door which was bolted to the floor. I took my handcuffs off. The concrete block had been cemented and bolted into the concrete floor, and should I manage to prise it loose it would be too heavy to lift. I tried to budge it again and again. I took a run at it and hit it with the flat of both my feet; it moved a little, and I began to get it loose by running at it and kicking at it. I managed to lift it up and drop it on to the wooden bed, which was shattered to pieces. I then tried to smash the cell door down. It made a terrible noise, and I could hear the warders outside panicking. They came rushing in to get me, but ran out again when they saw me with the huge concrete seat. They couldn't believe it – they'd been boasting about their new concrete seats and how secure they were. I heard them saying I was a nutter and that I should be in a mental hospital. I was crying with rage and frustration, and when they heard this they took the opportunity to speak to me like a human being, saying that if I came out quietly nothing would happen to me.

I came out without resisting and was put in another cell. They put another set of handcuffs on my wrists – this time of the bracelet kind that can be tightened till they dig in. After they'd gone I removed the handcuffs, and once again smashed the wooden door-bed with the concrete stool. They were demented, but they got me out without my resisting or their beating me up. They asked me how I'd managed to get the handcuffs off, but I only laughed and said that if they put them on again I'd take them off again. They then produced a body belt made of thick leather with chains and handcuffs attached to it and tied me into it, taking turns to pull at the belt and chains to make sure they were secure.

After they'd left I managed to slip out of the body belt and chains partly because I was so skinny, but also I'd learnt a trick. I pressed the emergency bell, and when the warder opened the spyhole I was standing there with the body belt held out like a present, and I said, 'Give these back to that fucking teuchter of a chief.'

The chief told me that he had asked the works to make something that I couldn't get out of, and that until it was ready staff would sit in the cell with me to prevent me doing any more damage. We sat there for about four hours, me in one corner and them in another. They seldom spoke to me, and each time I made the slightest move their eyes were on me. They complained that the works warders were taking too long, and that they felt like prisoners themselves, sitting there with a madman.

Eventually I made a deal with the chief and they left me alone with my few luxuries – tobacco and a mattress and a guitar. I was placed on governor's report for damaging the cells. I saw a civilian taking pictures which were to be sent to the Prison Department so that the authorities could see the damage I'd done.

26 THE BARLINNIE ESCAPE TRIAL

A lawyer and a Queen's Counsel came to see me about the escape from Barlinnie. They advised me to plead guilty in the High Court in Glasgow, but I refused. They told me they wouldn't be able to defend me since I was guilty no matter what I said. I told the governor I was citing him as a witness, so that he could testify that it wasn't me who had escaped. He asked me if I would like to see the gaol psychiatrist. I told Jim and Archie that the lawyers weren't going to represent me in court. They couldn't stop laughing when I said that I had told the QC that I had been kidnapped by them, and that that was how I became involved in the escape. Jim's and Archie's defence was that they hadn't escaped – they had fled for their lives, fearing more brutality from the warders.

It came as no surprise when our QCs stood up in the High Court and asked permission to withdraw from the trial. We were left to defend ourselves. Our first witness was Joe McGrath, but when he tried to describe the brutality the judge told him to shut up. That was the end as far as our witnesses were concerned. The authorities knew that we were prepared to put the system on trial and show it up for the monster it is, which was why they stopped Joe in his tracks and had him removed from the courtroom. The judge told the court that it wasn't the penal system that was on trial, but me, Jim and Archie. We did manage to say something about the brutal regime, and I believe the newspapers carried some of it. We

275

were all found guilty. Jim and I were both sentenced to three years in prison, and Archie to four years. Three years on top of the twelve I was already serving only made me even more determined to escape again.

Back in Peterhead, I was determined to find a way out of the hall. I was sitting in my pal Checker's cell on the top gallery one day and I had a good look at his ceiling, which was made of granite. I never said anything to him about it, but I talked to Jim and Archie about having a go at digging through it. They both agreed it was feasible – as long as I did the digging! If we got through the ceiling, it would take us up into the loft. From there we could make our way down the building under the cover of darkness during recreation time – and, with luck, we wouldn't be missed till lock-up time at nine p.m.

I agreed to do the ceiling myself, and slipped into Checker's empty cell with an iron bar. We'd thought about asking Checker to come with us, but we knew he would freak out at such a suggestion and he knew nothing of it. I asked one of the cons to make sure that he stayed out of his cell. In fact Checker and a few others were due to play cards that night, and the guys were prepared to give evidence that he'd been out of his cell throughout the recreation period.

There was a sink outside Checker's door and we left the taps running to smother any noise coming from the cell. I put on my home-made woollen hat to keep the debris out of my hair, and stripped to my shorts. I put some of Checker's belongings in his locker, taking care not to tear his photo-graphs as I took them from the wall. I had to stand on his locker to graft his ceiling, and the debris fell on to his bed. I put some blankets on the floor to stop any chunks of granite from falling heavily on to the concrete. I was almost blinded by the dust, and my eyes were burning. I had to sit down on the bed for a moment, and I got down on my knees to feel for Checker's basin of water so as to wash my eyes. Archie came in to see how I was doing and he bathed my eyes with clean water. That helped, and I tore into the thick granite ceiling again – but it was obvious that the hole wasn't going to be big enough in time. By now it was only half an hour until lock-

276

up. I couldn't leave the cell as it was, so I asked Jim to get me some plain paper and some glue.

By the time he returned I had cleaned up the cell. I had swept the boulders and rubble under the bed, shaken the dust from the blankets and put them back on the bed, and dusted the windows, shelves and walls with a damp rag. The only evidence that remained was a fair-sized hole in the ceiling. I cut the paper to size, but before gluing it over the hole I stuffed some newspapers in so that a dark patch wouldn't show through the paper. The paper blended in perfectly with the lumpy white plaster – no one would have known there was a hole above it. The only tell-tale sign was that the glue on the white paper had a shiny appearance, unlike the rest of the ceiling, so I squirted some Vim over it to make it lose its sheen.

The only other problem was that there was no way we could get all the boulders and rubble out of the cell that night – and if we left it there Checker was sure to find it and panic. I felt I had to tell him. There was no recreation for the next two nights, so it would be Thursday before I could get back in to work on the ceiling. It wouldn't be noticed by the warders so long as we got rid of the debris in the morning. On the top gallery there was a heap of granite and rubble which the works warders, who were fixing a pipe, had left for the passmen to clean up, and I thought we'd put our rubble in with the rest.

I went to find Checker to bring him in and break the news to him. He froze when he saw us, and there was a look of distrust in his eyes. I couldn't really blame him. I asked him to look at his ceiling and tell me if he noticed anything. He couldn't see anything wrong, so I stood him right underneath the hole and asked him to look again. Still he couldn't see anything. I stood on the bed and peeled back the glue-covered paper, and poor Checker had to sit down on the bed while I explained it to him. When I told him I wanted to come back the following Thursday, he agreed to help by pretending that nothing was wrong. I nearly laughed out loud when I asked him to look under his bed – Archie had to give him a drink of water to bring him round.

Next morning we got rid of the rubble, but on Thursday we

were told Checker was in the punishment block for attempting to escape! The warders had got to know about it. We knew he wouldn't grass on us but we had a guilty conscience about him. Rather than see him in the cells, possibly losing remission for nothing I thought that one of us should own up to it and get him out. We decided to draw straws and Jim drew the shortest. We made sure he had tobacco before he went. Jim walked down to the PO on the bottom floor and told him that they had the wrong man. I was sorry to see him go, but I was proud of him for not hesitating to take the rap for Checker.

Next morning Jim went in front of the governor, who said he admired Jim for not letting an innocent man suffer. Jim was locked in punishment for a week or two, and all the charges were dropped against Checker.

T.C. and Shadow had been charged with aiding us in the escape and in October 1980 we appeared in court, handcuffed and with an armed guard, as witnesses for them.

The newspapers, radio and television carried the news of T.C. and Shadow going free. They had been found not proven. There was a large photo of them both standing smiling outside the High Court in Glasgow.

27 THE CAGES OF INVERNESS

There was much tension in Peterhead, and after I'd found myself in more trouble a warder asked me how I felt about going to Carstairs state hospital for the mentally ill. I thought they were only trying to frighten me, but then I realised they were serious. I felt I'd rather die than go anywhere near such a place. I knew I was sane, and I hated the thought of being tagged as a mental patient.

My cell door opened, and a mob of warders beckoned me out. Once I was in reception they pounced on me. They handcuffed my hands behind my back and carried me off to a waiting transit van, which roared out of the gaol to be met by an armed police escort. When I asked where we were going the warders didn't answer, but then I heard one of them talking about the Cages of Inverness. I had heard a great deal about the Cages and the goings-on there. They were thought of by the prisoners as a miniature Carstairs for crazy prisoners, a place for degrading men the system couldn't control.

From where I sat, I could see people walking about the streets, and it looked like they didn't have a care in the world. Sometimes I had to close my eyes on the world beyond the van's windows because it hurt to see the things there. It was like falling in love with someone who you know has turned their back on you.

When at last we reached Inverness, I was surprised to find the gaol in a side street. As we drove through the huge gates the driver shouted out that they had one for the Cages. The

279

Cages are in a separate block, away from the other halls and fenced off by a twenty-foot fence, topped with razor-wire. Six warders were waiting for me – the ratio per prisoner in the Cages. The main corridor was L-shaped – the long part having three cages and a silent cell, and the smaller part two cages facing one another. At the end of the corridor were a steel sink, a toilet and a shower, and two sets of double doors leading out to the fenced-in exercise yard. Each cell door had two spyholes for the warders to look through.

I was stripped of all my clothes, and then taken inside a brilliantly lit 'cage'. It was a cell that had been divided into two with steel bars so as to make a cage within the cell. The wooden bed had been bolted to the concrete floor; the window had a frosted glass sheet over it to stop me looking out and others looking in, and it couldn't be opened. The ventilation system was a metal grille on the wall below the window. The walls were painted pink, the heavy bars a dark green, and the bed a mustardy brown.

I was the only prisoner in the Cages at that time, and I felt really lonely having no one to talk to. I paced up and down the floor, from one wall to the other. I could only take three paces either way, because they had cemented a huge concrete stool into the floor.

All I was allowed in the cage was a pisspot, a plastic mug and a book. Pens, pencils, soap, toothpaste and toothbrush were all forbidden – supposedly to protect the warders from being injured! Outside in the corridor was a lock which controlled the cage door: before the warders opened the cage they always came into the cell to make sure that I hadn't gone mad and wasn't about the attack them.

I couldn't eat my first meal – I couldn't even swallow the soup without taking a mouthful of water with it. I couldn't believe it when I was offered a choice of chicken or a chop! The chop looked good, but it was nearly all bone. I hid the bone: that night I began to work a brick out with it, but was discovered. From then the bones were taken out of my chops. I vomited all over the floor my first night there – I couldn't stand being in that small cage, like an animal.

280

Next morning I was taken to see the governor and informed of the rules. I was told I could expect to stay there up to three months. I could write one letter a week, and as for wages I was to make fish nets for £1.20 per week. Needless to say, the governor said he knew my dad. I asked to see the visiting committee to find out why I was in the Cages as I hadn't used violence. He told me I was here to be punished. When the visiting committee came to see me I asked them for an advanced payment since I had no wages or tobacco. They refused. One might have thought I had asked for the canteen shop!

The warders never let me out of their sight when I was slopping out or exercising.

A works warder spent a few minutes showing me how to make a fish net with a piece of S-shaped metal. He hadn't been out of the cage two minutes before I'd straightened it out till it was about ten inches long. I had to laugh – they wouldn't allow me a pencil, yet I'd been given a tool ten inches long. I bent it back to its S-shape again and sat till dinner time wondering what to do with it. I felt so depressed that I began to think about murdering one of the warders because I couldn't take any more. I put the S-shaped piece of metal in my pocket, and pressed the bell to go to the toilet. I had lost all fear of consequences, and felt no regard for human life. It was a strange feeling.

Once in the toilet, I pretended to be having a shit. I sat there with the weapon in my hand, picturing what might happen. The door on the toilet cubicle was only about two and a half feet high, enabling the warders to see the prisoner's head, shoulders and legs. It was disgusting and degrading: they stood there looking on, and it was even worse when they all stood there in silence, listening. I kept telling myself to go out and stick the weapon into the heart of the nearest warder, but although I felt I had nothing to live for I couldn't bring myself to kill anyone, or even attack someone with my weapon. I wanted to, but something held me back. I began to look on the warders as human beings, just like me. I had a thousand reasons for stabbing them, but I always found one reason not to. I had to do something, but escape seemed the only logical thing and it was easier to do than stab or kill one of the warders. Shaken, I went back to the cage with the concealed weapon and began to check the walls and the brickwork for weaknesses. I noticed that the beans on my dinner plate were almost the same colour as the pinkish paint on the walls, so when I started digging around one of the bricks I used the beans to cover up the hole. When I ran out of beans I had to stop digging. I put the debris into my chamber pot and emptied it. If I heard the slightest movement out in the corridor I pretended to be working. They found the hole one day when they came in to search the cage; they confiscated the tool and refused to let me work again.

My problem with eating was getting worse and I plucked up the courage to see the doctor about it. He came to see me, and he had to ask the warders to let him into the cage – they expected him to examine me through the bars. He seemed to be a gentleman, this tall, young-looking prison doctor in Wellington boots. I told him I couldn't swallow my food; he looked into my throat with his torch and felt my throat and glands, but said he couldn't see anything wrong. When I told him how I had to have water to help me swallow even liquids he seemed puzzled, and said he would consult his colleague.

The following day I was informed that the doctor wanted to see me in the governor's orderly room. I walked in, only to find an old man sitting alone at a desk in the middle of the room, staring slyly at me. He asked me to explain to him about my swallowing, and I waited for him to get up and give me a medical examination, but he never did. Only when he had finished talking to me did he tell me he was a psychiatrist! This scared me, and I thought they were going to certify me. But no – I was sent back to my cage, and the only help the psychiatrist offered was to tell me to chew my food longer than usual.

The warders kept spying on me, so I threw my food at the spyholes. They warned me that I could do my time the easy way or the hard way, and that hard cases like me soon gave in to them. I spat at them and they spat back.

My clothes were put outside the door every night. The cage was lit by a fluorescent tube about six feet long, and it made a constant buzzing sound. I tried to smash it with my plastic pisspot, but it was well protected by a sheet of Perspex. When I complained about it, the warders merely laughed.

I found a piece of pencil in the exercise yard and hid it among some shit in my pisspot so that the warders wouldn't find it. I started to write poems on pieces of toilet roll. I wrote and wrote, seldom tiring of it.

A priest, Father McDonald, visited me every Tuesday evening. He was good company and he laughed heartily when I told him stories about Ma and Maw. When I told him that Maw was blind, and would like to visit me, he immediately offered to pick her up in his car and bring her to the Cages. He used to sit outside the cage with me inside, and there was no warder present. We never said a mass, but I'd whisper so that the warders couldn't hear me confessing to him. Before he left he always shook my hand and promised to pray for me.

Two other guys were brought into the Cages, one of them a pal from Peterhead. It was great to have some company, and at night time we'd shout to each other and tell whatever news there was to be told. At seven p.m. we were allowed a radio on the outside of the cage for an hour. It was a small radio, and the warders had to chain it to the wall to stop anyone lassoing it into the cage.

After three miserable months in the Inverness Cages I was taken back to Peterhead and put in a cell in the punishment block until the governor had seen me. He commented on my swallowing problems, and asked me how it was. I never answered him. He wasn't so sure of himself now, and he said he thought I would have learned my lesson while in the Cages.

That day I was allowed into the hall again. Everyone said I'd lost weight and that I was the colour of death; my eyes had sunk into my sockets and my face had collapsed inwards. I never told anyone about my not being able to swallow my food at the Cages, but it took me some time to get round to swallowing food again.

The police who had arrested us when we were on the run came to see us. They wanted a statement about the warder in Barlinnie who was supposed to have taken the bribe, but they left empty-handed and furious. We decided not to give them a statement or help them with their inquiries in any way, because we would get too much hassle. They also asked me for a statement for the Procurator concerning Lana and the other two lassies who had been arrested for harbouring us, but again they got nothing.

Some time late in the summer of 1981, I received a citation from the Crown to appear at the Glasgow High Court as a witness in the trial of Lana and her two friends. We picked up Archie, who had been transferred to Aberdeen, and from there we were taken to Barlinnie.

We were never called by the Crown to give our evidence. We were told we weren't required, and although we demanded to be taken into court, we were refused. The lady who owned the house was found 'not proven', and Lana's pal was given a six-months deferred sentence and released there and then. Lana was sentenced to one year in prison for harbouring us, and her children were put into a foster home till she got out. I was heartbroken and cursed myself for getting Lana involved. I was now more determined than ever to escape.

I said goodbye to Archie at Aberdeen, and then I was taken away to Peterhead under armed escort. In Aberdeen a Highland prisoner made a snide remark about Lana. He was stabbed for it – and who should get the blame but Archie, who was moved back to Peterhead as a result.

28 SAVAGE STRENGTH

Have you clung to prison bars
With a madness never known,
Sought the savage strength
You need to see you through?
Felt like one of many failures
Trying to make it on your own
And one of them will make it – God knows who!

Not long after Lana's trial some cons asked me if I would like to join them in a riot. They were going to storm the cookhouse and smash everything in sight. They had had enough of the gaol's shitty food. I sympathised, but I wasn't interested in the food, however bad it was. I was more interested in trying to escape, and I said so to a guy called Franco, who had approached me about the cookhouse; and he agreed with me. Franco and I managed to talk the cons out of rioting in the cookhouse and into escaping with us.

It was a kamikaze escape, but we reckoned that at least some of us would make it. A new punishment block was being built next to the tailor's shop – rumour had it that it was needed because of the damage I had done to the old one. They hadn't laid down the foundations yet, but they had fenced off the area, and there were ladders lying around. Twelve of us would rush in and snatch the ladders while others held back the warders. This was to be done at the weekend, at three o'clock in the afternoon, during recreation. Although I was on strict security and wasn't allowed out in the football field area, I was to disguise myself and hope to get away with it. Failing that I would rush through the two massive gates that led to the football field, run down the Burma Road and crash through the wooden door into the compound where the new punishment block was being built.

A few days before we were going to escape I was called to the governor's orderly room and told that I was to be kept in solitary confinement. Franco was also to be locked up. We were both moved into D Hall to serve our punishment. I asked the governor why I had been locked up, and he told me, after giving me a long stare, that had I gone ahead and done what he had been told I was going to do I would have been a sorry lad. I would stay in D Hall till he was ready to let me out.

After a month the governor sent for me to have a talk before he allowed me back into circulation. He told me he was taking a chance in letting me back into the hall, and asked me not to cause him any more bother. He also said that he was going away soon to another prison, and he hoped I did not have any escape plans. I was eventually moved into a special security cell on the third gallery of A Hall. Franco was taken out of solitary confinement on the same day as I was. We never found out who had grassed on us.

In October 1981 I tried to escape again, hoping to get out of this hell. I started cutting through my bars and got plenty of background music from my neighbour, Skylark, to drown the noise of the cutting. My pal, 'Bald Eagle', wanted to come with me, as did a couple of other guys who had heard me sawing my bars. Each time I finished cutting a bar I filled it with wood filler and painted it over till it was unnoticeable I never cut the bars completely through – I always left them on a thread, so that when the warders shook them or hit them with their truncheons they wouldn't fall off. I only cut them through completely at the very last minute.

We planned to leave on a Friday night just when recreation

was starting, so as to give us a bit of time before they discovered we were missing at lock-up at nine. We had our clothes, a bag of chocolates and tobacco for our journey into the wilderness that surrounded Peterhead. Jim didn't want to escape any more, and was trying to settle down: I was glad of this and wished I could do the same, but I couldn't. He helped saw the bars.

By Friday night we hadn't sawn the bars as much as was needed. We were short of another half hour. Jim said the only thing was for me to go alone during the night, but the Bald Eagle and Burnsy pleaded with me to let them come too. I couldn't let them down after they'd put so much effort into cutting the bars and getting the plans made up, so I decided to wait until the Saturday. I knew I was taking a risk, and all that night I paced about, wondering if I should in fact go by myself, immediately.

I had painted all the bars; I had to stick back one that had come off completely, hoping it would pass inspection in the morning. I had no glass panes in my window frame, so I had to borrow some from guys who had managed to get them out of their own windows without damaging them. I stuck them on with cleaning paste and painted them over. Next morning I heard banging from outside the hall, and when I looked out of my window I could see warders with ladders checking all the bars and hitting them with a mallet. I quickly knocked on the wall and told Skylark what was happening. He put a mirror out of his window and saw some warders up ladders on our side of the building, only a window away from me. Everybody was at their windows, wondering what was happening. I pressed my bell to go to the toilet, from where I could watch the warders banging on the bars of my window with a mallet. My heart sank – and yet when I returned to my cell no one was there and the window bars were as I had left them. Skylark told me the warders hadn't noticed that my bars had been cut. How they missed them was a miracle. . . .

Jim and the Skylark advised me to hold off till the afternoon recreation period, as the warders were on their toes. The warder on my gallery was the one who was infamous for killing prisoners' pet pigeons, and on the afternoon that I was preparing to escape, I was told that the pigeon killer had been in my cell! I was talking to a pal at the time, and when I looked up at my cell on the gallery above I saw that the door had been locked. I wanted to lie down and die. I had spent night after night cutting the bars till my fingers were raw, blistered and bleeding, and I felt furious with frustration. Big John, my pal, sensed this, and tried to persuade me not to do anything crazy. I left his cell and walked upstairs towards my own. Everyone knew about my sawing through my bars, and they were all watching me. As I approached my cell I saw the pigeon killer coming up the other flight of stairs, staring at me with an evil grin on his rotten face. I wondered if that was how he looked at the pigeons. . . . I looked through the spyhole on my locked door and saw that one of the bars had been removed. The pigeon killer stood at the top of the stairs, only a few feet from me, and asked me to come along with him downstairs to the punishment block.

I later learned that the warder in charge had told the pigeon killer not to approach me until they had locked everyone inside their cells, but he couldn't wait. His expression changed when I said, 'There's no way I'm walking down the stairs with you – ya fucking grass!' The hall suddenly went very quiet – everybody was watching and waiting. The pigeon killer warned me that I would be sorry for this later, and I told him he would be fucking sorry – now. I attacked him then and there, at the top of the stairs. I kicked him, butted him with my head, and punched him. I felt others grab me from behind. I remember them all on top of me; one of them had me in a stranglehold and was choking me, while the others held my arms and legs. Then Jim appeared with a pool cue in his hand, demanding that the warders let me go. I managed to get one of my hands free, so I grabbed the pigeon killer's balls and squeezed them. Instantly he let my neck go. As I looked in his eyes and saw the fear in them, I laughed in his face and asked him who was sorry now. But before he got the chance to answer Jim had crashed the pool cue over his head.

By now warders were appearing from everywhere. I'd had

the shirt torn off me and I jumped on to the hotplate and started throwing steel trays and bowls at them. Two warders were on the floor with Jim, one of them the pigeon killer. I jumped off the hot-plate with a tray in my hand and ran to help Jim. I brought the steel tray down hard on the pigeon killer's head, and he let Jim go and crawled away. I jumped back on to the hot-plate. The riot bell was ringing, but I kept on throwing trays and bowls at the warders and screaming at them to fight me.

Some of the warders tried to calm me down, and Jim and the others urged me to surrender, but I couldn't stop: as far as I was concerned the Peterhead Mafia were getting a dose of their own medicine. And there was nothing to surrender for, except to go back to the punishment block.

Warders were lying on the floor, groaning, and dozens more were coming up the stairs – but they couldn't get near me. When I came to my senses and saw the pigeon killer, with blood on his face, holding his balls, and the other warders pleading with me to surrender, I suddenly felt sorry for them: I had caught a glimpse of what lay beneath their uniforms and realised that they were no different from us.

One of the POs said, 'I'll take you down, Johnnyboy, and make sure nothing happens to you.' I knew him from being locked up in solitary, where he was quite sympathetic towards me – he had passed me tobacco from Jim when I shouldn't have been getting any – and I decided to give myself up.

When I reached the double doors of the cells some warders came towards me as if they were going to beat me up, but the PO told them to leave me alone. They didn't seem too pleased at that. I was stripped of my trousers and pants and shoes, and thrown into a cell. I could hear thumps, and Burnsy and Big Tam screaming: I kicked at the door with my bare feet and shouted at them to leave them alone. It's horrible to be in a cell, listening to guys being beaten up and screaming. I was so furious that when the warders opened my cell door I ran out with two bits of my shit in my hands.

I refused to take in my bedding, and threw out everything in the cell, including the pisspot. A warder brought it back and told me I would need it during the night, but I told him that from now on they could clean up my shit and piss. When they came next they removed a pile of shit I had stored in a corner, and when I realised what they were doing I made a dive for it and tried to throw it at them. I refused to wear my clothes. I was sick of wearing drab grey clothing that didn't fit me and made me look even skinnier than I was. I put on a pair of large pyjama trousers, the old-fashioned type that tie at the waist with a piece of cord. I ripped them at the knees, and I wore nothing else. However uncomfortable I was, I enjoyed knowing that the bastards wouldn't have the pleasure of telling me to put my clothes outside the cell door each night. Nor could they take my mattress from me in the early morning; it went too. If I had nothing, there wasn't anything they could take from me, in a material sense. I knew the one thing they wanted was my spirit.

Next day I was taken to the governor's orderly room, where he told me that I was to be remanded in the punishment block for assaulting warders and attempting to escape. He was worried that I wouldn't stop fighting the system. I informed him that it was my sanity I was fighting for – not that he was interested. He seemed more concerned that I hadn't put on my clothes when appearing before him as a sign of respect. For me there was only one way out: my sentence was getting ever-longer it was up to fifteen years – and I was becoming more desperate.

A few days later I was taken away to the Cages again, still wearing my torn-off pyjama trousers. I was filthy black and stinking, and the warders argued about who was going to be handcuffed to me in the van. On the way out I laughed in the faces of the warders who were cleaning my shit off the floor, calling them toilet attendants.

Back at the Cages, I wouldn't wear gaol clothes and kept my pyjama trousers on. The warders expected trouble from me – not so much the violent kind, but refusal to co-operate and attempts at escaping. They searched me thoroughly, looking for concealed weapons – even as much as a plastic comb. I was put into a cage at the end of the long corridor –

it was a little bit bigger than those in the short corridor. One of the warders said I must like it there to have come back. I spat at him, and the others threw me into the cage and locked it before I could make another move. They shouted that I was an animal and would be treated as such.

On the wall outside the cage, facing the bars, was a small square mirror, and I could see myself looking out of the cage. I stared at my white face, and kept going back for another look. I wondered why the mirror was there, and whether it was a two-way mirror through which they could watch me.

A funny thing happened shortly after my arrival. The chief warder came to see me, and he asked me if I was innocent of the charges for which I had been sentenced to twelve years. I told him I was guilty, but he said he didn't believe me – I must be innocent, no man could cause as much trouble as I had if he wasn't innocent. He told me that if I wanted to study law, I could have pens, paper and law books in my cage, and that there were many good lawyers in Inverness who would help me take my case to the European Court of Human Rights and prove my innocence! I had to laugh.

About this time my dad had a massive heart attack, and couldn't do much for himself. I must confess I wasn't very upset when I learned of this. I couldn't really have cared if he died, but I was concerned for Ma, so I prayed that my dad wouldn't die too soon. He still wrote to me, trying to persuade me to be good. Ma came to visit me at the Cages with her friend, Mary Carroll, whom everyone mistook for her sister. As usual they complained about how thin and pale I was. I lied to Ma, telling her I felt fine and was eating my food. I had to keep repeating myself through the wire when talking to her – she had bad hearing, and it seemed to be getting worse. She told me that Maw was still going strong, and that she kept talking about me and missed me and cried over the thought that she'd never be with me again. News like this had me crying inside.

At night I'd get the urge to write some verse, and having no pen or pencil I used my excreta to write on the walls, just as one would write on a blackboard. By the morning I had written dozens of poems, and when it was time to write my weekly letter I would copy the poems on the walls into a book or on to a piece of toilet roll. The shit was horrible to handle, but I had got used to it by now: I had been living for so long like a caveman with nothing but raw intelligence to get me through each day. Verses were flowing out of me, and when the authorities realised that writing was keeping me quiet, I was allowed a piece of lead from a pencil and some paper.

Father McDonald continued to visit me every week, and sometimes I'd recite to him verse which I had written. I became very friendly with this wee gentleman. I told him that if I ever got out of gaol and was getting married, I'd like him to do the service. I even used to clean up my cage for his visits.

I was charged with assault and taken to Peterhead Sheriff Court. I pleaded guilty, and a further four months was added to my sentence.

I spent another Christmas and New Year in the Cages. The warders told me that they'd be glad to see me back at Peterhead because I caused them nothing but trouble. There was one warder there whom I hated in particular. As he walked, both his arms swung to and fro at the same time and it made him look like he had a humph, so that was the nickname he was given: 'Humphy'! Every time I saw him I'd say: 'Hi, Humphy!'

No sooner was I back in Peterhead than I was looking for a way out again.

29 SPARE THIS MAN

When I was very young and my dad was drunk he would say: 'When I die, son, I want you to make sure that I'm buried in the garden in front of our house.' But even though he was in such ill health, I couldn't imagine him dying. He couldn't walk more than a few yards without his walking-stick, and he had to get permission to be driven into the gaol in Mary's car when he came to visit us; but he still looked as smart as ever, and even more like Lee Marvin. I was sorry to see him so frail. He asked me to behave myself and not put my ma into an early grave by causing her worry. I found myself praying for my dad that night in my cell. I never saw him again. He died in March 1982, a few days before my twenty-sixth birthday. Jim and I were shattered and depressed, and I wondered how Ma would be able to cope on her own with Maw now that Brenda had married.

The governor told us that Ma wanted us out to attend the funeral, but that he couldn't get any warders to take us! It seemed the bastards were pleased to hear that my dad was dead. Some of them told me they were sorry, but I thought otherwise. Eventually the governor told us that he had managed to find six warders, none of whom had had any trouble with us, to take us to Dad's funeral, and he promised us that we'd be able to wear civilian clothes. He told us they knew what sort of people would be at the funeral – meaning that there would be many gangsters there from all over the country – and he warned us not to try to escape as there would be armed police present.

I had never been to a funeral, and I didn't know how I would react. Dad was to be cremated, and his last wish was that his ashes be scattered over the East End of Glasgow. There were hundreds of people there to attend the mass. Ma was helped in by Brenda and Lana – she was all dressed in black and sobbing her heart out – but Maw had to stay at home – she was too old and frail to come out. All my uncles and aunts and some cousins were there, and many people whom I hadn't seen for years. As the priest said mass I saw the casket containing my father slowly disappearing under the floor. I whispered goodbye to him, to the father I hardly got to know.

Father, spare this man
Whom you call son.
'Twas you drew up the master plan
Which produced us, one by one....

After the mass everyone in the chapel came past Jim and me to say how sorry they were and to wish us luck. We managed to speak to Ma in the back of the transit van for about fifteen minutes. We tried to comfort her, and she begged me to stop fighting the system and get out before she too was in her grave. We didn't want to stay much longer because all our relatives had gathered round the van and were trying to speak to us through the windows, so we said goodbye. We could see the police vans parked about the area, and we had been told by some of my dad's friends that the police were video-recording the people going into the chapel.

When I got back to A Hall, and went upstairs to my cell, who should be on the gallery but the pigeon killer, staring at me. I went into my cell and put my belongings into the cupboard. The door opened, and the pigeon killer came in. He warned me that he hadn't forgotten about my attacking him. Just then another prisoner, Bill, came into my cell. He had been a friend of my dad's, and he was the biggest con in the gaol – about six foot four, with the weight to go with it. The pigeon killer turned white when Bill walked straight up to him, never taking his eyes off him, and asked me if everything was okay. I said I was fine, gave him a wink of approval and told the pigeon killer to get out. There was an atmosphere in the hall, and everybody could sense trouble: but the other warders never interfered, and I found out that later some of them were disgusted at the problems they could do without.

The new governor told me any time I felt like cracking up or was having difficulty doing my time, I was to let him know and he would lock me up in solitary! The idea of this he said, was to save me from getting myself into further trouble. It hurt me to hear his solution to my problems, and getting up to leave I told him to fuck off. 'You're missing the point!' he called after me, and I answered: 'So are you.'

My dad's sister Mags came to visit me. I couldn't remember her as I'd only been a wee laddie when I last saw her. She showed me some photos, including one of her babysitter, Margaret. She told me that Margaret had been with my dad when he died, and had tried to revive him and given him the kiss of life. Mags and Ma had been on holiday in Spain at the time – he died the day before they arrived home. Poor Ma had stepped off the plane clutching the presents she had bought for my dad.

I asked Aunt Mags if she would ask her good-looking babysitter to be my pen pal. Mags said she couldn't wait till she got back home to tell her, and for the rest of the visit she boasted about how lovely her babysitter was. Margaret wrote and asked if she could visit me. She came with Mags, and she was indeed lovely looking, with beautiful green eyes. I could see she was shy, and must have felt awkward sitting across from me and having to put up with my staring at her. I felt shy and awkward too, but I wanted to make an impression on her, so I said some funny things which had her laughing. Jim was there as well: he told Aunt Mags that the babysitter and I were in love already, which had Margaret laughing shyly.

*

In May 1982, I was cited to appear at the Inverness Court to give evidence on behalf of a friend; so were Burnsy and two other pals of mine. We were told that we would be kept overnight in the Inverness gaol – not in the Cages, but in the main gaol. The warders there weren't too pleased to see us: they expected trouble, so they kept us locked in our cells. I'd smuggled in two steel rods and I passed one to Burnsy. We'd dug a hole in the wall big enough to put our heads through by the time the warders caught us. They took the rods and removed everything, but left us in the cells. On the cell floors at Inverness gaol there is lino, which I was surprised to see, for there's certainly none at Peterhead or the Cages. I lifted it up to see if anyone might have hidden a knife under it which could help us to tunnel through, but there was nothing. The lino, I noticed, had a kind of canvas material stuck to the bottom of it and it was so stiff that to try and bend it or roll it up broke it. I had an idea which seemed ridiculous: I broke a length of the lino off. It was about six feet long and four or five inches wide, just like a plank of wood. The cell walls were made of red house-bricks with half an inch of mortar between each one of them. I gave Burnsy one end of the lino through into his cell, and resting it on the mortar between the bricks, we started sawing – and it was doing the trick, though every little while we had to replace the lino with a new bit because it was wearing away with the friction. I had to stop because I couldn't keep from laughing at our luck. Suddenly, on the other side of the spyhole, we saw a warder who was shouting: 'I don't believe this!' I had managed to squeeze through in beside Burnsy where both of us, in our excitement and knowing we had fucked them, were doing a Highland jig around the cell. We agreed to take the rest of the wall down, so I went back into my own cell and put the lino through and sawed away. . . . They came in and dragged us both to different cells. I lost another fourteen days remission and got a fifty-pound fine. The Inverness warders were glad to see the back of us and I was told I'd never be allowed back into Inverness gaol again, for any reason.

*

One day we heard rumours that Big Tam had been badly beaten up after falling into a trap laid for him by one of the warders. My heart went out to Big Tam, but when I told the warder in charge, he just laughed and said that if Big Tam was being beaten up by the staff he must have deserved it. We rioted, chasing the warders off the third and fourth galleries, smashing what we could and throwing beds over the galleries on to the warders below. At the top of the stairs we made a barricade of toilet seats, sinks and beds to stop the warders rushing us in their protective riot gear. The governor came in while I was taking off a cell door, and asked me what it was all about. I told him that Big Tam had been badly beaten, and that we wanted an inquiry into brutality in the punishment block. It was hard for him to hear what I was saying because the cons were still busy wrecking the gallery. He told me I should petition the Secretary of State if I had any complaints about brutality, and that there'd be no retaliation if we surrendered – which, in the end, we did.

We went quietly, one at a time, to the punishment block, where we were stripped of our clothes. They came round later and beat us up for rioting and assaulting the warders. They had on their riot gear, so it was pointless to fight back.

So there I was, back in my pyjama trousers and without any bedding. I covered the cell in my own shit, and I would run out the door covered in shit and throw handfuls of it at the warders' desk. Every day the warders had to clean up the shit which had been thrown at them. It was a good weapon, and one the warders feared.

I appeared before the visiting committee in May 1982. For my part in the rioting and assaults I lost 365 days remission. I had hardly any remission left on my twelve-year sentence, so they took it from my three-year sentence. When I pointed out that they couldn't take remission from a sentence I hadn't even started, the governor said that the Secretary of State had accumulated all my sentences for the purpose of depriving me of my remission if necessary. I was fined twenty-five pounds and given twenty-eight days solitary confinement.

'I hope this will be a bloody lesson to you, Steele, once and for all,' one of them said as I was being taken away to my cell. It would be almost a year before I got out of the punishment block – but it wasn't a lesson, it was just another punishment, and nothing more.

At nights I was in agony from my stomach. I thought that maybe I had an ulcer. It was difficult to dig through the cell walls while holding my stomach with one hand. I had been complaining about the pain to the doctor for quite some time. I asked to be taken to the hospital for an X-ray, but they were reluctant to do this because I was a security risk. My Aunt Mary and Mick wrote to the governor, complaining about my health and asking for an 'independent' doctor to examine me. The governor told Mary that I had been thin and ill-looking for as long as he could remember.

If it hadn't been for Mick and Mary I wouldn't have had an X-ray – which gave me the all-clear – nor would I have been taken to the hospital to check me for an ulcer. Again I got the all-clear. The prison doctor told me the results, and I told him I didn't believe one word he said, so he let me read the results myself, and even then I called him a liar. His job appeared to me to be to see if I was fit for the punishments the governor handed out.

A few weeks after the meeting of the visiting committee the governor told me that I had had 365 days remission restored on a technicality. But a few days later he started taking some of the restored remission back again because I was, they claimed, going crazy. I destroyed every cell they moved me to, and I was destroying them faster than the works warders could repair them. They put in a new type of Perspex, unbreakable window-pane but I removed the first one to have a look at it while the warder was installing the second. They were right – it was solid and unbreakable, and I began using it to dig out a brick from around the window. It was better than some of the best tools that I had ever managed to get hold of. I was taking the brick out of the wall when they came in and dragged me to another cell.

*

298

Margaret continued to write and to visit me. I began to call her 'Honeybugs', soon we were talking love – which was crazy, because we couldn't possibly have a future together as I had years to serve. When Honeybugs and Aunt Mags visited me I was usually in solitary confinement or the Cages. I didn't tell them about the conditions I was in, but pretended everything was fine. Even though I had taken a shower and put on clean clothes before the visit, Honeybugs always said there was a funny smell – I told her it must be off 'them', pointing at the warders. I was in love with her, and I guess my Auntie Mags knew this, for she would say things like 'I think yous would make a lovely couple,' and we would laugh. I'd sit and stare at Honeybugs while she blushed and lowered her eyes, and after each visit I gave her a long kiss. My pal Franco made a huge teddy bear for her, and Big Bill, my dad's pal, made a jewellery box out of rosewood with the name 'Honeybugs' on it. She was very chuffed with her presents. Afterwards I would lie in my cell and wonder what Honeybugs was doing at that moment. I thought of her standing at her ma's cooker with her apron on making dinner, or I'd imagine her there beside me and off I'd go with her on cloud nine. Whenever I got a letter from her I had to light a cigarette before I read it, I was so excited. But being in love was just as bad as being in gaol. It was torture just to sit at a table and talk. It might have been better if I could have put my arm around her and gone for a long walk, but that was forbidden. I could feel my love for her growing stronger, which made doing my time seem even worse. I had to get away from love somehow: I knew that sooner or later we would both end up being hurt.

Because there was no heating in the cells I had to light fires to keep me warm, with matches smuggled in by the passmen. I always lit them immediately below my window so that the smoke would go up and out, but sometimes the wind blew it into the cell. The warders didn't seem to bother much. There was nothing to burn except some old books or newspapers. One morning the governor discovered me sitting at my little fire: there was a lot of blackish smoke because I had put my slippers on the fire to make it last longer. He said he didn't really mind the fires – considering there was no heating installed – provided I burned newspapers only. He wondered why, if I was cold, I didn't take my bedding in when I had the chance, or why I wouldn't wear my clothes. In fact I had ripped one of the sleeves off my jumper to use as a hat, and the warders had been told to remove any clothing I had damaged and not replace it. All my clothes were either torn or covered in shit. As a result, I was naked apart from a garment I had made from some floor cloths stolen from the toilet.

There were hundreds of flies in my cell because of the shit and stench, and they were breeding. They swarmed all over my food; when it was dark I could hear nothing except the flies buzzing around. I would spend hours killing them and throwing the maggots I found amongst the food slops in my cell out of the window. My food was always cold and insufficient, and they wouldn't give me plastic utensils because they said I could tunnel through walls with them. One of the cells I was moved to was crawling with lice, and had to be fumigated and left for twenty-four hours before anyone was put into it. The lice were everywhere. They seemed to come out from under the paintwork. To stop the lice from crawling on me I set fire to a piece of towel and let it burn out: then I took the burnt black material and rubbed it all over my naked body. I stayed like this until they fumigated my cell and rid it of the lice.

A warder from the surgery came to see me one day and warned me that if I didn't stop they would have to give me some injections for my own good. I knew the sort of injections he meant: the brain-numbing kind. It frightened me to know they were serious.

'What else can we do?' he said when he saw the expression on my face.

I felt fear of a kind I hadn't known before, and I told them that I would kill if anyone attempted to come near me with a needle. It was either kill or be killed. . . . After they had left me alone I gave much thought to my life – what it was all about and where it was taking me: I had cousins and aunts and uncles out there in the decent world whom I didn't know. I had hardly known my own family – my dad especially. I hadn't even lived. I had been running most of my life and couldn't stop. I promised myself I would make an extra effort to comply with prison rules and get to fuck out of this hell hole. But no sooner had I thought of trying to settle down when the panic came over me at the thought of trying to get through fifteen years and four months. I didn't have it in me to serve that length of time: for me to settle down was merely wishful thinking.

In the mornings, when the warders came to take me to the governor's room to be punished, I refused to walk – which meant they had to carry me, wearing surgical gloves to protect them from the shit on my body. They'd dump me on the floor of the orderly room while the report was read out.

One day a warder threw me a canvas sleeping bag. I tied this up to my window and jumped into it. When they came to take me away to the orderly room, I refused to get out of it, because at the bottom of the bag I had some bits of metal which I had taken off a steel grille on the outside of the window. I curled down at the bottom of the sleeping bag, clutching the tools – which I wrapped in a piece of towel to stop them rattling. The warders turned the bag upside down and shook it, but I had jammed myself tight inside it. In the end they had to drag me down the stairs and into the orderly room in the bag, which they placed in front of the governor's desk in an upright position, and I heard the governor ask them if they were sure I was in the bag. After he'd read out the report I heard once again: 'Have you anything to say to the charge?' and of course, once again they heard: 'Fuck, you, and your charge, you bastards.' I was dragged away in the bag.

They stopped putting me on report for a while even though I was still rebelling: the punishment block was out of commission because I had damaged all the cells in it.

They would make us go for exercise in the 'pens', come hail, rain or snow. I was in the third pen one day, and I heard Frank screaming. I told the warder on the catwalk to let me in, but he ignored me. I stripped off the pyjama shorts I was wearing and threw them over the wire at the top of the sixteen-foot wall and on to the corridor roof. I knew that the only way to get through the razor-wire was to go naked so as not to get one's clothes tangled in it. The warder on the catwalk was at the first pen, and had his back to me. Putting one hand on one wall and one hand on the other, I crawled up the wall through the razor-wire and on to the corridor roof, where I put my pyjama trousers back on.

The riot bell was ringing as I climbed on to the roof of the punishment block. I threw down slates and smashed some thirty windows. When I looked inside I could see warders running for shelter from the falling sheets of glass. The cons in the exercise yard and on the football field cheered me on. The warders were furious that I had got out of the pen – no one had ever done so before. They put it around that I was mad, and that only a madman would do such a thing. Eventually I came down of my own accord because – for the first time on a roof, I felt dizzy and frightened that I was going to fall off.

On the way to the surgery I felt like fainting, but I had to fight it. I couldn't pass out now: I was terrified that the surgery warders would give me an injection when I was unconscious. They had begun cleaning the cuts on my body with antiseptic when I saw the needles. They told me not to panic as it was penicillin. I could hear the high-pitched noise in my head and ears, the warning sign that I was about to black out. Still dizzy, I pushed the surgery warders away, saying I didn't want any injections. Apparently I was the colour of death. I managed not to pass out, and they took me back to the punishment block.

After this I was handcuffed to a warder whenever I was allowed out to exercise. Out of the blue one day the warder told me that there was a lot he could do for me if I would co-operate with him. I asked him what he wanted, and much to my surprise he asked me to be an informer for him, since no one in his right mind would ever suspect me. I refused to do it – I wasn't going to grass on anyone.

Whenever I went to the orderly room and started screaming

abuse, they would put on a tape-recorder and hold the micro-phone to my mouth! This was meant to put me off shouting and cursing, but it didn't. A warder then told me that the tape-recordings were being analysed by psychiatrists, but that didn't stop me either. I knew the warders were having a lot of meetings about me, and wondering what they could do with me. It was even suggested that I should be left in the exercise pen all day with a huge lump of granite and a hammer and chisel.

One day, when I was coming back from the exercise pen, I saw some works warders smashing the window-panes out of three cells near the warders' desk. Three of us were moved into these cells, from which everything had been removed, including the paper plates and the pisspots. Not even a sheet of paper was allowed in. The absence of window-panes didn't bother me at first, but one night I almost froze. I wasn't allowed a blanket at any time, night or day – all I had on was my pyjama shorts and a pair of slippers. I sat below the window so as to keep the bitter North Sea wind off me: if I sat down and put my bare back to the wall, it was like being touched by an ice cube. I tried walking to keep my blood circulating, but then the wind got at me. I cowered back into the corner below the window like a frightened animal, fearing the worst. I took off my slippers and sat on them to stop the cold concrete getting into me, and I tried to rub my feet with my numb hands. Too weak to kick the door for help, I shouted for the warders through the broken spyhole. When they eventually came to see what I wanted, I asked for a blanket, but they refused, on orders. I tried pulling my head down into my shoulders and rocking to and fro, but that didn't help. Again I called on the warders and asked them for something to keep me warm, even a sheet of newspaper – but no. I was in agony again from the pain in my belly, and they agreed to get a surgery warder. By now I was shivering violently, and the wind was howling in through the window. Then I had another idea. I squatted and leaned right back till my head was almost on the ground and my body arched; then I urinated over my belly and chest so that it ran warmly down to my shoulders and neck. The heat felt great – but it didn't last long, and before long the urine had frozen.

The surgery warder was a decent type. He told the warders to give me my bed – but they said they had been left strict instructions to give me nothing, not even a sheet of newspaper to wrap around me. The surgery warder then went away, and came back with a huge tin in his hand. In the tin was a deep-heat rub ointment, which he rubbed all over my body. He warned me that I would feel as though I was burning, and he was right. It felt as if I was coming back from the dead, and I could have cried with joy.

About a month after I had been charged with assaulting three warders while on the roof, I was again charged with assault. The incident had happened in August 1982. There had been five or six warders on duty, and they were known throughout the jail as the 'dog squad', because they acted like dogs and treated us like dogs.

I had walked up to Frank's door and looked through his spyhole to see if he was still there as he had been very quiet. I saw him on the floor, cuffed by his legs and arms; he was gagged around the mouth and it looked as though he couldn't breathe properly. I went berserk and attacked the warders. I managed to get away from them, and I ran into the toilet cubicle, where I jumped on to the seat and started kicking them. I managed to rip out the ballcock from the cistern and used it as a club, raining it down on their heads. The toilet cubicle was pretty small, making it difficult for them to get at me, so they used a mop to try to throw me off balance. They had all lost their hats as they fought with me. But before long they got me, and I could feel the blows from their truncheons as they dragged me back to my cell. Blood was pouring from a head wound and running down my face, but I couldn't feel any pain – and then I fell unconscious.

The three of us were moved from the windowless cells to cells that was almost pitch-black. Once my eyes had got used to the dark I saw that a huge steel sheet covered the entire window, blocking out the daylight. I felt around the cell. There was a mattress and bedding on the floor, a cardboard table

304

and chair, and a pisspot. In a hole above the door there hung a dim light-bulb which lit up part of the ceiling. In front of the light bulb was a sheet of unbreakable Perspex to stop me from getting at the bulb, or climbing through the hole. The heating had been fixed and hot air was coming in through the ventilator high on the wall: a huge sheet of Perspex outside the window prevented a breeze from getting into the cell, which was boiling.

Some tiny holes had been drilled in the steel grille, but I covered them with food slops and shit till no light got in at all; and with a match I had been given I set fire to the sheet of Perspex, which melted easily enough, so that I could reach through and break the bulb. The cell was now in complete darkness. I ripped my foam mattress into thousands of small chunks, and the table got torn up as well.

When the warders opened my door next morning they couldn't see a thing. They came back with a flashlight and shone it round, but they couldn't see me lying under all the bits of torn-up foam. They prodded it with a mop handle to find where I was.

I seldom emerged from my 'cave', though I had to read my letters in the exercise pen. The governor told the warders to leave me alone, and they did. I was in one helluva mess, and in my 'cave' I could shed tears without fear of being seen. Sometimes crying helped, and sometimes not, but singing always did, and I went through most of Jim Reeves' songs as I lay in the darkness of the cave.

'Eddie', the passman, told me that they were using the darkened cell as an experiment – and that they were livid because it had backfired, and they didn't know what to do with me any more.

I don't know how many weeks I was kept in the dark, but they soon tired of not being able to see me, and put me back in an ordinary cell before my case came up at the Peterhead Sheriff Court. The governor had often told me to get myself a lawyer, but I knew if I did I wouldn't convey the full story to the court. He said I wasn't capable of presenting my own case, but that if I pleaded guilty, he would write a plea of mitigation to give the judge. I told him he was also cited for attempting to pervert the course of justice by trying to influence me into pleading guilty. He was raging at me when he got a citation to appear as a witness at my trial.

At Peterhead Court I was approached by a lawyer who said he had been appointed by the court to defend me. I told him to fuck off – I didn't need him or anybody else. I had five assault charges against me, all on the one indictment, but I didn't realise that I was on an indictment: I thought it was a Sheriff summary, in which case the longest sentence I could get would be six months. I had no desire to go through with a trial – I just wanted to plead guilty and get it over and done with, even though I hadn't done half of the things the warders said I had.

I was taken in handcuffs to a little room in which the Sheriff and the Procurator Fiscal were sitting. While the charge was being read out I butted in and told the Sheriff that I was pleading guilty, but he told me I couldn't make a plea or declaration at this time as I was only there to be fully committed. If I wanted to plead guilty I should write to the Procurator Fiscal. I then realised I was on indictment, which meant I could get anything from two years to a remit to the High Court for a longer sentence.

Outside the Sheriff's room the Procurator Fiscal approached me and confirmed that I should send him a letter stating that I was guilty. I guess I was crazy for thinking of pleading guilty in the first place, but that's how I felt at the time: apart from thinking I was on a summary, I didn't want to have to listen to the warders coming into court and telling lies against me. But instead of writing a confessional letter to the Procurator Fiscal, I turned up at court again with a list of more than eighty witnesses and a plea of not guilty.

On the 18th of January, 1983 the jury were sworn in. It's normal practice in Scottish courts to object to 'certain' members of the jury; most lawyers would like a jury full of working-class people because they believe they will give their client a fairer hearing than, say, a jury full of bank managers and shopkeepers who can see the authorities do no wrong. I was given a list of all the jurors and their occupation, and the judge explained that I had the 'right' to reject members of the jury if I felt it necessary. I told the judge that I wasn't rejecting any, regardless of their occupation. The P.F. again handed me the list and I threw it back at him. He was raging because I wouldn't reject any jury members – I even turned around and faced the eighty-odd men and women waiting to be picked for my jury, and I told them I had no reason to object to any of them being called.

During the trial I had to stand handcuffed in the dock while defending myself and taking mental notes of what was being said by the warders who were taking the oath and lying my life away. One warder in particular told lie after lie to get me convicted. I stood there helplessly, raging at this bastard who hated me. When my turn came to cross-examine him I simply told the judge and jury that he was an out-and-out liar, and that I had no intention of cross-examining him. I told him to get out of the witness box – 'You've been telling lies all your life,' I shouted.

After about half a dozen of the warders had given their evidence they sat behind me in the courtroom to watch the rest of the trial. Whenever I stood up to cross-examine a witness I could hear them laughing and sniggering behind my back. I could only imagine they were trying to make me look a fool in the eyes of the jury. I turned round and said, 'Hey! You're not in your fucking governor's orderly room now, ya turnkey bastards!' The Advocate Deputy then stood up and looked at the warders; he told the judge that there were too many warders in the courtroom, and asked if they could be removed. When the judge told them to leave they were livid – still more so when I turned round and smiled at them.

The lassie who was taking down the proceedings in shorthand sent the court clerk over to ask if I could speak more slowly. It must have been nerves on my part: I tried to do so, but whenever I looked across to her she waved a clenched fist at me. She had a smile on her face as she did so, and I fell in love with her! We used to say hello and goodbye every day. Normally I hated anyone to do with courts, thinking they were

307

all bastards with no human feelings, yet there I was in love with this girl because she smiled at me and seemed friendly. As I was getting dressed up in my civilian suit to appear in court I would try to look tidy for the jury, but soon I started dressing for her benefit. I'd try my hair in different styles, wondering which one she would like best.

I think it was on the second day of the trial that Jim sent word down to me that a newspaper had carried an article about my assaulting the warders, in which I was referred to as a 'killer' and a 'murderer'. In court I reported this to the judge, saying I feared it would influence the jury against me. Next day the reporter responsible for writing the articles found himself sitting alongside me in the dock. I asked him where he had got his information from and he replied that some warders had told him – but he told the court that he had had a brainstorm, and he was fined £500.

One warder accused me of punching him to the ground and hitting him on the head with a bolt. He had tried to jump over the wire to get at me on a flat part of the roof across from the punishment block. I asked him not to as I had no intention of surrendering to him, but he wouldn't listen – his feet caught in the wire and he fell on all fours in front of me. I told him I didn't want to fight with him as he had taken me to my dad's funeral, but when he got up he began to circle me in a threatening manner with his truncheon in his hand. He took a few swipes at me and I ducked, but then I caught him on the side of the head with my fist – after which I turned and walked away.

The lies he told in the witness box about my assaulting him when he was on all fours made me wish I'd jumped on his head, and I cursed myself for being too soft with such ruthless bastards.

I had cited Jim, Checker, Dez and Frank as witnesses. I felt sorry for Frank when he was giving evidence. Like me, he had been locked up so long he didn't know what was what. He got the various incidents mixed up. I had to stop and tell him which incident I was on trial for. 'Come on tae fuck, Johnnyboy, you've mentioned dates to me – and there's that many incidents – ah don't even know what year this is!' he replied. Although his face was all screwed up in the way that usually made me laugh, I couldn't laugh this time – it was true what he said about there being so many incidents, and his head, like mine, was so fucked up.

So the war of hate between warders and prisoners went on in the courtroom. When warders gave evidence in the governor's orderly room, they were never cross-examined and their word was taken for granted, but here they had to mend their ways. To tell the truth, everybody lied. The warders lied to get me convicted and given more time, and to get compensation for their alleged injuries; and most of my witnesses lied to stop them getting a conviction against me.

On the fourth day of the trial, when all the witnesses had been heard, the Advocate Deputy started his summing-up to the jury, asking them to bring in a verdict of guilty on each charge against me.

When my turn came to sum up, I had barely got four words out when the judge stopped me and said he couldn't hear a word I was saying, and he didn't think the jury could either. I thought this was a tactic to put me off my speech and make me feel nervous. I told the judge I had a cold sore in the corner of my lips which made it difficult for me to speak. 'Do you mind if I come out of the dock and stand directly in front of the jury so that they may hear me more clearly?' I said. He seemed confused at my request, but then said, 'Oh, very well then!' I walked right up to the jury with the warder handcuffed to me, and I began my summing-up to them, looking them all in the eye as I contradicted the evidence the warders gave. I asked the judge if I could be given the pile of slates that I was alleged to have thrown at the warders, so that I could pass them to the jury so that they could feel their weight and sharpness. Again he seemed puzzled, but he agreed. I asked them if they thought it possible that such weapons, if hurled from a roof some forty feet high, would only have bruised the warders? They shook their heads from side to side. I then looked at a jury member, and I said to him something like: 'Sir, if I were to throw this slate at you from where I stand –

and not from a height of forty-odd feet – would you expect it to leave only a *bruise*?' Again their heads were going from side to side. When it came to the fight with the warder on the roof, I told the court that I hadn't assaulted him because he was one of the few warders who had volunteered to take me to my dad's funeral. As for the other fight in the toilets with the warders, I had no witnesses on those charges, because there were none – only the warders. They had lied when they said Frank wasn't in his cell: I said he was, but handcuffed and gagged. One of the warders admitted he had hit me on the head with a truncheon to subdue me. They admitted the cells had no sinks or toilets for us to slop out, and that we were on a dirty protest. I admitted to punching one of them as they ran forward to manhandle me.

With the trial at its end, I felt I was going to miss all the members of the jury, whatever their verdicts. I had got to know some of their habits: and at least they had listened to me. This was the first time in my life I had spoken to an audience for so long – and with so much to say.

The judge then summed up after I had finished. He told the jury that even though I hadn't been represented by a lawyer, I had presented my case very well indeed. The jury then left, and when they returned to give their verdict the court was hushed. I was found not proven for assaulting the warder on the flat roof and for hitting another on the leg with a slate. On the third charge, of hitting another warder with a slate, I was found not guilty. On the two charges of fighting with the warders in the toilet and assaulting them with the ballcock, I was found guilty.

I was happy with the verdicts. I noticed one wee woman in the jury was crying, and the shorthand girl laughed and waved to me as though I was her long-lost brother. Even the judge showed his approval by giving me a wink and a nod, after which he lowered his head and continued to write. The Advocate Deputy looked at me with his eyebrows raised, and a wee forced smile crept over his face. I gave him a look as if to say 'Tough luck, mister.' I even felt I had gotten to know him during the four days of the trial. The only time I felt real anger

310

towards him was when one of my witnesses was in the stand giving evidence for me, and the Advocate Deputy kept calling him a liar. Big Dougie rose to the bait and stood up to his full six feet something. 'Who are you calling a liar?' he growled. I managed to calm him down by telling him that the Advocate Deputy was winding him up, and that he shouldn't bite back, as it would only damage my case.

The judge asked me to stand while he passed sentence. I prayed he would let me off lightly – and he did, sentencing me to four months consecutive. I thanked the jury, and waved my pal the shorthand girl goodbye. I was driven back to Peterhead under armed escort and locked up in the punishment block. The warders were furious at the verdicts, but when I told the guys in the punishment block they started cheering.

I'm not sure if it was before my trial or just after that the governor told me that he was going to rescind all punishments, except loss of remission. That meant that I was to be given a wage for tobacco, and be allowed a radio, a mattress and bedding, a cardboard table and chair and books in my cell. I couldn't believe it, and thought he was up to something devious. He said it was the only way he could see of stopping me from getting into further trouble now that they had tried everything else.

It was great to have everything back. It seemed like a decade since I last had such luxuries, and I began to think the governor was a decent enough guy. But before long I couldn't accept it. It meant lying down and accepting solitary confinement, and I wanted out. The governor came into my clean cell with a smile on his face, but he wasn't smiling for long as I demanded all my punishments back, and then told them all to get to fuck out of the cell. I threw away the bedding and radio, and started smashing up the cell.

They refused to give me back my punishments – they wouldn't even put me on report for digging at the walls or cursing them. 'Just leave him,' they said. I was told that there was no way they would risk letting me back into circulation, and that the Secretary of State for Scotland had ordered them to keep me in solitary confinement until further notice. I was an embarrassment, and I had more punishments and reports than any prisoner in the penal history of Scotland. I was twenty-six years old, I had served three and a half years of my sentence and had twelve still to serve: I was incorrigible, it seemed.

About a week after the end of my trial they took me away to the Inverness Cages once again, and I remained there for three months. The warders at the Cages had heard about my 'caves' at Peterhead, and they reckoned I would be glad to be in a cage rather than a cave; but it didn't make me feel any better.

I arrived back in Peterhead in April or May 1983 and went into A Hall. Franco gave me two little pigeons, only weeks old, and I had to mouth-feed them. Every day when I came in from work the wee birds were still there. They'd come running over to me flapping their tiny wings, and I often shared my food with them. One day I was emptying my basin of water when Franco told me I was being followed. I looked behind me, and there were the two wee birds. When they were old enough to fly I let them out of my cell window to roam, and I found myself worrying about them if they stayed out too long.

One Saturday evening I was sitting in my cell, which wasn't unusual. What was unusual was that I had with me two crowbars, a ladder, a tool-kit of spanners and screwdrivers of all sizes, a hacksaw blade and a civilian suit. I was still on strict security because of my continuous attempts to escape, but although my cell was searched every day they had failed to discover my escape equipment. The wood I needed for a ladder had been provided by the authorities – the hardwood frame of two poster boards, three wooden lockers and the framing underneath the table top. That evening I put the ladder together with over fifty nuts and bolts that a pal had stolen for me from his work shed. I drilled all the holes with a huge screwdriver. It was hard work and I was soaked in

312

sweat. I'd covered my spyholes with paper – had the warder come to my door I would have told him I was having a shit. The ladder was up against the wall with the spyholes on it.

My door had two steel bolts on the outside as an extra security measure. I broke off the two end prongs of a steel fork I had stolen and slipped it into the tiny gap in the door so that it was touching one of the bolts. I then pressed the fork on to the bolt, spreading the two prongs till they had a firm grip on it; after which I turned the bolt towards me, freeing it from its safety bar, and shoved it to the left till it was clear of the hole. I then did the same with the other bolt. After that I took one of the thick crowbars and worked on the cell door. There was a sheet of metal on the cell door to stop anyone digging their way into the lock, and another sheet of steel on the door frame. I wedged the crowbar into the gap and began forcing the door open. Wood was splitting and snapping, so I stopped to listen for the warder before I continued.

I removed the steel plate from the door frame and dug my way through the wood behind it; but behind the wood was a steel bar, and behind that I could see the 'sprung' tongue of the lock. Before I could get the door open I would have to get the steel bar off – and I couldn't do that because it was part of a steel frame bolted into the side of the door frame. I tried sawing through the bar with my hacksaw blade but had to give up because of the screeching noise it made, which echoed through the hall. I had nothing to worry about from the guys in the other cells since I knew they wouldn't grass. They knew what I was up to, and while I was working on my door they played loud music to drown the noise.

Once again I wedged the crowbar into the gap between the door and the wooden frame, working it up and down and making the gap wider. At one point the bottom half of the cell door had bent and buckled inward, but the lock and the bar still held. I could see out into the gallery and to the cells across the way from me. I worked non-stop, heaving and forcing with the crowbar – and then, as if someone had put a key in the lock and turned it, it opened! I had ripped the whole jamming device out of the door frame.

I crawled out on to the gallery on my belly, making sure no warders were on the 'third', where I was; looking over, I could see them in their office on the bottom floor, by the hall entrance. I pulled my cell door closed and drove the bolts home. The damage couldn't be seen from outside, and with the two bolts holding the door shut the warders could walk up to my door and shove it – as they always did – to make sure it was locked.

Then I crawled along the gallery on my belly to my pal the Bald Eagle's cell door. I rapped three times to let him know it was me. He had taken the steel plate off his door frame and dug out the wood till he could see the steel bar holding the sprung tongue, which he had cut through with a hacksaw blade, but he couldn't get his bolts open – that was my job. I heard him cursing, thinking his door wouldn't open. I sat with my back to the door, placed my feet on the gallery railings and pushed the door as hard as I could – and it gave. We spoke in whispers, congratulating each other. So far so good – but then someone pressed their bell, so we had to hide in one of the arches while the warder went to find out what the guy wanted. Peter pushed his cell door to and shot home the two bolts. The warder passed our doors, gave them both a shove and moved on to check the other security prisoners before going back downstairs.

We both slipped upstairs to the top landing, but no sooner had we got started with a jack on the bars of the huge window at the end of the hall than someone else pressed their bell a few feet from where we stood. We removed the jack from the bars and slipped quietly past the cell doors and into the arch, where we waited while the warder came to see what the guy wanted. In the arch were toilets, showers and sinks, and two slop-out sinks. The arch was, in fact, two cells knocked into one; there was no door or grille to it, so there was no need for a warder to go there. It seemed an age that we waited there in the darkness.

I knew Big Shug, the guy who had pressed his bell. When the warder reached his door they argued for quite some time. As soon as the warder had left we began to make our way back to the big window – and then Shug pressed his bell again. Once again we slipped back to the archway and waited. I felt like asking Shug to leave off pressing his bell, at least until we had got away, but it was too risky. The warder came back to the cell door and spoke to Big Shug once again, and then some surgery warders came upstairs to his cell. I wondered what was wrong with him. Time was getting on and we couldn't afford to hang about much longer. We had never thought to tell the guys on the top floor not to press their bells if they could help it.

Once the warders had left Big Shug's cell, we continued back along the gallery only to hear one of the warders coming upstairs on his rounds. Yet again we got into the arch. He was at my cell door, and I heard him call my name. I was almost above him in the arch. I had butterflies in my belly and an ache in my heart.

'If you don't take the paper down from your spyhole, you're going to the cells!' I heard him say. I could have killed myself for forgetting to clear my spyholes before I left my cell. 'Are you listening to me in there?' he was shouting through my door.

We tried to figure out what we should do next. It was obvious we were caught, so I took the hacksaw blade out of my pocket and hid it inside my underpants – if they found it, too bad, but if they didn't I could use it on the bars in the punishment block. We could hear other warders coming upstairs and heading for my door. A warder pulled back my bolts, and was about to put the key into the lock when he discovered that it wasn't locked. They quickly pulled the door shut and fastened the bolts again. One of them then ran round all the security cells, turning out the lights, never bothering to look in the cells. They didn't want to alert anyone to trouble in the hall. They thought I was still in my cell, even though they knew the lock had been burst open, because the bolts were still in; once they were in my cell they searched for me under the bed and in the tiny cupboards. We could hear them calling me, asking where I was. I looked through a small window into the gallery, where I saw a worried-looking warder holding a flashlamp and gazing at the skylights on the roof high above him. He came into the arch, shining his lamp – and when he saw me with the crowbar in my hands, laughing at him, he dropped his lamp and ran away, shouting for help.

I ran after him, but he got down the stairs five at a time and on to the third gallery where the others were. They too ran downstairs, but when they realised I wasn't chasing them they stopped on the bridge of the second gallery and looked up at me standing there calling them all the bastards under the sun. One of them ran to the phone, while the others asked me to give myself up and put the bar down. Two of those there were well known for beating up prisoners, and one of them began to make his way upstairs towards me. I raised the bar and warned him not to come any closer. He stopped when the Bald Eagle came out of the arch, warning him not to come near. They panicked again, not knowing he was out of his cell – or how many of us were out.

I told one of the warders that we were surrendering and would come downstairs with him as long as the others stayed away. They couldn't have been nicer, and it was Johnnyboy this and Johnnyboy that and 'You're doing the right thing in giving yourself up, Johnnyboy.'

When I reached the double doors of the punishment block I froze, frightened of what lay behind them. I was shoved into a cell and they closed the door on me, telling me to calm down. I took the hacksaw blade out of my underpants and hid it outside the window. Then they asked me to take off my clothing so they could search me. They came back in and told me there'd be no brutality since none had been used on them, and one of them asked me if I had any tobacco. When I said I had none he took out some of his cigarettes and threw them on the floor, asking me to keep quiet and not smash the cell up. That night I started cutting my cell bars with the hacksaw blade, singing loudly to drown the noise. Alex had put his radio up at his window to help drown the noise.

The next day I was taken to see the governor and charged with attempted escape. He was very embarrassed at my having broken out of a security cell, and having so much equipment.

When he asked me where I had got the crowbars and toolkit from, and what the ladder was to be used for, I laughed in his face. And so I was taken before the visiting committee for the sixth time. They sentenced me to twenty-eight days solitary backdated; I forfeited thirty days remission, and was ordered to pay a fine of twenty-five pounds.

The governor thanked me for not causing problems with the visiting committee. He was delighted to say that the Bald Eagle and I would be going back into circulation within a week's time; but I knew – as everyone knew – that they didn't want me in the punishment block, hence the small favour.

The warders were so embarrassed at my breaking out of the cell that they locked up Big Shug in the punishment block, and charged him with aiding us in the escape! They claimed that he had deliberately rung his bell to cause a diversion. I told them over and over again that Big Shug had nothing to do with it, and that if it hadn't been for Shug ringing his bell we might have got away. I went and saw the governor about it, and Big Shug wrote to the Grampian and Highlands Chief Constable and lodged a complaint. A short while later he was taken off the 'strict security' party. The chief warder wanted me to tell him where I had got the crowbars and other implements, but I wouldn't help him. (In fact I had got them from my pal Frank, who had taken them from right under the warders' noses.) He then asked me what the ladder was for, since it obviously wouldn't have reached the top of the wall. I refused to tell him that either. He was right: it wasn't meant to reach the top of the wall, but was an extension to another piece of ladder that had been hidden outside the hall because it was too big to hide inside.

Honeybugs had written me a letter with the hint of a proposal in it. I read it over and over, and thought so much about its contents that it brought a tear to my eye. She didn't know the mess I was in and I didn't tell her. I knew she was good for me, but I knew I'd be no good to her because I couldn't stop doing what I was doing. Much as I loved her, I couldn't marry

317

her under these circumstances – it would have only made me more determined to escape – so I wrote her a long letter of explanation and asked her to forget me and find someone who could offer her a better life. It wasn't an easy letter to write. I kept tearing it up and rewriting it. She wrote back: it seemed she was quite hurt, but she told me she could understand and wanted to continue being my friend, if nothing else. I cut off for my own sake as well as hers, but I didn't cut off completely – it wasn't that easy. At nights I would think about her and wonder what she was doing with her life, and I'd often ask Auntie Mags how she was keeping. Sometimes I changed my mind about marrying her, and I'd put pen to paper and sit there for hours telling her how I felt about us; but the thought of how I had hurt everyone I ever loved made me change my mind again, and I ripped the letter up.

30 DYING WITHIN

One week after getting out of solitary I was cutting a set of bars in another prisoner's cell – with his consent. It was the only thing I could do; I couldn't even sneeze in my own cell without the warder peering through the spyhole. There were cameras outside my cell window, and a warder was permanently seated outside my door. Every night, when I got the chance, I would go into the guy's cell alone and cut through his bars for about fifteen minutes. The guy who let me cut his bars wanted to escape – in fact, there were quite a few who wanted to. Dez was there now – we had finally gotten into circulation together – and he was in on the escape plans. Micky was in on it, and so was Frank, though he wasn't going to escape: instead he and some others were going to climb on to the hall roof and distract the warders, so they'd think we were all on the roof. Frank told me he had managed to get me some civilian clothes to wear and a few other useful odds and ends.

Next Saturday morning a fight broke out on the ground floor of A Hall over a game of pool. I was cutting through another bar when I heard the commotion, some warders ran over to break up the fight, and they were being a bit rough on the guys. Dez and a few others, including Micky and Frank, ran downstairs to stop the warders. When I saw what was happening, I left the guy in the cell with the hacksaw blade and went downstairs. Dustbins and billiard balls and brushes were flying everywhere, and the riot bell was ringing throughout the gaol. I didn't want to get involved, but I couldn't stand there and watch Frank being dragged about the warders' office. As I moved to pull Frank clear, someone hit a warder with a pool cue and Frank got away. Someone else said the riot squad were coming and there was a panic.

I had no option but to get out of the way, because if they saw me they would automatically assume I was involved. We all moved up to the top gallery, and everyone started smashing sinks and toilets and windows. I stood by and watched them. I was shattered to be caught up in this situation: my mind was on the bars I'd been cutting.

That night a mob of warders rushed into my cell, dragged me down to reception, handcuffed me and threw me into a van; and once more, for the fourth time, I was taken away to the Cages, as were Micky and Dez. I was told I was to be remanded for assaulting a warder with a pool cue, but I kept thinking about the half-cut bars.

In Inverness once again, I paced up and down my cage till I was exhausted and fell asleep. The newspapers had made a big deal out of it, and there was a hue and cry about our being put in cages. The Cages were unpopular with the media, and the National Council for Civil Liberties had been trying to get them closed for ever on the grounds that they were inhumane.

I felt sleepy all the time I was at the Cages and Micky and Dez said they felt the same. I wasn't there long before I had a visitor, and when I walked into the visiting room Auntie Mary let out a scream: she had her hand to her mouth and stared wide-eyed at me as though she was seeing a ghost. She kept saying, 'What have you done to my boy?'

I asked her what was wrong, but this only seemed to make her worse, and she started bawling that I had been drugged and that my speech was slurred. I didn't feel as though, I'd been drugged, but I didn't feel right. The warders denied that I had been drugged, but Mary wouldn't believe them. I began to fear that the bastards had put drugs in my food. Aunt Mary said she was going to the National Council for Civil Liberties – and she did. Its Scottish general secretary, David Godwin,

320

told the story to the newspapers and asked for a public inquiry into conditions in the Cages.

After that, I was careful what I ate, as were Micky and Dez. We started throwing our food and shit at the warders. Humphy was there, causing trouble as usual – he was a master at persecuting prisoners. Some of the warders had told him to ease off and not bother us, but he wouldn't.

'I hope you enjoy your food now – don't be thinking that any of us nice warders would put anything in it,' he'd say, with an evil grin on his face.

They wouldn't let us out of our cages, so our food was slipped under the bars. Somebody had urinated into our food. I even found some shit on my plate, and when I reported it to Humphy he asked me how I knew it was shit. I told him I'd tasted it, at which he grinned and slammed the door.

One day I asked to be let out of the cage, promising not to attack anyone. I told them – especially Humphy – that I'd had all I could take, and wanted to settle down. The grin crept up his face and he ordered a warder to open my cage. They were dressed in riot gear and carrying baseball-type riot-sticks, and they warned me not to do anything. I promised again I wouldn't. I stood by the sink brushing my teeth and looking in the mirror I could see Humphy behind me in the corridor. I squirted an entire tube of toothpaste into my mouth and turned to face Humphy, holding the toothbrush and empty tube out to him. With a grin on his face, Humphy reached out to take the brush and tube, not knowing what I had in my mouth. My lips almost touched his as I spewed the toothpaste into his eyes and mouth. I remember laughing, and then being knocked to the ground by the riot-sticks. But it was worth it to see him running about, holding his eyes and screaming.

They beat me all the way into the cage and left me there on the floor. Humphy appeared, holding a wet handkerchief to his eyes; he looked as though he was satisfied that I had got what I deserved. I couldn't get up – my knees and shins were aching from where they had hit me – so I crawled over to the cage and, just to get back at Humphy, I asked him to let me out of the cage and promised not to cause trouble. He stared right through me, humming the same nonsensical tune he always hummed, and then he left, slamming the cell door with considerable force. I knew this was to annoy me, so I told him he hadn't slammed the door hard enough. He opened it and slammed it again. 'That's more like it,' I called after him.

David Godwin arranged with the Prison Department to come and see me and the others. He seemed a nice guy, and not just because he wanted to close the Cages. He had worked hard over the years in dealing with prisoners' complaints about brutality and ill-treatment. While I was talking to him through the wire, the chief warder came in and asked him if he wanted a cup of tea or coffee. I told him not to in case they put something into it.

Not long after the incident with Humphy and the toothpaste, Micky, Dez and I were summoned to appear at the High Court in Glasgow on behalf of Big Tam, who had been charged with assaulting warders at Barlinnie. I was dressed in rags and told the governor of the Cages that I was going to court that way. Micky and Dez were covered from head to foot in shit, and in the van the warders wore boilersuits so it wouldn't rub against their uniforms. I needed to pee, so I pissed where I sat. I could feel the wet running under my arse and dribbling on to the floor. The warder who was handcuffed to me was wet as well, but he never said anything. The warders opened a window to let some fresh air in: I was shivering in the back of the van wearing only a loincloth and two bits of grey woollen blanket wrapped round each foot.

We were to stay the night at Barlinnie, and when we arrived at reception everyone stared at us because of the condition we were in. We had to clean ourselves – there was no way we could appear as witnesses for Big Tam dressed as we were. They took us to one of the halls, making sure that no prisoners got talking to us. There were warders outside our doors at all times. But when the guys I knew heard that I was there they called to me from their cell windows. One of my pals told me that my young brother Joseph was in Barlinnie serving three months for a petty offence, and that he would try to see me before I left.

The governor came to see me. He asked me how I was keeping, and when I was ever going to settle down. He was a strange character, remarkably young-looking and in good shape for his age. He was hated and feared by most of the warders at Barlinnie, just as he had been at Peterhead. He said I should try to put on some muscle next time I came up against the system – that way they wouldn't look so bad. He felt my biceps and laughed. He told me he would do what I was doing if he was locked away under these conditions. Before he left he said Ma could come and see me while I was at Barlinnie – 'That's a promise.' I wasn't supposed to get any privileges during the stay, yet here was the governor telling me I could have a visit from Ma. Ma and my Aunt Mary squeezed into the little cubicle and were peering through the glass at me like they were looking for bruises. I was trying to answer their questions one at a time, but they were too fast with them. One wanted to know if I had been beaten up and the other was asking if I was covering myself in shit to protect myself from the warders. I denied it. 'Don't you sit there and tell me lies,' Ma said with an air of authority, and Aunt Mary said even the cats and dogs in the streets knew what was happening. They said they had heard I was being carried into the governor's orderly room in a sack or had been put into special caves – and I told them it wasn't me but Jim. It was easier to put a bit of humour into the answers than to throw myself at them with a dead weight of truth.

When I walked into the court handcuffed to a warder I saw Big Tam sitting in the dock, looking pale and thin. I shouted out to him and asked him how he was feeling; he said he was okay. I took the oath, and told the court about Tam's experiences at Peterhead, and how they had him on drugs so that half the time he didn't know who he was or what he was doing. Apparently the warders at Barlinnie had him on medication when he committed the assaults. I was surprised

323

when Tam's lawyer asked me to describe the Cages to the court.

'It's just a human zoo,' I said. I saw a lassie in the jury laugh when I said this, but wasn't sure if she was laughing at me, or laughing at what I said. Micky and Dez were also called – and then it was back to the human zoo with us.

The three of us were still at the Cages when there was a full-scale riot at Peterhead. We were pleased for many reasons, one of which was that the authorities at Peterhead always tried to cover up their troubles there by saying that they were caused by a small group of hard-core prisoners. We also heard that the guy who had let me saw his cell bars had managed to get out of his window, but was caught between the wall and the outside fence.

My piece of hacksaw blade had no teeth now – they had worn away rubbing against the bars of my cage – but I kept going till my fingers were raw and bleeding. I was more than halfway through when they moved me to another cage. I had some razor blades in my mouth when I came back from Barlinnie – I had wrapped them in silver paper and rubbed away the sharp edges so as not to cut myself – and in my new cage I started cutting a bar with one of the razor blades. I made the edges of the blade ragged so that it would bite into the steel bar, but to finish the job I needed more blades. I spent most days and nights working on the bar, and Micky was in fits of laughter when I told him what I was up to. The policy in the Cages was not to tell prisoners when they were being taken back to their own gaols. I kicked my last meal up in the air the day they told me I was being taken back to Peterhead. The walls of my cage were covered in shit and food slops, and there were maggots amongst the filth. Across the wall I had written 'Man's Inhumanity to Man' in shit in huge letters. I was glad to be getting away from the Cages even if it meant going back to punishment.

We had travelled only about twenty miles out of Inverness when the van was stopped by the police, who told the driver we wouldn't get through because of the snow. I was shattered at the idea of going back to the Cages. Humphy laughed when he saw us again, and said with his usual grin that I had made history by being in the Cages not four but five times. . . .

There was shit in my cage and I knew it wasn't mine – it was of a lighter colour. I knew that one of the bastards outside had done it. I picked it up, intending to rub it on to the bars and walls along with my own shit – it would help stink out the cage even more badly since it was fresh, and as long as those bastards suffered the smell I didn't care. I had it in my hand when Humphy opened the cell door, and the grin on his face made me sicker than the shit in my hand. He asked me if there was something wrong. I wanted to grab hold of him and ram the shit down his throat, but the way he was standing suggested that he'd be able to close the door rather too quickly. I could feel the hate surging up inside me. I asked him which one of them had shat in my cage. He asked me how I knew it wasn't my own. I halved the shit with my bare hands, told him it was pointless arguing whose it was, threw half of it at him, saying he could have half, I'd keep the rest. I don't know if it hit him, but he was screaming at me from outside the cell door.

Humphy came back in with some other warders to give me a security search. He was acting like a supersleuth, humming his nonsensical tune as he checked the bars on my cage. He started kicking the bars, and the other warders were banging the brick walls and the roof and floor of the cage with their truncheons. When the others had finished their search Humphy was still strutting up and down, looking at the bars. Once he was satisfied, he told his warders to leave the cage. As he was leaving I asked him to let the chief warder know I wanted to see him immediately, and that it was very important. Humphy wanted to know why, but I refused to tell him.

When the chief came in I asked him if he would like to buy a hacksaw blade for an ounce of tobacco and cigarette papers. Without hesitation he said he would. There was silence in the cage. Humphy laughed and told the chief I was fooling him, but the chief never took his eyes off me. He asked me where it was.

'Open this cage,' I said. The warders around him were laughing as if it was some sort of joke, but I could tell by the

325

expression on the chief's face that he was taking me seriously.

'Open the cage!' he ordered and I walked out, telling them to follow me to a cell in the short corridor. Humphy was looking worried now, and he told the others I couldn't possibly have a hacksaw blade. They opened the cell door and we all went inside.

'Open the cage!' I said. I was enjoying giving orders, and made a meal of it. I turned to Humphy and said, 'Come on, you! I haven't got all day waiting on you!' When the cage door was opened I went inside, pointed to the bottom long bar and said the blade was jammed in the gap where the weld was. The chief told one of the warders to check it out; he poked his penknife into the gap, and the blade fell out on to the floor, wrapped in a cigarette paper. I picked it up and handed it to the chief, who unwrapped the cigarette paper. He was biting his bottom lip.

Humphy wasn't humming now, but he was quick to say that such a small blade couldn't cut bars. I told Humphy that the chief must be the judge of that, and peeled back a piece of paper to reveal the half-cut bar. The chief had taken his hat off and was banging it on the outside of his leg. He told the warders that somebody's head would roll. Humphy broke the silence by telling the chief that he hadn't been on duty when I was in this cell – and that if he had been he would have found it. The chief wasn't impressed, and neither was I. I accused Humphy of neglecting security precautions.

'Shut up, Steele!' he spluttered.

The chief raised his eyebrows and asked me if I had cut any other bars elsewhere. I reminded him that Humphy had warned me to shut up.

'Never fucking mind that idiot and show me, please,' the chief said.

'Follow me!' I called, loud enough for Micky and Gary to hear, and they followed me back down the corridor and into the cage I had just come from.

I broke the silence again with something like, 'Aye, ye wir saying, Humphy, about you no being oan duty when the bars wir being cut?' and peeled back a piece of paper to reveal the

326

half-cut bar. The chief asked me where the hacksaw blade was: I told him there had been no hacksaw blade, but I gave him the well-worn razor blade, and told him that they should think themselves lucky that I wasn't the 'madman' they said I was, otherwise I could have had a field day slashing them.

The chief said he'd be grateful if I told him where I got the blade from. You could've heard a pin drop. I pointed my finger at Humphy's rotten red face and said, 'He gave me them!'

I laughed my head off as I heard the chief arguing with Humphy as they vanished up the corridor. I shouted to the chief through the ventilator, 'If you don't send me the tobacco you owe me, I won't tell you about the hatchet I've got hidden!'

Surprisingly enough, the chief sent down half an ounce of tobacco, and Humphy brought it into me. I don't think they believed me about the hatchet, but he asked me if I really had one. He had the sleekit detective look on his face, as if he wouldn't have put it past me to have one. I told him I had buried the hatchet long ago, but he didn't get my meaning for he started looking about the cage for hideaways, and left looking hurt when he realised I was laughing at him.

They were too embarrassed to put me on governor's report for the blades or cut bars. There was nothing more I could have done to the bars with the blades – they had quite worn away and were of no use except for slashing the warders with. Next day they told me that the roads were clear and that I was going back to Peterhead, where Micky and I were put in the punishment block.

I think it was late January when Micky and I came back from the cages. A few weeks later I was sitting at my window when I heard screaming, and fighting, and a cell door slamming. 'I've been framed, ya bastards!' echoed throughout the punishment block. I called on whoever was screaming to come to his window, and he said that he was covering himself in shit before the warders came back. I didn't recognise his voice. It was the done thing to cover ourselves in shit under those circum-

327

stances, because it reduced the chances of the warders beating us up. But not everyone did it – some thought it disgusting, and that it only degraded us in the eyes of the warders. The guy who had been screaming came to his window again, and I saw it was my dad's old pal Toe Elliot.

That night we talked at the windows of our cells. Toe told me he had been out on parole when my dad died, and that he went to pay his last respects in our house in Garthamlock. He told me he had given my dad a kiss as he lay in his coffin. It hurt me more to hear about my dad's death from Toe than to have been at the funeral. He spoke of my dad like he was speaking of his own father, about the love he had for him and the skulduggery they had been up to.

I told him how to make a hammock to save him from lying amongst the shit and piss. He had been charged with involvement in the A Hall riot about a month after it happened. Everyone knew that the governors and warders had manufactured evidence against him. Toe had the gift of the gab. All we had there was each other for company, and as the months got worse, the authorities took everything away from us – everything that is, except each other.

Almost every day I was put on governor's report for not standing to attention or for being on a 'dirty' protest or for digging holes or for destroying prison property. One day I asked one of the governors why it meant so much to him that we should stand up for him, and he told me it was a sign of respect. I was standing there in my loincloth, covered in shit, and I was amazed to hear this rat demanding respect – the same rat who had stripped me of my clothing, and left orders that I wasn't to be allowed anything in my cell, and told the works warders to break and take out all my cell windows, and thought it funny to see me in a darkened cave.

One day I told the governor that I wanted to see the police, and that I had some information for them. His eyes lit up – he must've thought I was turning canary. When the detectives came to see me in the governor's orderly room, I told them about how the governor had fought with the prisoner all those years ago in the punishment block. I said I was coming forward

328

now because I was frightened the bastards would do the same to me. They took a statement from me and said they would investigate it and get in touch. I then told them I would like to press charges against the present governors for ill-treatment and brutality, but they said I would have to write to the Secretary of State and make a complaint before they could interfere. The warders were livid at me for having told the police about the governor, and for trying to have the present governors charged.

Conditions got worse, the dirty protest got worse, the punishments got worse. Once again the warders took away our pisspots so that we had nothing to throw the shit in. But it didn't deter me. I made the shit into balls about the size of tennis balls and threw them on to the walls outside the cell. Others started to do the same. Each time the shit made contact with the granite walls everyone in the punishment block would cheer. It kept our spirits up, but it didn't do the morale of the warders any good as they constantly tried to clean the shit from the walls.

In the end even the warders rebelled against conditions in the punishment block; for three days they refused to clean up the shit that had been thrown everywhere – especially the stairs, since the governors had to walk up them. I burned the Perspex above my door and kicked out the steel sheet so I could see out into the gallery. Soon most of us had removed the Perspex and steel sheeting. Apart from talking to each other through the hole, we could lie in wait for the governors.

A warder came into my cell to try to persuade me to stop my rebellion. He said I was only degrading myself living this way. He stood in my cell among all the shit: he didn't even bother to use the stepping-stones I had made from some granite bricks I'd removed from the wall. He was crying as he told me that when he went home he had to change his clothes in the garage, and that his family could smell the shit, which humiliated him. I cried as well, not because of what he'd told me, but because I saw him for a brief moment as a fellow human being, and I began to feel as if I had taken a liberty with him. I promised him that I wouldn't throw my shit at him and he thanked me.

Every night, whatever the weather, we could be found at our cell windows talking and having sing-songs to break the monotony. I don't know what I would have done without my window – I was forever looking out of it. One night when it was Toe Elliot's turn, he sang 'Take these chains from my heart' and we all joined in, just as if we were at a party. Toe was forever asking me to recite my verse – he told me I had a talent for writing, and should make a book of my poems.

Every day I looked forward to getting out of my cell, if only to go to the governor's orderly room. I started carrying my shit bombs with me because the warders were stealing them from me when I left them in the cell. Sometimes my door would open and there'd be no one there. It was a strange feeling – and a good one – to step out into a gallery and not have warders follow my every move. I would strut up and down in my loincloth and home-made blanket shoes, picking targets to aim at. The warders would hide till I had thrown my last, then they'd come out.

The governors stopped me taking my letters into my cell – I had to read them in front of the warders, because I was always lighting fires – and keeping warm wasn't a good enough reason for the fires. I wasn't allowed a book – not even a Bible – or any paper whatsoever.

I came off exercise one day, and instead of being put back in my own cell I was taken to another, clean cell. I refused to go in, saying I wanted to go back to my own cell, but they dragged me into the empty and newly washed cell and left. I was furious – and frightened, because it reminded me too much of a cell, with its yellow-painted walls, and a door painted blood-red on the inside. The bare, clean cell brought one back to the reality of it all, and somehow I had to get away from it.

I shouted to my pals, and told them that I had no shit to put on the walls or throw at the warders. I was so angry that I asked the others if I could borrow some shit from them. They thought I was joking at first, but when they realised I was serious they lowered some down to me. One guy said if he gave me one of his shit bombs he wanted two in return! God knows it was horrible to do what I was doing, but I was determined to fight back with everything and anything short of physically harming the bastards. Within an hour of being in the new cell I had covered all four walls in shit, and whenever I vomited violently I smeared that on as well. At one point I was on the verge of pressing the bell to get out of the cell and away from the smell and thought of other people's shit, but I fought against it. I kept some aside for throwing into the warders' area. Eventually I did press my bell, and when the warders came to see what I wanted they found the cell walls completely covered in filth, and me with shit in my hands. They forgot to close the door in their panic to get away, and I threw some shit at them. I could hear them whispering outside my door. I thought they were going to beat me up when the door opened, but instead they stood there with shit in their hands, which they then threw at me. Far from ducking and diving out of its way, I grabbed it and threw it back at them.

Early in May I was out in the exercise yard in the same pen I had climbed out of before – only they had cemented the corners to stop me from climbing out that way again, and had put roll upon roll of razor-wire at the top. The warder on the catwalk hadn't been all that long in the gaol. He was an ex-marine and was recognised as a decent guy who never bothered anyone, and for this reason no one threw shit at him.

Some time before, my Aunt Mary and her young son, Martin, had come to visit. When the visit was over Mary found that her steering wheel had jammed and she couldn't unlock it. A warder came over to help, and while he was doing so Martin wandered off on his own, broke into a car and stole cassettes, a tape-recorder and some other equipment, which he hid in the boot of Mary's car. The police were called when it was discovered that the car had been broken into: Mary's car was searched and the stolen items were found. The car belonged to the warder who had been helping to unjam Mary's

331

steering wheel. Martin was charged with breaking into the car, then they were both allowed home.

The chief warder informed me of the incident the following day. He was furious that one of my visitors should have broken into a warder's car. Most of the other warders were equally angry, but the only one who bore no ill-will or malice against me because of this incident, was the warder the car belonged to: the one who was on the catwalk now. He said he hadn't wanted to press charges against Martin, since he was only a kid, but another warder had phoned the police. I apologised to him on behalf of Martin. When I next saw Martin I asked him why he had done it, and he said it was because of what they had done, and were doing, to me.

The warder must have sensed something was wrong with me as I paced back and forth in the pen in my underpants. It was a beautiful day, too good to go back to the punishment block. Everywhere was covered in filth: it was driving me crazy. By being sent to Peterhead I had been classed as a hard case, yet they were the ones who had made me into a hard case after which they had tried to break me and use me as an example to others.

I told the warder on the catwalk I was going to get out of the pen because I couldn't face going back to the punishment block. I told him I wouldn't do him any harm. He pleaded with me not to try it as I would rip myself to pieces on the wire. I was afraid that what he said was true, and that I wouldn't get out: I began to panic, and could feel the madness creeping up on me again. I felt trapped like an animal, with nothing to live for but to be punished again and again; I felt my belly turning, and I wanted to scream out for help – a jag, shock treatment, anything to get me away from the reality of this bare existence. I could have asked for medication, but when I thought of myself being locked up in a mental hospital and living a life prescribed by psychiatrists I decided I would do better to be torn apart by razor-wire than by doctors.

I took a run from one end of the exercise pen, clambered up the wall, and pulled myself through the razor-wire. I became caught up in it, and I could hear Toe and Dez calling me from

332

their windows, pleading with me not to struggle or I would bleed to death. I saw the warder on the catwalk run and press the riot bell, but I was out of reach of any warders who might try to pull me down. I was wrapped in wire, and it was worse than being in a cage or cave: everywhere I turned I could feel the needles sticking into me.

'Don't move!' the warder on the catwalk called, but others were there cheering and saying they hoped I would bleed to death. What also frightened me was that I was covered in shit, and if I cut myself I might poison my bloodstream. But somehow I managed to get through, and I ran on to the roof of the punishment block.

The chief warder was shouting at everyone to go back to their halls. I ran up and down the roof to make sure the warders weren't trying to sneak up on me. Some slates came loose, almost making me lose my footing and fall off, and again I felt dizzy at being so high up. I saw Jim in the crowd below staring up at me: I wanted to ask him for help, but I couldn't bring myself to do it – he had been out of trouble for some time.

Jim walked over and stood below me, and I could see he was upset by the state I was in. He asked me if any of the warders had beaten me up, but how could I possibly have said yes? If Jim had attacked the warders, it would have meant his losing all he had: a half-decent job and the training hall.

The chief warder shouted at me not to cause any problems for my brother and the others who were still in the yard – he was well aware of the tension there.

Jim said that Ma would have a nervous breakdown if I did anything crazy. Standing there with open arms, looking up at me pleadingly, he told me he was getting home leave to see Ma because Maw wasn't well. I was shattered. I couldn't see Jim getting home leave if there wasn't something seriously wrong. I dreaded hearing this sort of news.

Wee Smiddy came towards me, and when a warder tried to stop him he shoved him away. He winked, said 'Here, pal,' and threw me a tobacco tin and a cigarette lighter. I was grateful to Wee Smiddy and the others, not just for the tobacco, but for risking punishment by going on strike and remaining in the yard against orders.

Fearful that I would fall off, I started crawling on all fours. I felt as if I was swaying to and fro and was about to blackout. I lay down on the roof, holding on tightly. Toe warned me that some warders were coming up for me, and that they had a rope. I warned them not to come near me or I would dive off and take one of them with me. I turned to the guys standing in the yard and asked them to go back to their halls, and we waved and said our cheerios. I assured Jim that I would be all right and that I would come down without hurting myself or any of the warders – but I really wanted to scream, 'Jim, help me! Don't leave me to die!'

I crawled to the other side of the roof and lay out of sight, crying for Maw and remembering how she walked about with her arms outstretched, feeling her way about the house. Then I crawled on to the roof of the archway, where I could see the guys in the punishment block looking out at me from their windows a few feet away, unrecognisable, covered in their own shit. I was choked with tears to hear a big friendly country guy say, 'Could you spare a couple of those cigarettes for your big pal?' – and to see that when his arm came out of the window it too was covered in shit. I reached out and gave him a handful of tobacco, and I heard him singing away to himself.

The warders said they were coming up to get me, but they didn't have to. There was no fight left in me. They took me to the surgery and cleaned my cuts – again I refused the penicillin injections – after which I was taken back to the punishment block. I expected them to beat me up, but they didn't. The chief warder sent for me and thanked me for not smashing the roof and windows or assaulting his staff. He told me I could keep the tobacco as long as I didn't start any fires.

An MP came to Peterhead as part of an all-party penal affairs group, and he asked to see me. He asked me humorously if I was *the* Johnnyboy Steele who had been causing so many problems for the authorities. I didn't find it funny, and told

334

him so. He told me that Mick and Aunt Mary had often written to him, complaining about my health and the conditions I was being kept in. I didn't like his attitude – and still less so when he claimed that the authorities were trying their best to help me. I thought he was only saying this to please the warders, and so I accused him of taking sides without even listening to my case. He stood up, grabbed his briefcase and said in a high-pitched voice, 'I'm not talking to you – you've accused me of taking sides!'

As he headed for the door I called after him, 'You're running away because you're afraid of the truth, you old bastard!' He sat down again while I told him about the governor fighting with the prisoner and the brutality and the Cages. I could see he was getting nervous, and was ready to leave in a hurry. He was up again with his briefcase, and kept repeating, 'I'm not sitting here listening to this – you've accused me of taking sides!'

'I bet the bastard governors never told you about the fucking caves they had me in when they were telling you about all the trouble I was causing them!' I shouted. He looked at me as if he couldn't believe what he had heard.

'Caves? What caves?' with a worried look on his face.

I had no sooner started telling him than he jumped up again and said he had no intention of listening any more. I was screaming at him as he left the visiting room: the warders jumped on me, but they couldn't restrain my anger and I cursed and spat at the MP. Next day the governor told me to give in, since the outside world couldn't give a damn for me or any other prisoner. I told Toe that things couldn't get any worse, and he agreed.

That June one of the prisoners from A Hall told me something that made me fall back from my window on to the filth and urine on the floor: Joseph, my young brother, had been arrested and charged with six murders. T.C. and the Shadow had also been charged, along with the three others. A fire had been lit outside a house door in Ruchazie, and the fumes had killed six members of a family. I wasn't worried by the warders shouting to me that Joseph was a mad dog like me – I was too hurt thinking about Joseph and Ma, who I knew must be going crazy. I lay there thinking about my little brother: I could clearly remember the day he was born, and the silver I had pressed into his tiny hand to bring him good fortune in the life ahead of him. . . .

Ma came to see Jim and me not long after Joseph's arrest. She was helped in by one of my aunts, and I could see the tears in her eyes and the mark the shock had left on her face. I fought back my own tears for her sake – I wanted to grab her and hold her tightly, and I've no doubt she was thinking the same. She couldn't compose herself, but she eventually got some words out: 'My wee Joseph was in his bed when that fire was lit.' I could hear the high-pitched noise in my ears again. Mental and physical exhaustion was making me black-out, but fear of every kind had me fight it. Jim told Ma that Joseph wouldn't be taken to court for the murders because the only evidence against him was police verbal, but I reminded him that my dad had had explosives planted on him in our house by the police. It wasn't easy for me to say, but I told Ma to expect the worst in Joseph's case.

Jim disagreed, and told me not to tell Ma such things and make her feel worse. Ma was more inclined to believe what Jim said – that Joseph wouldn't get done. I felt bad about arguing with Jim during the visit, for I knew he was shattered too, and like me was holding back the tears: I knew he was right in his way to tell Ma that Joe couldn't get done, but I also knew I was right in telling her to prepare herself for the worst, because I knew too many men in gaol serving long sentences – including life – for crimes they hadn't committed.

It was the worst visit I ever experienced. Some time later I received a letter from Ma in which she said she was worried about me, having heard from someone about the conditions I was living in and my ill health. Whoever had been talking to Ma told her about the brutality in the punishment block, and she knew I had worn no clothes for months. I cursed whoever had told her, as it only had her worrying more than she could

336

handle. I decided to write back and tell her that I wasn't that badly off, and that I had no clothes because the fat rat governor had removed them.

The following day I was told that the governor wanted to see me. He was sitting behind the desk when I walked in in my underpants, covered in filth. I noticed he was turning a letter over in his hand and looking at me all the while. I hated this man, this subhuman who thought *me* an animal – we hated each other, and when we met we screamed abuse at each other. Holding it up he told me he had read my letter to Ma, and that even though there was truth in it I shouldn't send it. He said that Ma was being attacked by her neighbours because of Joseph being arrested. I was numbed by the shock as I stood there, helpless, imagining Ma being beaten up by people she'd been friendly with. I took in every detail of the governor's room for the first time: a golden sunbeam that ran along the wall and across the desk till it reached the governor, the bare walls that seemed coated with intimidation and fear. I had to lean on the desk to stop myself from swaying, and that high-pitched sound was back again.

I asked the governor where he had got his information from, and he said, 'Steele, as governor it is my duty to know what goes on in prisoners' families.' He held up my letter again and asked if I still wanted to send it. For some reason I said I did.

I don't remember going back to my cell. Perhaps I dreamt that Toe Elliot leaned over me and cradled my head on his lap. His face was covered in hair from his thick black beard; he was smeared with filth, and he was crying. I remember him saying, 'Don't believe the bastards, Johnnyboy!' but I hadn't been dreaming, it had really happened. The guys in the punishment block told me later that I had broken down when I told them about Ma. Toe had asked if he could go into my cell to comfort me.

I wrote to Mick and asked him if there was any truth in what the governor had told me, and he wrote back to say that it was a load of rubbish. Ma then wrote to say that the governor was simply trying to get me to crack up.

Jim was granted his home leave. When he got back I went

337

to see him in the governor's orderly room. He showed me some photos he had taken, including one of Maw lying on what looked like her deathbed – but then I noticed that in one hand she had a small glass of whisky and in the other a cigarette, as if to say she was going out of this world in a blaze of glory. I had to smile.

The orderly-room door opened and the governor came in with a mob of warders.

'I have some bad news for you,' he said, 'your grandmother, Mrs Elizabeth Padden, died yesterday.'

I looked at him, hoping to see something in his face that would tell me he was lying again; I looked to Jim, but he turned away from me; and then I broke down completely in front of them all. I wanted to die, but I was too weak even to will myself to die in this fucked-up world. Warders were holding me up, but I pushed them away. I couldn't contain my tears, and I didn't want to. The governor said that since Maw was like a second mother to us we would be allowed to attend her funeral. He asked me if I would like to go, and I said I would – but then I declined, because I wasn't sure if I could trust myself, and I didn't want to cause a scene at her funeral by running away.

Next day the governor said he would like to see me again. He stared at me for a moment and then he said, to no one in particular, that they had finally broken my spirit. I didn't answer, but did ask if I could go down to Barlinnie so that I could see Ma and comfort her. He asked me if I was ready to stop fighting the system, and I said I was. He told me he hadn't come across anyone quite like me, and wanted to know what made me tick. I couldn't answer him. He said I had broken all penal records and caused them terrible embarrassment and trouble. The chief warder, who was also there, told me I had matured ten years over the last few days.

Back in my cell I could hear the guys talking about me. Andy Mac was telling the others – warders included – that it wasn't the warders that had broken me, but nature itself. I was touched by their sympathy. 'Slop out, Steele!' – and I walked out with my pisspot, emptied it down the slop-out sink and went back to my clean cell. 'Stand up for the governor's visit, Steele!' – and I stood up when he came in. 'Morning, Steele, how are you today?' I told him I was fine, and said I wanted to apologise for all the abuse I'd given him through the years. He smiled and thanked me.

At Barlinnie I was allowed into the halls with the other guys: the first time I'd been in circulation for nearly a year. I was put into B Hall, third gallery. The news that I was back was all over the hall within minutes of my arrival.

I saw Ma, Auntie Mags, Aunt Mary and many other relatives and friends. Honeybugs had written me a note to say how sorry she was about Maw, and asking if she could visit me. It was good to see her again – she was a mother now, with a baby daughter. She asked me how I was keeping, and I told her lie after lie, pretending not to be as hurt as I was.

Joseph's trial began, and every day the newspapers carried horror stories of how the family, including a baby, had died. Ma and the others were convinced that Joseph would be found not guilty because they didn't believe he could have committed such a crime, and the police themselves said they didn't believe that whoever had set fire to the cellar outside the house had meant to do more than frighten the family.

Maw's death had taken its toll on Ma. She looked very pale, and was ageing fast. She and Brenda were in the little cubicle, with its armour-plated glass and wire: she turned her back to me and leaned backwards, resting her head on the little shelf, her eyes closed. I stood up, wondering what was wrong with her, and Brenda peered down at Ma with a frightened look on her face. When I asked her how she was feeling, she said she was simply resting her head.

Brenda told me about Maw's last days, and how she kept demanding whisky and cigarettes. She said Maw was always talking about me, and that the family had to read my letters to her over and over again. When she began to lose her senses she would call out, 'Where's my wee Johnnyboy?' thinking I was there. Whenever I thought about this, it hurt me terribly

339

to think that I had wasted so many years in and out of homes and gaols, being away from Maw and the family for so long. I began to think about God and his heaven, and wondered if Maw was there. . . .

I was due back at Peterhead before Joseph's trial ended, but I needed to have more time with Ma since I sensed from the headlines that Joseph would need to be Jesus Christ to be found not guilty. I asked the governor if I could spend a bit longer at Barlinnie so as to be with Ma. It was embarrassing to have to ask him – after all, I had put the police on to him only months earlier.

'Why should I do you any fucking favours after what you've done to me?' he shouted, calling me a grass for sending the police to investigate the fighting. I could hardly believe my ears. He leaned over his desk, cursing me. I didn't back off but leaned over the desk too, arguing back and the chief warder had to keep the two of us apart. The governor asked me why I'd decided to get in touch with the police after so long; I told him it was because I was being tortured by his pals at Peterhead. He denied they were his pals, adding that they didn't know how to run a gaol – I had to agree with him on that. Before I knew it I had told him to forget about my request for an extension, but as I was walking away he called out, 'You can have the extension, but only because your ma needs a shoulder to cry on.' I thanked him under my breath and left.

While the jury was out, Ma was at home preparing a meal for Joseph, his girlfriend Dolly and his solicitor – she was that sure he'd be found not guilty. Dolly had taken the radio into the toilet and was listening for a news flash of the verdict. There were quite a few people in the house at the time – which was just as well, because when Dolly ran in, shouting that Joseph had been found guilty and sentenced to life, Ma went berserk. She had to be held down and have a bread knife taken away from her after she had threatened to go to the Easterhouse police station and stab the police for manufacturing evidence against Joseph.

An appeal was lodged immediately. The newspapers and television were full of it. Some papers carried stories about

340

how Jim and I were serving long gaol sentences, and how our dad had been a well-known Glasgow gangster who had connections with the Kray twins – painting as black a picture as they could, as if to justify Joseph's sentence.

Joseph was sent to Barlinnie and put in the same hall as me, on the second gallery, so I got to talk to him each day at work, and at nights in his cell. He was shattered and couldn't stop crying. He said he had had nothing to do with the deaths of any of the fire victims, and vowed that he would fight the case for the rest of his life if necessary.

I was in my Barlinnie cell one evening in November when I heard smashing of windows and screams for help coming from one of the other halls. Shortly afterwards, while I was washing and shaving for a visit from Ma and my sister Brenda, I was told that someone had died in a fire during the lock-up period in C Hall. On the way down to see Ma I stopped at Joseph's cell. He had been put into solitary confinement for punching and kicking a warder who had called him a murderer; he had been charged by the police, and was waiting to go to court. As I passed C Hall I saw a blackened cell window, and could still smell the smoke.

I spoke to Ma and my sister, and promised to stay out of trouble. They knew about Joseph assaulting the warder. Ma said she was writing to the Queen about his being sentenced to life for murders he hadn't committed, and my sister said she was going to write to the Pope and ask him to intervene.

On my way back I was approached by a guy named Alex Fullerton, an old pal from St Joseph's and St Andrew's. He had a strange look on his face, and told me he was very sorry.

'Sorry at what?' I asked.

'Didn't the bastards tell you that your Uncle Atty was the man who just died in the C Hall fire?' he blurted out.

I collapsed on the floor: I wasn't unconscious, I just couldn't stand up any more. Alex helped me to my feet and leaned me against a sink. I kept thinking of Ma and how it would affect her. I even began to wish she was dead so that she wouldn't have to suffer any more, and I could kill whoever I wanted to without torturing her. If Ma *had* been dead I would have

341

slaughtered a warder – any warder, governors, chiefs, I hated them all. They knew Ma had been seeing me yet they never informed her of her brother's death, never even told me or Joseph.

Either they were playing psychological games, or Alex had been mistaken. I asked him who had told him that Atty had died in the fire – I hadn't even known he was in Barlinnie. Alex told me he had heard the warders talking about it.

All that night I paced my cell, thinking, crying and praying for Atty. In a sense I was happy that he had died, but sorry about the way if had happened. For most of his life he had been in a mental hospital, and I knew it had tortured him and that he always wanted out.

Next morning everyone was talking about Atty's death. It seemed that Uncle Atty had been arrested for a breach of the peace and remanded in Barlinnie. He was receiving medication and should have been in the hospital wing – but Barlinnie is full of guys who should be in hospital.

On the Monday night I had a visit from Ma and Brenda. I couldn't bear to look at Ma – I felt too emotional and upset. She told me they had learned of Attey's death from the television. Brenda warned me that Ma had to be watched carefully in case she tried to commit suicide, and begged me not to do anything crazy.

31 PSYCHO-
LOGICAL
CONTROL

My extension over, I was taken back to Peterhead. In the shower room I was searched, and one of the warders said he had found a hacksaw blade in my shoe. I told the bastard he must have put it there. I was taken back to the punishment block and shoved into a cell. The first things I noticed were the silence, and that there was no smell of filth. I wondered what was happening. I was determined not to fight back now: I just wanted to get back into circulation as soon as possible, and settle down if I could.

An hour or so later my cell door opened, and I was told to follow some warders through the double doors, down the corridor and into B Hall. For months B Hall had been empty, with the noise of hammering and drilling coming from it all day long. The bottom landing had been renovated, new steel doors had been put on each cell and all the walls had been reinforced to stop us digging through them. Looking up through the safety net, I could see that the other galleries were empty. It looked like a condemned building up there, with paint peeling from the walls, but down here it was brightly lit and the walls had been newly painted.

I was stripped and given new gaol clothes, and then locked in a cell. Each cell had three sets of bars and a steel grille on the window; a steel bed which had been bolted to the floor and cardboard tables and chairs. I spoke to Toe and the others, who told me that B Hall was the new psychological control unit. We were to be kept away from the other prisoners in the

343

mainstream of the prison and kept locked up alone for twenty-three hours a day under Rule 36. We were divided up into twos or threes and let out in groups to work during the day and to walk about or watch the black and white TV in the evening. There were no games, and the only hobby we were allowed was a jigsaw puzzle. The authorities had kept the regime of the control unit a secret and a hospital screen covered the double doors to stop anyone seeing into the hall. At night some of our pals would shout to us from A Hall and ask what they were doing to us and when we were getting out. We sat at our windows till morning, talking quietly: all we had was each other for company.

I was taken to see the governor and charged with having a hacksaw blade. When he asked me how I pleaded to the charge, I merely smiled at the stupidity of such witless persecution. I told the chief warder that I had had enough punishment and only wanted a chance to settle down, and would he please get me out of the control unit and back into circulation. He patted my shoulder as I sat there with tears in my eyes. He said I had caused so much trouble that no one thought I was capable of settling down and accepting prison life; if I started talking about settling down it would only make the staff more suspicious of me. I was trapped again: they were keeping me locked up indefinitely because they believed me to be incorrigible.

Jim was allowed in to see me before he was transferred to Perth Prison. We cuddled and cried together; he told me I was showing real strength of character by not reacting to the brutal regime, and that he was glad about this because he'd been afraid I would end up getting myself killed by the warders or being sent to the nuthouse. With Jim gone from Peterhead I was glad for him, but I missed him very much.

Alone in my cell I told myself they would never give in tormenting, and brutalising and degrading me, and that I was a fucking sucker for allowing myself to even think about settling down. I was at times so confused. We were exercised in a new cage at the back of the control unit, some of the passing warders seemed to think it funny and would make a

344

barking noise like a dog, so I started barking back at them.

I spent another Christmas and New Year locked up in punishment, but in February I was told I was being transferred to a new ten-man unit for troublemakers on the other side of the gaol. I was told that I would spend an indefinite period there, and that if I made progress they would consider letting me back into circulation.

The ten-man control unit was a cellblock, but from the outside it looked like a bungalow. Next to it were three huge cages for exercising, and a larger exercise area surrounded by a high wall with cameras on it. As in B Hall control unit, there was a camera inside watching the cell doors. When I arrived there were only two other guys there, but more soon arrived. I was put in a group with a guy called Frazer. Alex and Toe were in the other group.

The cells were smaller than the other cells in the gaol, apart from the 'iron lungs'. Each had a steel toilet and sink in one corner, a steel bed bolted to the wall and floor, a grey cardboard table and chair, grey waxcloth on the concrete floor and grey walls. Everything was grey except for the bed, which was asylum blue. Having sinks and toilets in our cells meant we were kept longer in our cells, as there was no slopping-out period and no need to go out for water. It was just like sleeping in a toilet.

I'd been there a few days when a warder asked me if I would like to attend a staff meeting. He said the purpose of the meeting was for us to try to get to know each other better, and to try to solve each other's problems! I found this hard to believe – me attend a staff meeting? I wondered what they were up to, and told him to go away and leave me alone. He did so, but asked me to think about it. There had to be a catch somewhere, I couldn't trust them.

He came back later and again asked me to attend a staff meeting. He said they wanted to get to know my problems, and to try to make life easier for me; I could put forward my views on how the new ten-man toilet should be run. Some warders came in and sat down next to me, taking their hats off as they did so. Somewhat alarmed by this, I moved away and stood by my window. They called me 'Johnnyboy' and offered me cigarettes and tea. I wondered if they thought I was a lunatic to be treating me like this. 'You cannot possibly go on as you are,' they said.

I agreed to go to the meeting so as to find out what they were up to. They asked me how I thought the unit should be run, and I had to laugh. I told them I wasn't there to help run gaols, but to run away from them given the chance.

They reminded me that this was my new home, indefinitely. All I could suggest was that I should be allowed to work in the garden instead of sweeping the corridors. They said this was a great idea. Then one of them asked me, in a sort of friendly way, where I had got the crowbars and the toolkit when I escaped from my cell with the Bald Eagle. . . .

'Fuck you!' I said, and I got up and went back to my cell.

That night Alex and Toe and I sat at our windows, trying to figure out what they were up to. I told them we were in a miniature nuthouse, and that the bastards were experimenting in psychological warfare.

The warders showed us the silent cell in the ten-man toilet. It was a cell within a cell, with nothing inside it. The lights were on the outside of the wall, and shone through thick frosted glass; there were no heating pipes but heat was provided by lamps on the outside. Each wall had a spyhole. One of the governors asked me if I'd be frightened to be locked up in it. 'It frightens me to be locked up in any cell,' I told him.

A couple of days later I noticed that the warders' attitude had changed again, and it was, 'Right Steele' or 'Right, you, out to work!'

I was out on exercise with Frazer one day when I noticed a man in one of the three huge cages, and I stopped to look. I was told to keep on walking, and think myself lucky that it wasn't me who was in the cage, but I paid no attention and went over to him. He was crying. I couldn't bring myself to walk round while this guy was in a cage. I spat at the warders and told them I had had about all I could take of their fucking psychological torture. I then walked back to my cell.

I started kicking my door and shouting at them to get me

out of there. I stripped off my clothes and covered my body and my cell in shit. I wrenched a tap off the sink and used it as a hammer, smashing everything I could. A warder told me I was on governor's report: I told him I couldn't give a fuck for the governor or his reports, and that I wanted back all the punishments that the fuckers had rescinded.

Next morning I heard the others being given their breakfast, but no one came near me. I managed to smash the spyhole and push shit through it into the corridor. By now the cell was flooded with water from the tap I had broken – I was almost up to my knees in it – and when they eventually opened the door the water surged out and soaked them. They rushed in and some of them grabbed me, while others kicked into me, I couldn't feel any pain, only fear as they dragged me into a van.

I didn't know what was happening, or where I was going. They drove me to the punishment block and dragged me into the silent cell. It was as dark as ever in there, and the window was covered in bird shit. I was glad to be there, away from the gaol and all that went on in it. Singing helped, and I sang every day, often composing my own songs. I didn't want to go on living in that hellhole of cages, punishment blocks and psychological control units. They kept me there for three or four days. I didn't know what punishment the governor had given me, or even what the charge was – I kept my fingers in my ears and whistled whenever he tried to talk to me.

The 'Bear', who had slept through the riot in 1979, was back in the punishment block. He'd been told he would stay there unless he volunteered for the B Hall control unit. He told me that he wasn't going to any control unit, whether on a voluntary basis or under orders. 'Dae ye think that because I've been in Carstairs I'm an idiot!' he used to shout at the governors and warders.

He was right when he said he wouldn't go into a control unit, for he took his own life down in Barlinnie, where he'd gone on visits. They found him hanging behind his cell door.

The governor came into my cell soon after I had heard of the Bear's death, and he said 'All right, Steele?' I lay on the floor, looking at him and wondering what made him tick.

'Yes, I'm all right,' I told him – and just as he turned to leave I added, 'But you're fucking sick!'

I cut off one of my bars, but the warders heard me digging with it. I barricaded the cell door by jamming the bar between the door and the bottom of the concrete bed, and I laughed at them as they tried to get in, and couldn't. The warders on the catwalk were unaware that I had removed the outside bar, since I made a dummy to replace it. Mick and Mary had bought me the *Encyclopaedia Britannica*, Volumes One to Twelve, and I used them to help barricade the door. I knew they could have burst down the door with a jack, but they didn't – their idea was to leave me there, and if I didn't want to be fed or exercised that was fine with them.

Joe, who was in the cell next door, asked if he could have my breakfast. They were only too glad to give it to him, hoping this would torment me. As soon as the warders had gone, Joe threw me a line out of the window and passed over my breakfast in a plastic bag that he had kept hidden. He did the same for dinner – he had only the one bag, so as soon as I had finished with it I gave it back so that he could refill it. They were at my door again with the governor asking me how I had barricaded my door. I told him it was with my Encyclopaedias. I could just imagine his face, for when I received the Encyclopaedias from Mick and Mary, the governor told me I couldn't get them in because of my behaviour. Then he had said sarcastically that they would be of no use to me anyway as I'd been to a special school for mentally handicapped and backward children. 'The whole world is against you!' I said sarcastically to him through the door. I don't know if he got my meaning. They all left.

In the end they forced my door open with a jack. They searched me for the hacksaw blade with which I'd cut the bar; one of them told me to bend over so that he could look up my arse. I refused and was ready for them to attack me, but they didn't. I was taken away to the silent cell again.

I had spent about five weeks in the punishment block since my removal from the ten-man toilet. One day I was slopping

348

out and brushing my teeth when two warders started talking to me, I was told that I wouldn't be allowed into circulation unless I agreed to go back into the ten-man toilet for a spell, and that I'd be guaranteed a year's remission if I did. I wrote to the governor – it was easier than looking at his face – and he summoned me and confirmed that I would continue in solitary confinement if I declined to go back to the TMT. I turned my back on him and walked away, saying that if I had to stay in the punishment block I would rather be in the silent cell, away from them all. And so it was the silent cell again.

One day I was reading my book – I had been given a copy of *Les Miserables* by Victor Hugo – when I heard a voice say, 'Are you going to hide away in here for the rest of your life, Johnnyboy?' I looked up and saw one of the governors standing in the doorway. I hadn't even heard the door open. He asked if he could come in. I had never heard him be so friendly or polite before. He said things were different now in the TMT: only Toe and Alex were there, and I would be allowed out with them every day for exercise, work and recreation. I could work in the garden too, and get plenty of fresh air. Again I was told I wouldn't be kept there too long. I asked him where the logic was in giving me better conditions for no more than three months and then putting me back into circulation under worse conditions. Instead of answering, he told me he was throwing me a lifeline by taking me to the TMT, of which he was the governor. I gave in and went back to the TMT.

As soon as I arrived, Alex and Toe were allowed into my cell to make sure that I was all right. They confirmed that the TMT had changed and that the warders didn't seem to bother with them. In fact, some of the best warders in the gaol were there.

The three of us used to sit in the garden during the day, and sometimes we'd dig it for something to do. The warders were growing vegetables, and using the silent cell as a hot house!

At night Toe and I used to sit at our windows, talking into the wee small hours. From him I learned more about my dad than I'd ever known before. Toe said he was one of the best guys he'd ever known. When I told him about the punishments he gave me as a kid, Toe laughed and said his father had done the same – all the older mob believed in beating their sons to keep them in line. He said how my dad often worried that I would follow in his footsteps and spend my life in and out of prison. Toe told me things that made me think twice about my dad and the hatred I'd felt for him. I couldn't make sense of it, so I started to write about my childhood experiences, putting down all I could remember, trying to analyse myself and catching only glimpses of the gentleman Toe referred to when speaking about my dad. All I could remember was a man I feared, hated and hardly knew, who was not only forever punishing me and saying it was for my own good, but on many occasions told me I wasn't even his child.

'If, as you say, my dad always boasted that I was his favourite, why all the witless beatings and punishment?' I asked. Toe said it was obvious my dad was doing it to try and stop me from doing wrong, no matter how trivial. Why, then, had Jim never been hit for the trivial things he did as a kid? Toe had no answer. I reckoned that Jim was his favourite son, and that – as my dad always said – I wasn't his. I couldn't find any other reason for what he did to me. I let Toe read the hundred-odd pages of self-analysis. He sent it back to me with a note saying that I should turn all my sufferings and misery into something constructive by writing my life story, which could be very beneficial to society and save other kids from being brutalised. Because of my song-writing and verses Toe reckoned, as others did, that I was quite a talented writer, and tried to encourage me. When it dawned on me that perhaps I had a hidden talent I felt a sense of pride. Toe often said he knew I wasn't evil, but that if I didn't do something positive with my life the authorities would turn me into a killing machine sooner or later. He was right – I wasn't evil, but I did wonder how long it would be before I used a knife on one of the governors or warders.

The ten-man-toilet allowed me more breathing space. On sunny days I worked in the grounds stripped to the waist. We saved our wages to buy tomatoes, cucumbers, tinned pilchards and pickles. We got potatoes from the cookhouse, and I stole the odd lettuce from the garden– the warders looked on, telling me to hurry in case I was seen by anyone else. Alex made up a salad each night, and the warders let us use their cooker and pots. I told the governors that I would sooner stay in the TMT than go back into the mainstream of the gaol, where I wouldn't survive long. They said they had noted my progress.

After about five weeks, I was told to pack my kit since I was going back to A Hall. I asked about the year's remission I had been promised, and was told I would have to earn it by long periods of good behaviour. I was also told I would be working in the mailbag party.

I told the governor that I wasn't going back there to be persecuted. I went back to my cell, and when they came for me I wouldn't let them in. Toe and Alex put up a fight on my behalf, but I told them it was okay and that I would just have to go back and make the most of it. I shook hands with them and left.

I didn't know many of the prisoners in A Hall. That afternoon I was taken to work with the mailbag party, in a cold and dirty shed. When I was given some filthy mailbags to mend, I refused and threw them on the ground at the warder's feet. Everyone stopped working. He threatened to put me back into the punishment block if I didn't get down to work. Eventually it was decided that I would get no wages for refusing to work.

My first day back in circulation hurt me just as much as my first day in gaol – nothing had changed, it was still as ugly to look at and to be trapped in. The warders wouldn't let me out of their sight, and there were many new warders whom I'd never seen before.

I was about to take my clothes off and put them outside my cell door that night, when one of the cons told me that he had overheard the warders talking about my being taken back to the punishment block. I put my clothes on again and walked downstairs to the double doors and out into the damp and empty corridor. I was taken to the silent cell in the punishment block at my own request. It was peaceful there in the darkness and I could relax. With no window to sit at, and cut off from everyone else, I took to thinking about my life.

Early next morning one of the chiefs came to see me. He said that they weren't going to allow me to lock myself away from the world, and that it was time I got a grip on myself. He added that they didn't want to see me being punished any more, and that they would all go out of their way to help me. I took this with a pinch of salt, and reckoned they must be furious about my walking into the punishment block, which was supposed to be so frightening. Again I was asked if I would like to see the prison psychiatrist, and again I refused. I agreed to go back to the hall that afternoon and try to fit into the regime once again. But the witless persecution started again and I was put on governors' report for having my hands in my pockets in the exercise yard, and locked up in the punishment block for three days. I talked to T.C. in the punishment block. He was fighting his case and studying law. He had no option but to be there, because the authorities were persecuting him and making it difficult for him to fight his case. He had been on hunger strikes and was so thin I hardly recognised him.

When they put me back in circulation once again, I decided to get away from it all by trying to escape. A guy called Midnight offered to help, after failing to talk me out of it. I knew that there was a huge ball of twine which was used for mending the mailbags: it was very strong, and could be used to make a rope. In the mailbag party was an old lifer called Pat, who was in for murder. I asked him if he could smuggle out the twine, since he wasn't searched as thoroughly as the rest of us. He knew right away what the twine was for and asked me if he could come too, but I said he was too old to climb. He went off in a huff for a few moments, but then he gave me a bear-hug and said he would help.

Midnight and I cut lengths of twine, which Pat then rolled into small balls and hid under the cap he always wore. At night Midnight made the rope in his cell. I managed to get some iron bars off some sewing machines with which to make grappling-hooks; these were smuggled out in a tea-can, which

352

was collected every morning and taken back to the cookhouse. They were then passed to Wee Smiddy, who was a passman in A Hall, and he hid them till I got in from work. Rather than risk sawing my bars, I decided to dig through the ceiling of a cell on the top gallery, and I managed to get hold of a five-foot crowbar for tunnelling through with.

The gaol was full of new warders, which gave me the idea of dressing up as one of them in order to get across the exercise yard and round to the back of C Hall. We made a warder's hat, and Midnight stole one of their plastic raincoats. I also made, with Midnight's help, a minister's vest with dog-collar attached, and someone made me an imitation fur jacket, with a hat to match. I had found a small hole behind a steel plate inside the showers, where some pipes went up into the loft, and stashed the rope up there.

Joe the Meek was one of the passmen in A Hall, and over a few mugs of tea at night we reminisced about my family. He told me about Ma as a schoolgirl, and how some of them called her the wee innocent lassie of the Gorbals. I told him about how my dad used to tell me that I wasn't his son, and how Ma and Maw would argue with him and shout at him that I was his flesh and blood. I stopped to look at Joe's face – a hard-looking face like a boxer's – and the tears were streaming down his cheeks. He asked me if I knew that my Ma had been married before she met my dad! I was shocked to hear this, since it seemed to confirm all my suspicions. 'No, Johnnyboy,' Joe said, his arm round my shoulder like he was supporting me. 'You are his son – it's Jim who isn't.'

I was more shocked than I'd ever been in my life before. No one had ever told me that Ma had been married before – or that her first husband was doing a long-term prison sentence in this very gaol when she divorced him.

'The reason your dad never as much as laid a finger on Jim was because he wasn't his son,' Joe told me. He asked me to think about the life my dad had been living, and how he must have feared I would follow in his footsteps and be victimised for the things he had done. He said I should never forget that my dad had taken Maw to live with him when he needn't have, and treated Jim as his son when he needn't have, and done the same for my young cousin, who had been orphaned. If ever I'd needed my dad to speak to it was then, if only to tell him that I forgave him for all he had said and done.

For days and nights I thought about what Joe the Meek had told me. I tried to analyse my life as I paced up and down my cell and it started to make sense. I had been wrong about my dad all my life, hating him for being so cruel, for the beatings and for sending me to bed. I remembered how Maw had told me that one day I would understand my dad and how much he loved me. As for the escape plan, I couldn't stop now. I was still doing what I had always done when faced with hardship – running.

While we were preparing for the escape, some guys in the punishment block got out. A dummy gun was used and a hostage taken, but they gave up. A few days later T.C. was rushed to hospital with a broken spleen that he got from a beating.

I managed to get into the top gallery cell and started to tunnel through the ceiling with the crowbar, making a hole big enough to get my head through. I was stripped to my shorts, and there was dust and debris everywhere. As soon as I had finished for the night I gave a couple of knocks on the pipe and Midnight and some others came in with mops and pails and paint and paint-brushes to cover up the hole. But the guy whose cell I was grafting told the warders about the hole in his roof. He didn't grass any names, though he knew I was responsible. He told me that it was too heavy for him to get involved in, as he had only six months of his sentence left. He was right – it was heavy for him. They put him on protection over in the surgery where no one could get at him, but no one wanted to get at him.

The next day two guys who were supposed to be involved with me were locked up for subversive activities, and soon I was taken away to the B Hall control unit to await a governor's report for having forbidden articles in my cell. I told the governor that I had never had any forbidden articles in my cell, but he said that he knew I'd been heavily involved in the escape plot, and I was given fourteen days solitary.

T.C. was in the cellblock. He couldn't hold his food down since the operation. He looked like a corpse. He was still fighting his case.

When I got back to A Hall I went to see the governor about T.C.'s health and about him being moved to hospital for proper treatment. I was told to mind my own business. Soon after, my workshed went on strike to protest against the brutality being used on T.C. in the punishment block, and to have him transferred to hospital where he could be looked after properly. I was the last to be called to see the governor about it. I had barely walked in when he got half out of his seat. He was leaning on his desk, his face almost scarlet. In a fit of rage he screamed: 'You, Steele! Get into B Hall control unit!' There were more warders around me than normal, and they formed a circle to stop me from getting to the governor. I told him my reasons for striking, but was cut off by him sceaming: 'Get him out of here!' I tried to hold on to the framework around the door and screamed back at the governor that he was an animal and worse than any of the craziest prisoners in the fucking gaol. The warders hauled me away, and over to B Hall control unit.

32 A HOPE
IN HELL

In February 1986 I was sent yet again to the Cages: it was the sixth time I had been there. When the cage door had closed on me and the warders gone, I sat down naked, and buried my face in my hands wondering what my life was all about. It was 1986 – the year I should have been going home. I didn't know where the years had gone. I never thought I'd live to see 1986 when I was first sentenced back in 1978. But I still had almost another eight years to serve. I felt I'd never get through them. I didn't want to, it was too frightening; I couldn't stay out of trouble, and I couldn't settle down. My sanity couldn't hold on that long, and I'm not sure if I wanted it to. The authorities thought me a nutter, but in my heart I knew different.

Next morning the governor came to see me after I had refused to go and see him. 'Welcome home, Steele,' he mocked me. I couldn't even look at him: I just lay down on the floor shouting 'Fuck off!' till he left.

I managed to cut off one of the bars in my cage. My pal Bill, an Australian, had done the same, and we jammed them back on so that the warders wouldn't notice. We decided to tunnel our way through our wall outside the cage. It must have been about ten o'clock one evening when I removed the bar from my cage and crawled through. I began digging at the wall which led to the outside yard, removing the cement from around the brickwork as quietly as I could. A guy called Ben listened out for the warders: when I heard him singing a certain line in a song I knew the warders were coming, so I brushed the bits of cement behind the cell door so that they couldn't see them, crawled back into the darkened cage, jammed on the cut-off bar and pretended to be asleep. The warder came to my spyhole and put on the light, but when he saw me there he went away again. Then I heard him ask Bill what he was up to – he'd noticed that Bill's wall was damaged. The warder ran away to get some help, so I grabbed the bar and went mad on the wall with it. I could hear Bill doing the same. There were dozens of bricks all round me, and I was choking on the dust, but I kept on smashing down the wall. It was a mad dash for freedom. I could hear dozens of warders running down the corridor, and the blare of their walkie-talkies. Soon they were at my spyhole, shouting at me to stop. I was crying with rage and frustration. They shouted that the perimeter wall was surrounded by police with dogs, but I kept on smashing till I collapsed exhausted on a heap of rubble and bricks. The door burst open and they rushed in in full riot gear and grabbed me. A surgery warder handcuffed my arms behind my back.

They carried me along the corridor to a punishment cell. As soon as they had closed the cell door I took the handcuffs off and started digging a hole in the wall. They came in, snatched the handcuffs from me and dragged me off to another cage, where they handcuffed me spread-eagled to the bars and left me standing in the dark.

My eyes soon grew accustomed to the dark, and I could just see my reflection in the mirror on the wall outside the cage. I kept looking at myself and thinking about what I saw there. With my boyish face I looked much the same as ever: but I didn't feel like a boy, I felt old. I laughed and cried and cursed and screamed; I prayed to God, then I cursed him, then I prayed again. I imagined doing all the things I had never done with my dad – camping and fishing and laughing all the while, just like fathers and sons should do.

In the morning they took me down from the bars. My hands and wrists hurt badly; as I moved them slowly to my sides the pain went shooting through my arms. In the daylight I could see I was filthy. They passed me my breakfast but I kicked it

357

out again: I was sorry I did for I was starving, which was unusual for me. After the warders had left I put one of my legs through the bars and pulled in a slice of bread.

I noticed there was a foul smell in my cage. It smelled of shit, but I wasn't on a dirty protest at the time. I assumed that the cage hadn't been properly washed and thought no more about it. That night, as I lay on the floor, I heard a noise. Remains of food were splattered all over the outside of the cage, and eventually I made out what looked like a rat with a slice of white bread. I threw something at it, and it scurried away down the hole which led to the exercise yard from the outside of the cage. In the morning I put my hand into the hole and discovered an open pipe that smelled of the sewers. I was furious and demanded the doctor. I explained to him about the open sewer and the rat, and he promised to investigate. Some of the warders said it was only to be expected that rats would come up the sewer and into the cage as long as I left food slops lying around.

I wrote a petition to the Secretary of State. I got hold of one of my Encyclopaedias and discovered that it was illegal to have an open sewer in an inhabited building. I quoted this to the governors and doctors. About a week later the warders came in and blocked up the hole.

One of the assistant governors asked me which gaol I wanted to go to, but I said I wanted to go home. The chief warder then told me that the governor of Peterhead didn't want me back – nobody wanted me, and certainly not them. The only places left were Carstairs or the Special Unit at Barlinnie.

'Is there any difference?' I asked.

One evening the governor came into my cage and told me that the Prison Department and the Secretary of State had asked him to investigate the possibility of my being moved to another gaol. Something had to be done because too many people were asking embarrassing questions about me. I said I'd like to stay in Inverness gaol in the mainstream – that this way I might be able to settle down away from Peterhead. He told me there was no way that he or his warders would accept me. He said, half joking, that they would go on strike if I was transferred to their gaol, and that I wouldn't be able to cope because the regime was stricter than Peterhead's. He said the Secretary of State wondered whether I would like to go to the Barlinnie Special Unit. I said I wasn't volunteering to go to any loonybin.

I began to think that maybe there was something seriously wrong with me. Maybe I was a madman thinking I was sane; maybe I was incorrigible, for I couldn't stop doing what I was doing, and I couldn't settle down. I looked at myself in the mirror, trying to find a clue.

Ma and Brenda came to visit me, but I didn't even feel like seeing them. I was drained mentally, and had nothing much to say. I sat with my head against the side of the visiting-box and closed my eyes. Ma asked me if I wanted them to go, and the way she said it almost had me crying. I sat up straight and told them I was sorry and that I didn't want them to leave.

In late July 1986 a psychiatrist, a governor, a chief warder and a PO came from the Barlinnie Special Unit to interview me. A warder opened my cage and told me that the nutcrackers were waiting for me in the orderly room. When I got there I found a tall man on his own: he introduced himself as the psychiatrist. I told him about my fear of psychiatrists and their power to have me certified, but he made me feel at ease by telling me he wasn't here to certify me, and that I wasn't insane. He wanted to see if there was anything the Barlinnie Special Unit could offer me to help me stay out of trouble. He told me that he had deliberately asked to see me first so that he could give me a few guidelines before I saw the other unit members; he said I should ask them for help, since it made it easier for the unit team if they knew that someone really wanted to be helped. I said I would try my best to settle down if given the chance, and he shook my hand before I was taken back to the cage.

After a while my cage opened again, and I was told that the other unit members wished to see me now. There were three guys sitting in the orderly room, and as I came in they stood up, shook my hand and introduced themselves. The atmosphere was altogether different, and they seemed quite unlike any other warders I'd had dealings with.

The chief warder began by telling me that they had read about me in the prison files, but they wanted to hear my side of it. There was a lot of talk about the Special Unit and how it worked, about the trust that would be placed upon me and the responsibilities I'd have as an individual and as a member of the community. Staff and prisoners worked as a community; if one had a problem he could call a meeting at any time and the other members would all attend, regardless of what they were doing, and do their best to solve the problem. They told me that I could escape from the unit any day of the week if I wished to do so, but they hoped I wouldn't. They guaranteed that I wouldn't be put on any medication at the unit: no one was unless they requested it, and even then they preferred not to give it. There was no brutality, no governor's reports, no violence of any kind.

For me to be told this was weird – and, even though I thought it might well be true, I wasn't so sure that I wanted the punishments stopped or the violence to end. They had been part of me for a very long time. But I listened to their talk about my stepping into another part of the system which was geared to helping me rather than destroying me. I didn't want to trust them or to like them or to stop rebelling, yet somewhere inside I wanted to do all these things. When the chief warder reached out and pulled my chair in closer to him, I felt threatened, yet at the same time I knew they didn't want to harm me.

They told me that my family and friends could visit me there every day and that they could get involved with them as well, helping me to piece my life together and getting me out of the mess they had found me in. It was an offer I couldn't refuse, nor could I abuse it: although it was just another gaol I was being interviewed for, it sounded better than what I had known so far.

I was aware of them watching me as I told them about my life. I explained to them about the brutal conditions I had been subjected to and the punishments I had endured, physically and mentally, and how to rebel was the only way I knew to survive and keep my sanity. To my surprise they listened with interest. One of them asked to see a cage, saying he had only heard of them. I imagined they wouldn't want to hear me talk about the prison system and its faults – most warders don't like to hear this kind of talk because they are part of it and try to cover up its bad aspects – but they told me they knew about its abuses, and were trying to stop them, to help prisoners and staff rather than ignore problems which needed to be confronted and dealt with more humanely. I didn't cover as much ground as I would have liked, but they told me that I had presented my case very well. No one in my position would have believed such a conversation possible – there's no room for such compassion or humanity in the old prison system. And I've no doubt that many warders and governors think that there's no compassion or humanity in most prisoners. Occasionally when I told them about my feelings, I regretted it and cursed myself for opening up to them. To have done so made me feel insecure, but then I felt better to know that they too had opened up and said what they felt about the prison regime.

They couldn't decide there and then whether I would be accepted into the Special Unit: they had to inform the community and get the views of its members and decide whether they could trust me not to smash the place up or escape, after which a recommendation would be sent to the Secretary of State. They guaranteed me an answer within a week to ten days. One of them asked me if I thought I could handle the pressure of the Unit. I felt insulted, for it seemed like asking me whether I could live a normal life.

Ten days passed, and I heard nothing. I refused to ask the governors what was happening, though every day when they came round they stayed longer than usual, hoping I'd say something to them. I could only assume that they had decided not to take me. I was no longer even sure if they were who they said they were, and I began to wonder if they weren't really warders and psychiatrists out to certify me. I cursed myself for agreeing to see them. How could I have trusted the

361

bastards? How could I have allowed myself to think they wanted to help me? I thought that maybe they were going to keep me in the Cages permanently – I had been there almost six months already. I overheard some warders saying something about the Carstairs Mental Hospital. I couldn't eat anything, so certain was I that I had been certified. If it were Carstairs I was going to I wasn't sure if I'd try to escape or just kill myself. I thought about the times I'd visited Uncle Atty at the Gartloch mental hospital, and how he had complained about the electric shock treatment he was receiving. I thought of living a life prescribed by doctors – at least in gaol I was in control of my mind for most of the time, but in Carstairs I'd have no say in the matter. In the end I wrote to the Unit board, asking them to inform me of their decision.

On the nineteenth day after their visit the warder in charge of me came into my cell. He stood looking at me for a while, and then he said, 'There's a team coming from Barlinnie in a couple of hours to collect you.' I didn't believe him, and yet I wanted to. I still had a one-inch piece of hacksaw blade hidden up my arse in a small sheath to stop it from cutting me: it was the only comfort I had, and wherever the bastards were taking me it was coming with me.

The cage door opened, and I saw one of the warders from the Barlinnie Special Unit, plus a couple of others. I was handcuffed to one of them in the back seat of a car.

I was really glad to be out of the Cages, leaving what seemed to be the worst behind. They kept talking to me, but all I really wanted was to lie down and rest. I felt drained, physically and psychologically: part of me wanted only to go back to my cage, to be away from everyone and everything. I didn't feel right being away from the hell I'd been taken from, nor did I want to settle down.

'What the fuck is the matter with me?' I wondered. The warder leaned over and took off my handcuffs.

'Just relax, Johnnyboy,' he told me.

POSTSCRIPT

Fourteen years have now gone by and I find myself released from gaol and happy to be in the big, wide world and spreading my wings, and the world seems even more beautiful than I remembered. The past, for me, has been an experience which I would want to share with others in the hope that they can learn from my rights and wrongs. There's nothing attractive in crime or punishment and this is what today's youth must learn, or I fear that they will become tomorrow's gaolbirds.

It is only right that I add a personal thanks to Governor James Cameron Stuart, who eventually took me to his open prison at Noranside and gave me great support and help in preparing me for my release. And to all the staff and trainees at the Adult Training Centre at Forfar for allowing me to work with them and for their trust and support. But most of all to my mother, whose struggle was longer than my own.

And last, but not least, to Freddie Anderson, the Glasgow poet and author, who provided me with pen and paper, and great encouragement to write this book.

John Steele was released from Prison on 6.3.92.